# CILLA
## THE BIOGRAPHY

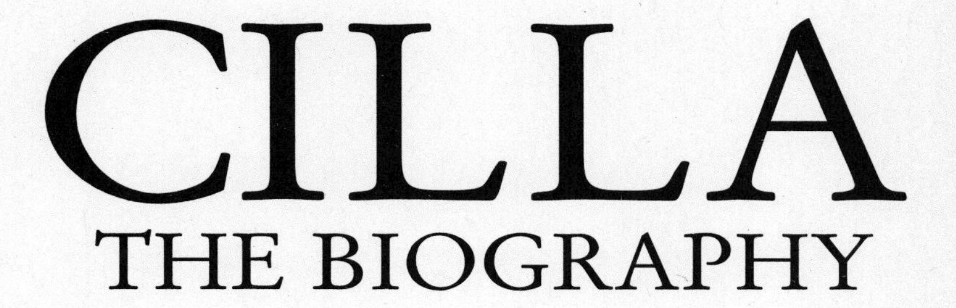


DOUGLAS
THOMPSON

Published by Metro Publishing Ltd, 3 Bramber Court,
2 Bramber Road, London W14 9PB, England

This edition first published in hardback in 2002

ISBN 1 84358 041 1



British Library Cataloguing-in-Publication Data: A catalogue record for this book is available from the British Library.

Design by ENVY

Printed and bound in Great Britain by CPD

1 3 5 7 9 10 8 6 4 2



Papers used by Metro Publishing Ltd are natural, recyclable products made from wood grown in sustainable forests. The manufacturing processes conform to the environmental regulations of the country of origin.

DOUGLAS THOMSON is the author of eighteen books. A biographer, broadcaster and international journalist, he is a regular contributor to major newspapers and magazines worldwide. His books, published in a dozen languages, include the television-linked anthology *Hollywood People* and bestselling biographies of Madonna, Clint Eastwood, Michelle Pfeiffer, Dudley Moore, Leonardo DiCaprio and John Travolta. His 2002 collaboration with Christine Keeler resulted in another instant top-ten bestseller. He lives with his wife and daughter in a farmhouse near Cambridge and commutes regularly to California.

For Dudley

**Bobby's Girl**

*When people ask me*

*What would you like to be*

*Now that you're not a kid, anymore*

*I know just what to say*

*I answer right away*

*There's just one thing, I've been wishin' for*

*I wanna be Bobby's Girl*

*I wanna be Bobby's Girl*

*That's the most important thing to me*

*And if I was Bobby's Girl*

*If I was Bobby's Girl*

*What a faithful, thankful girl I'd be.*

Words and music: Henry Hoffman and Gary Klein.



Original US recording: 1962 Marcie Blaine

Original UK recording: 1962 Susan Maughan

*'None of us could really sing but some got the breaks and some didn't'*

– Alvin Stardust aka Shane Fenton, on the hits and misses of the Merseyside music boom.

# CONTENTS

# ACKNOWLEDGEMENTS

It's been a long and winding road but made even more enjoyable by rediscovering the past in Liverpool, Manchester, Belfast, Edinburgh, Glasgow, London, New York and Los Angeles. The survivors of the 'Sixties and early 'Seventies now live worldwide and although their hairstyles have changed – in some cases vanished – their memories remain intact and invaluable. It helps to have talented friends. I thank them all.

## *Prologue*

# BOBBY'S GIRL

*'Ours was a great love. We were at one. Yes, I know my Bobby wants me to be strong, but at times I cry so much I can hardly breathe.'*
– Cilla Black, 2001

Cilla Black is a star reborn, an incredible survivor. Just look at her in the 21st Century. She often appears in figure-hugging, leather or dark denim pants with fitted designer shirts and the beloved black stiletto boots from Gina. Her hips are narrow, not matronly, and for certain outfits she parades a chunky gold belt draped across them.

For her, there has always been a reason for everything – motivated, at first, by understandable ambition. she has fought the odds to remain the highest paid woman on British television, (£60,000 an hour in the summer of 2002), but negotiations remain in place, along with an overwhelming fan loyalty.

She was never been one for a cavalcade of self-acclaim. But it is hard to avoid. Cilla Black, like time, has moved on. Her hair has gone from geranium to Titian, her spirit less carefree, more conservative and protective. She has stepped into a world of *Sir* Cliff Richard, *Sir* Elton John, *Sir* Bob Geldoff, *Sir* Jimmy Saville and *Sir* Paul McCartney. What heresy thoughts of such titles would have been when she was checking coats and moving weak cappuccino around the Merseybeat clubs a lifetime of yesterdays ago. They were all just kids having fun. Knights you found in Camelot, not Liverpool......

Now, she has her own 'gong'. She was awarded an OBE in the 1997 New Year honours. She should have collected it on the same Tuesday as Paul McCartney was knighted by the Queen at Buckingham Palace. But Cilla had television concerns about mislaid relatives: she did *Surprise, Surprise* on Tuesdays and please could the Queen reschedule? Her OBE was nudged into the Birthday Honours List and she went to the Palace on July 16 that year to receive her pink-ribboned with white stitching validation as a national treasure.

As with everything in her professional life, it was all carefully rehearsed. Her limousine driver checked and rechecked the driving time from the Savoy Hotel in the Strand in London to the gates of Buckingham Palace (he made it a dozen minutes) so she would not be a moment off schedule. Her coordinated cream coloured outfit was tried on again and again. The Honours are given out alphabetically so she was one of the first, 'The Queen was on the podium but then I supposed it is *her* show. It was a good job I was up there with the Bs. I never thought I would get an OBE. I thought, maybe, an MBE at the most. I wouldn't shut up and her Majesty glazed over. Not a nasty look – just "Oh, God, if I don't stop her now she's going to bang on forever." I can take a hint. It was like visiting your favourite auntie – one who might leave you something in her will.'

There is a very real hope and prospect of a 21st Century Dame Cilla. She has regarded her royal connections as endorsements of her place in British life. As a young pop singer she met the Queen at the Royal Variety Performance in 1969 and has since met other royals at charity events. When her OBE was announced, among the telegrams were those from Princess Diana, Prince Andrew and the Duchess of York. Cilla was not shy about it, 'I know they are fans of the shows but it was a great thrill to receive their personal messages.'

When she celebrated her thirty years in the entertainment business Cilla had raised a glass of champagne and toasted, 'Here's to the next thirty......!' It was what you would expect in the circumstances and if the clock would allow, she would do just that, carry on regardless. At that time, filling up the champagne glasses, protectively watching over every moment, making every deal, was Bobby Willis. He was the publicly silent partner in one of the most remarkable showbusiness careers ever. They were holding hands before there was colour television. He was with Cilla as she nervously travelled from Liverpool to London to sign a record deal organised by Beatles manger Brian Epstein which saw her go on to become – and remain in 2002 – Britain's biggest record selling female singer.

And for almost four decades he had been with Cilla: caring, checking, looking after, nursing her career along with a combination of love and faith and absolute belief in her talent. He always put it bluntly, 'She's like a good Hoover. I'm not selling poor goods. She performs.'

He was there for her from the start. Suddenly – there were not hints, no serious warning signs – he was diagnosed in 1999 with inoperable lung and liver cancer. The weeks vanished as if minutes. Bobby fought but it was only for the family. He knew he couldn't win but he suffered, with its dreadful side effects, chemotherapy treatment at the Royal Free Hospital in London. Cilla and their three sons who, idolised their father took him home on August 7, 1999. He died on October 23 that year. Cilla had every reason to collapse, to lose it in grief and self-pity. She did none of that. Maybe it was because she had been loved for what added up to for ever for her. Bobby insisted that she go on working while he was ill. He knew he was dying, but that Cilla and the boys carried on living was what mattered to him. 'I thought it was very cruel of him to make me go and do the shows. I said to him, "You're asking too much," but Bobby knew that if you fall off a horse, you have to get right back on. Otherwise the fear gets bigger and bigger.' Cilla, with enormous character, followed Bobby's longtime mantra that time was not an enemy but an opportunity.

It was a curious irony, which Bobby, with his sense of humour and belief that we create our own destinies, would have understood, that Cilla was wearing black as she presented the pre-recorded *Moment of Truth* on ITV, the awful Saturday that he died.

It was the television series Bobby discovered for Cilla who was his world, his everything.

Millions were watching as the evening news announced that Bobby had, after his valiant but vain fight with cancer, succumbed to pneumonia brought on by a chest infection. For Cilla it was like her support being kicked from under her. She was the upbeat Liverpudlian – in life as on screen – who had survived in the fickle world of showbusiness. Candidly, she had always admitted that she was able to do so, to turn herself into a millionairess and a British institution, because of the unswerving support of the man she met in a Liverpool nightclub some generations ago. She was Bobby's Girl, 'Even after all the years of marriage we would still sit on the sofa, holding hands, watching the telly and having a hug. There was nothing better for me at the end of a long day than cuddling up to Bobby.

'We had never spent a night apart since we got married. I couldn't bear being away from him. Even if he went to play golf, I missed him terribly. I got very anxious if he was five minutes late and he went bonkers if I don't get home at exactly the time I'd said.'

They were the 'strongest marriage in showbusiness', a cliché they enthusiastically proved. It was, perhaps, because they had the same ambition, the same finishing line: Cilla's stardom. That is not said unkindly but here was that rare thing, a man in a cut-throat business who was prepared to sacrifice the spotlight for someone else; his adoration of Cilla was boundless. On *Blind Date* and *Surprise, Surprise*, the crews would joke about Bobby's overprotective influence, but it was successful. He took care of the detail. Sometimes, it overwhelmed him: once during an episode of *Surprise, Surprise* he had to send out for Kleenex he was so caught up in the story of an emotional reunion.

He never missed a recording of Cilla's – a TV show, a pantomime, a week at the seaside. On *Blind Date* he was there in the recording booth watching Cilla's hemline, her nail polish – the right shade, no chips – and her attitude.

If she was too sharp with contestants he would tell her. He said their marriage was a compromise in that she went along with his ideas and he with hers. Mostly, it seems, he went along with hers but improvising and polishing them. His role as this sort of rough diamond cutter is reflected in Cilla's words about him before he died, 'Bobby always says nothing in the world can replace a hug. He is very much a security blanket, the rock I cling to. When I am upset he'll put his arms around me and give me a big bear hug. He pays me compliments all the time, boosting my confidence.'

Bobby was always likable, but always shrewd. He would talk about his budgies, pour champagne, and it would be the next day that everyone found out about the multi-million pound TV coup. He was an operator, but always more comfortable at their luxurious ten bedroom home in Denham, Buckinghamshire. The house and the grounds were extensive enough to require fulltime help. This was easily afforded. Staff were hired. But there was one condition of employment. The staff had to call Cilla by her 'real name' – Mrs Willis.

Also, having spoken to so many people around her and Bobby, it is clear that she would have thought it an affront to Bobby's decades of work for her if she had not gone on. It was his life's work. He was never Cilla's Svengali. He was her supporter. Mr and Mrs Robert Willis beat the statistics against marital longevity in showbusiness unions, where the temptations and separations are more prevalent than in the nine to five life. They led their lives almost like Siamese twins, never spending a night apart, other than for the births of their three sons, since their wedding on January 25, 1969. They are not unique in having a long, successful marriage. But it is so rare in a business where ego often edges love out of arrangements. But what is extraordinary about the Cilla and Bobby partnership is that they exclusively belonged to each other. Cilla's close friend Sir Paul McCartney lost his wife Linda to cancer. That couple's devotion to each other was complete. But there were others in both their lives. Watching Bobby and Cilla together or talking to those who worked with them and you knew there was no one else either could turn to.They loved and trusted each other. He finished her sentences. She started his. There were no other true confidantes. It was like telepathy.

They knew what was right for one another. It was not a grand, *Gone With Wind* romance but a wonderful, down-to-earth marriage, the sort of union that eludes so many. Despite their tremendous success they were so 'ordinary'. Of course, they could afford a lavish lifestyle, but there was not much that was 'precious' about them and so much that could have been. There has been great sadness for Cilla in the lonliness that followed Bobby's death. They had done everything together. But she has emerged from that as a 'new' woman, an independent, and still determined to succeed person. She admitted, 'I enjoy being single but I do miss Bobby terribly. He is my first and last thought of the day.'

Other than Bobby, the most important influence on Cilla's live was her mother Priscilla – 'Big Cilla' – who was 84 when she died. Despite her enormous success Cilla never lost the need for the approval of the mother she loved so deeply. Of the show she did the day after her mother died, she said, 'I wasn't being brave. I was being very much a coward. I was putting it off.' Now, both of her strongest supporters have gone. But she has her three sons. There is a pride amongst those of Cilla and Bobby Willis' generation in dealing with adversity with dignity. This pride has been evident in Cilla's achievements since

Bobby's death. Of course, Cilla and Bobby would think they would be letting each other down if they had behaved differently. Bobby Willis never disappointed Cilla Black.

Cilla is still proving herself worthy of his faith just as she always has. She did it when, in 2001, their eldest son Robert Junior, who had then taken to wearing a beard like his father, married his girlfriend, Fiona Crane at the same church where his father's funeral had taken place. The host of 'Blind Date' took on many of the preparations for the marriage at the family home of Robert to Fiona, a computer specialist. There were 130 guests and Cilla admits that Bobby Senior was tearfully missed, but she said, 'It was was a long and lovely day, and the youngsters finished with a fish and chip supper in the early hours. Fiona involved me in all the arrangements and I know Bobby would have been in his element seeing his eldest son tie the knot. Now, Robert is my best friend and my support. We never fall out. He keeps me in shape.'

As her manager, her son does just that. But it is a personal trainer who has helped he lose weight and tone her body – thanks to her son:

'It was Robert who found her. He was so embarrassed because he 'phoned a local fitness centre and asked for a recommendation for a personal trainer. But he said, very firmly, that it had to be a woman. It was only when he realised that they thought he was being a bit odd that he admitted it was for his dear old mum!

'I did not go on this health kick for vanity. It is as much for my sons as for me. When they lost their dad I realised that I as all they had left. I wanted to look after them. I didn't want them to become orphans. I need *all* of them to be married and settled before anything happens to me. I'm single and I'm a grey babe which is sort of cool. I'm much braver now because I have had to be. I thought I was invincible, infallible, but you find out you are not. It happens to all of us. And there is a good in that for it helps you face all your fears head on.'

On October 23, 2001, Cilla delivered another impeccable 'Blind

Date' performance at the London Television Centre which sits a golf chip away from the Thames. It was the second anniversary of the death of her husband, ' I was nervous. If anybody had said, "How are you feeling?" I know I would have lost it and we wouldn't have had a show. I thought that nobody had clicked what day that was. I thought, "Nobody knows what I am going through." They all did but they were such great actors they didn't let on. It turned out that the show went well. That night I went out to dinner with Joan Collins. We had a wonderful evening. When I got home I knew I had cracked the grief problem. I was pleased with myself and I knew Bobby would have been proud of me. Three days later had lunch with a girlfriend who had lost her husband. I was supportive saying all the right things. When I came home I just went and the tears swelled again. I had to go to bed. It was the worst day since Bobby had gone. I was annoyed with myself for I thought I had overcome the grief. I know now that I never will. I've resigned myself to understand that it will always be there and I'll never know when it is going to hit me. When it does, I just need to be left alone.

'Bobby did everything for me. All I have ever had to do is put on false eyelashes and go out and perform. When Bobby died I had to grow up very quickly. I used to say that I would retire if he died because I didn't want to do sub-standard work and I thought that, without him, I would quickly become sub-standard. I never thought I could do it without him. But I can and I do. It's what Bobby would have wanted. I was so loved and looked after. I didn't even know how to switch on the garden lights. I remember the day that I was told that Bobby had an inoperable tumour. I had gone back home and that night I had to walk the dogs, which was something I had never done before.

'I called Bobby in hospital and confessed, "I don't know how to walk the dogs." He said, "Don't worry. They know the way. They'll walk you."'

In 2002 she was re-recording *Step Inside, Love* a song written for one of her early television series by Paul McCartney. 'I practise my singing these days in the swimming pool house. I thought it was far enough away from the world until Robert came in and told me to keep down because the whole village could hear me'. But it was not her bestselling voice of the past, but her 21st Century personality, which yet again won over the moneymen at ITV in the same year. Astonishingly – well, certainly to the programme planners – their early evening football schedule, despite being hosted by the talented and popular Des Lynam, was a flop. The soccer was getting an audience of around four million viewers. When the panic stopped the ITV bosses invited Cilla to return to her 7p.m. Saturday night slot with *Blind Date*. The viewing figures doubled. Cilla, in her seventeenth year with the show, had shown up the Premiership. ITV1's overall Saturday evening peak-time audience also increased from 5.8 million to 7.2 million, which the network said was explained by the return of *Blind Date*. Cilla, as always, played the diplomat. She argued that her show's return to its peak-time slot was a victory for women viewers who wanted light entertainment, not football, on Saturday evenings. She admitted she was a keen football supporter herself, but suggested early Saturday nights were perhaps not the ideal slot for women who wanted to relax in front of the television.

In the Spring of 2002 *Blind Date* was regularly enjoying an audience of more than eight million viewers. And, like the series, Cilla says she has no plans to retire, 'The future's so bright, I'm wearing sunglasses.'

The image always arrives by chauffeured Rolls-Royce, for that's the sort of transport a national treasure requires – and no one has worked harder to become just that than Cilla Black. Sometimes it seems she is on television more than the news.

Often, she is the news. Her power, gained through the popularity of her television programmes, has made her a major player in the behind-the-scenes corporate world of showbusiness. Her extraordinary energy turned her into Mrs Saturday Night – the ratings heroine of what remains one of Britain's most watched programmes, *Blind Date*.

There have been other series, like the odd mix of candy-coated-bathos and sometimes controversy – *Surprise, Surprise!*, as well as seemingly endless guest spots and award shows and live pantomime and summer seasons. But Cilla's greatest claim to fame has been earned by her inspired hosting of a show arguably centred on whether or not a couple brought together for the prurience of millions of viewers *will or will not have sex*.

And if not, why not? And if so, how so? And how good? Or, in that marketing heaven of television coupling, how bad?

Always willing to have a giggle at herself and at the show's absurdity, with *Blind Date* Cilla Black established herself as one of Britain's wealthiest and most recognisable women; earning £65,000 an hour in 2002.

A showbusiness commuter for nearly forty years, Cilla has made all the right stops. During the 1960s, she was a pop sensation who had seventeen records in the UK hit parade. Her first hit, Lennon and McCartney's *Love of the Loved* reached number 21 on Elvis Presley's personal jukebox at Graceland, even though it only got to number 35 at home. She made fun and music with The Beatles – John Lennon saying unspeakable things about her white knickers, Ringo jiving with her mum, George Harrison and Paul McCartney writing special songs for her ...

Those were the heydays of London's King's Road and Carnaby Street, and Liverpool's clubland scene, where 'dolly birds' ruled the roost, with their lacquered, backcombed or Sassoon-scissored hair, gravity-questioning stilettos, startled Mary Quant eyes and plastic raincoats often set-off, not always happily, by the new mini-skirts. Other faces from those days surface every now and then for TV nostalgia trips or documentaries; some are fêted for still recalling how to do their Sixties make-up, others for the victory of simply being alive. Many have fallen victim to varying forms of over-indulgence, from designer drugs to designer Buddhism.

And yet Cilla is still here. In this world where anything and anyone can be yesterday's news before it even gets to midnight, there is no question that she is an ongoing phenomenon: as brassy and lively as ever.

'When I became a star at the ripe old age of twenty, I thought I had at most three years at the top,' is how she remembers it.

Others gave the stork-legged Liverpudlian six months – some, six weeks – and it was really only the tragic Brian Epstein, the man who made The Beatles and created the early Cilla, who had an inkling of the longevity of his 'girl singer'.

She was, he told anyone who questioned his judgement, 'the Edith Piaf of the future'. And famously he turned on an associate who in 1963 questioned her potential, telling him angrily, 'She is going to be one of the biggest stars in this country for the next thirty or forty years.'

If Cilla Black retires at sixty, in 2003, she will have fulfilled Epstein's prediction. It would have delighted him. To Epstein, she was the fifth Beatle – one of only five people he loved outside of his family. He said he would die for her, and in a way, he did, for her first television contract was in his arms as he slipped away in 1967 in his still-debated drug death. She maintains that the hugging of her contract proves he did not kill himself. He, like Cilla, wanted to go on for ever.

Cilla Black has undergone a remarkable metamorphosis since the days when Brian Epstein tried to devote as much time to her as he did to his other rather profitable enterprise, The Beatles. Although she never quite became an Edith Piaf figure or matched Shirley Bassey in the Divine Diva stakes, in her time Cilla was selling 100,000 records a day.

Now, on *Blind Date* the more swaggering contestants will try to put her down with wisecracks like, 'I hear you were once a *pop singer*.'

Without the pop and the culture that went with it, there would never have been Cilla Black. She was an integral part of one of the most potent eras of British entertainment – the Swinging Sixties.

The 1950s were all about restarting after World War Two, about *getting back* to the values and lifestyles which Hitler had so rudely interrupted. Pretty soon, however, there was a collective revolution against turning the clock back, and instead an unstoppable move to press the forward button into the 1960s – an era where everything seemed possible. At its most superficial, the 1960s proved a turning point in television: news readers were no longer required to wear dinner jackets or evening dress. What is more, the traditionally upper-class tones of broadcasting were also being invaded by the regions, by accent. Talking *differently* was not yet an asset – it just wasn't such a handicap any more.

The Liverpudlian accent, unfortunately, did not go down too well in London or Manchester or elsewhere. Cilla herself recalled, 'People outside hated us because of the way we spoke, specially the fellows, who were very guttural. If you asked for a drink in Blackpool or North Wales they'd throw you out of the pub.'

From early days she learned to speak differently.

Today Cilla Black doesn't sound like the Cilla Black we expect. When she talks about a 'lot of laughs' it is almost always transcribed in newspapers and magazine profiles as *a lorra laughs* – but this is in deference to what is expected rather than what is said. When her close friend Frankie Howerd died, certain newspapers reported that she had said goodbye to him in her local patois, 'Ta-ra, then, Chuck.' And if she had not, they reasoned she should have.

Cilla Black admits she is two different people. In this, at least, she is true to her stars. Respected astrologer Peter Watson, who works with the London *Evening Standard*, gave a rundown:

'Gemini is the butterfly of the zodiac, flitting from one experience to the next. The first of the air signs, it is associated with natural communicators who can take an idea at a moment's notice – and make it work.

'The razor-sharp Gemini mind can provide lightning responses and swift words or action. But one idea is often impatiently abandoned in favour of another.

'When they find their true vocation, however, they stick to it.

'They have a youthful approach to life and think on their feet. There is, however, a more secretive side to the typical Gemini that few people see. True, they can be party animals and like to be in the thick of things. But once the door is closed and they are within their own private world, they like to remain there, undisturbed and well away from prying eyes.

'They are popular, and although one side of their character is suited to a fairly sophisticated lifestyle, the other side is happier in a more down-to-earth environment.

'For a typical Gemini, look out for the fast reader, an easygoing personality or the person with beautiful, darting eyes. Look out too for someone who likes to combine the best of all worlds – fish and chips with champagne could be the perfect meal.

'At best a Gemini is enquiring, versatile, witty and friendly. At worst, deceptive, fickle, gossipy and cool.'

Peter Watson, who also does the star charts for the *Sunday Mirror*, explained: 'That is a general picture of a Gemini – and Cilla certainly fits.'

Her zodiac characteristics also match her times – fast to move forward and to change, and then a need to wonder about the wisdom of it. Astonishingly, she has not only taken her public with her, but has added to them. A couple of generations grew up with Cilla Black, while another couple still are doing so – some even planning their babies on television with her. For many of us she is a persistent reminder of all our yesterdays.

It takes a very special person to do this. *And continue to do it.*

Of course, success has its costs.

Tony Barrow was the Press Officer for Brian Epstein and worked with The Beatles and remains close to Cilla. He has always argued that the more you peel away the Cilla Black veneer, all you find is more Cilla.

She is a shrewd woman who has always been happy to play her part – if the price was right. We have been indoctrinated over the years, have been *told* that she is what we see: the working-class daughter of a docker and a market-trader, a pure pedigree Liverpool lass, a genuine Scouser and liver bird from the Catholic stronghold of Scotland Road – not like that John Lennon who came from upmarket Strawberry Fields. Of Strawberry Fields she says, 'That's the posh part of town – where I bought my mam her house. It was Paul, George and Ringo that were common like me.'

Such roots are an essential part of Cilla's career CV. Despite unfortunate early film experiences, she has developed into an exceptional actress, a consummate professional, and has kept it going. Her audience really believe they *know* her.

Oh, they know she's rich, that she's been a millionairess since she was twenty-five – when she celebrated by getting a new nose – that she rides around in a Rolls-Royce, drinks Moet and Chandon champagne, has a 17-acre 'garden' in Buckinghamshire and a mansion with enough loos for *Coronation Street* – or '*Correrś*' as she calls it, herself an avid fan. She explains to them 'When those electronic gates close behind me, I am just an ordinary housewife and mother.'

What makes her position today even more impressive is that she is self-educated in the politics of showbusiness. Her classroom was her family's front room, where she belted out *The Good Ship Lollipop* for the neighbours after the pubs closed on a Saturday night; her college, the madcap music scene of the Swinging Sixties.

In those days, her unmistakable voice was remarkably successful.

When Burt Bacharach was working with her and legendary Beatles producer George Martin on the recording of *Anyone Who Had a Heart*, he did twenty-three takes before Martin enquired:

'What are you after?' Bacharach replied, 'That little bit of magic.' The exasperated Martin told him, 'Oh, I think we got the magic on take three, don't you?'

Cilla had two number 1 hits and fifteen chart singles in the days when you had to sell 100,000 copies of a record a day to achieve a Top Twenty position. On *Juke Box Jury*, when asked to offer a verdict on *Anyone Who Had a Heart*, Pete Murray said her voice and the record were somewhat awful. But he voted it a 'Hit', saying 'Everyone in Liverpool will buy it.' He was wrong. The whole country went for it. Critic Johnny Rogan decided as late as 1997, 'If Cilla Black had died in 1967, she'd have been regarded as one of the greatest British singers of all time.'

Some have argued that there is no great secret to Cilla Black: what you see is what you get. Of course it's not that simple. In 1998 it is her hair (beneath the dye) that's white and her name that's Black. She has lived on her wits since she was a youngster who worked on her mother's secondhand clothes stall and was paid in sweet tea and buttered toast. The market-trader banter learned in her formative years pays off on *Blind Date*.

The contestants – the 'blinders' – can rarely get the better of her. What they don't know is how well she disguises her disdain for some of them. Or did until she got caught at an emotional awards evening jokingly cailing them 'idiots'. Of them she says publicly, 'Ninety-nine times out of a hundred they hate each other. They are all very flash, competitive types.'

What would be an apt description of her? Her biggest frustration is that she can never change how she looks. No matter how much money she makes, she will always be that working-class Liverpool lass, 'our Cilla'. It's there in her face and her figure – in her genes. She has great legs but a dumpy midsection. Close up, what's startling about her is her blue eyes. They're bright – and they never miss a trick. But as she flips through the glossy magazines and catalogues every night, the chic, well-bred images and lifestyles elude her. Money can't buy her that.

She is philosophical. And clever. When a Sunday newspaper published photographs of her on holiday – her figure flopping out of an inadequate swimsuit – she was mortified. Her anger was incredible. But on stage that same evening, she used it to advantage: 'I'd like to thank the *Sunday Mirror* for publishing my holiday snaps. It saves me getting mine developed at Boots ...'

A marvel at catching the moment and shaping it in her own favour, Cilla is an expert at triumph over adversity – but that and her increasing perfectionism has taken a heavy toll on her, and her family. She is a complex, sometimes troubled woman.

And always a contradiction. She says she saves butter wrappings (now more often low-fat spreads) to grease the baking trays at home, but she also loves expensive baubles and gems. And both loves and saves her memories, 'I just happened to make it in the Sixties and be mates with The Beatles who were ordinary guys.' With them she shares an *extra*ordinary story.

Of course, The Beatles disbanded. But Cilla sailed – and sails – on. Even though she is now a multi-millionairess, she would still be happy to open a supermarket every day – if her management didn't advise that it might be just a little over the top ...

Her fortune, fame and future are entwined with *Blind Date*, but she is there because of what she was, as much as who she is and who she still wants to be. When George Martin first met her all those yesterdays ago, he marked her down as 'this dolly rocker from Liverpool.'

Knighted Sir George in 1997, he now admits that Cilla proved him wrong. Very quickly. Cilla has been surprising people for four decades. The chauffeured image is of a British institution, an icon, a lovable figure. On British radio, broadcasters will introduce her records with, 'Here's Cilla' – reflecting a familiarity similar to Sinatra's glory days in Las Vegas when the billboards read: *He's Here*. Like Sinatra's fans, Cilla's public feel she's their best friend. Over the years she has learned to play that role.

The power of her popularity enables her to bargain with the major decision-makers of British television which, with the digital revolution going on, is ever-changing and greatly in need of mass audiences. Programming, marketing and advertising decisions involving millions of pounds are made around Cilla Black, her wishes – and her demands. The television world accepts and mostly admires that, although one TV executive – albeit with a smile – revealed that she and her husband Bobby Willis could be a handful to deal with.

Willis, her teenage sweetheart, was there for her from the start of her career; with their three sons they made a strong family unit. She has always said that she could never have achieved what she has 'without Bobby'. He provided her with much needed support. They existed for each other. There is – she says it is apocryphal – a story that when she's working she even calls the camera 'Bobby'. The pair both grew up in Liverpool, he gave up his songwriting for her, and as a team they conquered almost everything for which they strove. They both claimed that work and marriage were hard but rewarding work. They always gave their all, were ultimately professional, and asked for the same in return. Sometimes that resulted in a *demanding* image.

In the Sixties, Brian Epstein, or 'Eppy' as she called him, first encountered this 'demanding' trait in Cilla, the girl who wanted to pull off that clever trick of living her life and understanding it. At London Weekend Television, it is the same story. LWT is Cilla's corporate 'home', it broadcasts *Blind Date* – one of the most valuable properties on television and, like its host, part of the national heritage. Cilla says of the series, 'It's what makes Britain great.' An LWT executive allowed: 'She can be a monster. But she gets her way and she always will while she delivers the audience. And she keeps doing that. They try other people, other acts and formats, but no one comes close to the numbers she gets.'

Cilla's peers take a different view. They see her as a winner – and a loyal friend. Cliff Richard, (as a teenager she says she lusted after his 'raw sexuality') believes their friendship is important, 'What we have should never be mucked about with. We all go through our lives and have relationships which work or fail or change, and we learn to live with it.

'Most showbusiness friendships are pretty loose, but Cilla and I are compatible. We've worked together a heck of a lot but we don't socialise much so it's based on our mutual respect as artistes. In our industry that's not a bad way to start a friendship.'

With Cliff Richard, she has worked for charities, notably for the orphans of Chernobyl. In 1997 she led a successful appeal for Wycombe Hospital near her home in Buckinghamshire. All who know her well, and most of them have stayed around over the decades, applaud her loyalty. When her close friend Frankie Howerd was seriously ill in hospital, she tried to get into the Harley Street Clinic in London without being spotted by the Press crowd waiting for details of the comedian's condition. She was brave about the imminent death of one of her dearest friends, 'He must be all right because he tried to kiss me. I am praying for him.'

She *is* loyal. And she says she is true to her Gemini star sign. But has she been and is she true to *herself*? And to a Britain that she says she – and her values and television productions – accurately reflect?

For a great chunk of the 20th, and now the 21st,century she has been a mirror of mass popular tastes, from the innocent days when she says The Beatles wouldn't swear in front of her to today when, cynically, we might argue that there is no innocence to applaud – or to lose. Cilla Black and her vehicle, *Blind Date*, are loud, brassy and powerful manifestations of the times – a part of modern history.

Of the people on her most popular show she says, 'Every bone in my body aches for them. Number two might look like Quasimodo but have an incredibly, sexy velvet voice and you *know* she's going to pick him.'

Hard-headed, professional, money-minded but also faithful to her modest roots, caring and big-hearted, a devoted mother, wife and friend, Cilla then emphatically points out:

'Having said that, I'm in the business of making a good television show and the audience just love it when she *does* pick Quasimodo ...'

## *Chapter One*

# THE SCOUSE THAT ROARED

*'Fame is all I wanted since I was three years old.'*
-CILLA BLACK, 1994

Cilla has always been businesslike. Her life roars along like a movie script, and the way she talks of her Liverpool childhood it sounds like an Ealing Studios comedy, and perhaps there's something to the spirit of that. The city was cruelly hammered by German air raids during World War Two but the blitz on Merseyside was over by the time Priscilla Maria Veronica White was born at the city's Stanley Hospital on 27 May 1943.

Scouse resilience and humour had kept the city and families like the Whites together. Depressed housing conditions had been aggravated by the bombs, with thousands of homes destroyed or damaged, utilities regularly ruptured. They say you have to be a comedian to live in Liverpool and it certainly helped then: it's the place Ken Dodd calls 'Mirthyside'. In the 1960s, the once world-renowned seaport was known for the Grand National, football, The Beatles and Cilla Black. Liverpool is a city remembered by those who have escaped it with a rosy glow. Like ex-pat Scotsmen who want to put a kilt on everything, those who have left Liverpool want to recall it as one party of laughs after another. Bleak memories of poverty in a city scarred by war, of long working hours in poor conditions, are lost in jokes and fondness for an exuberant place that has triumphed against the odds – like Cilla herself.

It was Liverpool Docks that gave birth to the blues – and lots of other music, but most importantly for Cilla Black, it was what gave the Merseybeat the edge,
made it the 'happening' sound as the 1950s noisily began rocking into the 1960s.

She grew up with her older brothers George and John listening to 78s of Sinatra and Dean Martin on the ten-stack record player (younger brother Alan sang along with his brothers' musical choices) in the comparatively large front room of the family home at 380 Scotland Road. 'Scottie' Road was a colourful environment with a massive, outgoing Irish-Catholic population in a rough and tumble area of the city. It was 1954 before the Council put a bathroom in the family house, and until then, the Whites made do with an outside lavatory and a tin bath in front of the kitchen stoves – or the 'wash all over' at the nearby Council run Borough baths, with endless hot water available on Monday, Wednesday and Friday for men and Tuesdays and Thursdays for the ladies. The Council didn't work at weekends.

Cilla had been named after her mother, so she was 'Little Priscilla', a lively toddler bouncing around in rooms above a barber's shop and with a Chinese laundry next door. This precocious little girl still stood out in a neighbourhood which had a pub, and customers, on every corner shouting for attention.

Some with long memories recall she 'had more cheek than anyone' and 'could talk people into anything' and 'was a devil until she got her own way.' She admits, 'I was a horrible, horrible child.'

Her father John, a docker's docker and a man's man of few words, with his own chair in the front room and his own way of doing and dealing with things, adored her. His catch-all way of protecting his family from harm was, like so many of their friends and neighbours, an insistence that they all went to Mass *every* Sunday.

Cilla's father had worked in construction for eight years in London; he helped build the Dorchester Hotel, where his daughter would years later be fêted at tea and sumptuous dinners. John White, a strong, handsome man, was known as a character, a 'bit of a lad'. His wife would smile at their children and say, 'I don't know what your dad got up to in London.'

London then was like abroad, like the Moon, a long way away. But John White, nine years older than his wife, had the confidence of a man who had been places. He was a creature of habit: every Sunday morning the family went to Mass; every Sunday afternoon he and his wife locked their bedroom door. Later, when his daughter changed her surname from White to Black – the reason still a piece of Trivial pop Pursuit – he goodnaturedly accepted the teasing of his workmates, who taunted him with, 'He doesn't know whether he's coming or going, whether he's White or Black.' It was his mixture of warmth and stoicism which allowed Cilla and her brothers a good atmosphere to grow up in:

'I had a very happy childhood in Liverpool and never realised how poor we were until much later because everyone else was in the same boat. The barber's shop next door (via a connecting staircase) was really our front door. I remember my mother sitting on the stairs crying because the Council came round to the flat and said they could do the place up. That meant we weren't getting a council house and my mam always longed for her own front door.' Years later when Cilla bought her a house, her mother complained because there wasn't a bus stop outside!

'They talk about women's lib but my mother was a forerunner of that. She brought up four of us, ran a business and she always seemed to be there. At home I only ever remember laughter even on Monday mornings when Mam was doing the washing in the big sink. You couldn't call it a kitchen, it was more a passageway. She used to wash all the sheets by hand, put them through the mangle, and she'd be singing away in this incredible soprano.

'But I wanted to be a film star. Well, we didn't have any famous singers then, did we? And in our family we only saw television once in a blue moon, like the Coronation or something. I was always up for a star turn and singing provided the spotlight – I sang in the dockers' Christmas show until they banned me for winning three times in a row ...

'The Protestant school used to run a play centre after school. It was only attended by Catholics. Every day they had a talent competition with a real microphone and I'd get up and say: "My name is Priscilla Maria Veronica White and I'm going to sing *When The Moon Hits Your Eye Like a Big Pizza Pie*. (Dean Martin's *That's Amore*) I thought it was *piece of pie*, which made sense to me. I just wanted to sing – and I'd still do it today for nothing I got so much pleasure – and I could win prizes.'

Winning things was easier than buying them, 'I'm not used to money. And I can't bear to handle the stuff. If I push a credit card across a counter it makes it easier for me not to think about the amount I am spending. I was brought up with total thrift. Those are my roots, my standards. And no matter how rich I become, I will never get away from them. When I was a little girl I remember my mother scraping the butter off the paper until it was bone dry. Then she would fold up the paper and keep it for lining a baking tin. When I'm abroad I still haggle in the markets. I've got all my clothes, going back to the Biba days, in an extraordinarily big loft. I'm a hoarder. At school we were always taught about thrift.

'My first day at school was horrendous. I couldn't understand why my mother was dumping me off at this strange place. As the only girl at home, I was spoiled and kind of clingy, so it was all extra traumatic.

One of my plaits came undone and it seemed like the end of the world. I was crying, "Please don't leave me, I don't want to go." Though I should have been used to it, because I'd gone to nursery school.

'Like my brothers, I went to St Anthony's, a Catholic school near Scottie Road. We had to give donations for the privilege of attending and buy all our own books, pencils, everything. I was there from the age of five till I left at fifteen. Sister Marie Julie, the headmistress, was a tiny old lady, like a penguin in glasses, the terror of the school. I was always fighting to be one of the boys, but they didn't want to know – I'm still more comfortable with men than women. But from the age of eleven we were taught separately and had different playgrounds. I was quite popular at school, very much a tomboy and always the practical joker.'

The nuns did not always appreciate the humour, especially Sister Marie Julie who was in charge of discipline. Cilla thought if you can't beat 'em ... 'I did think seriously at fourteen of becoming a nun. We'd been to a nuns' convention and I'd admired their serenity and calmness.

'I soon realised I was just attracted by the outfit – dressing up and having people being sort of reverent towards you. I was a natural show-off and must confess to experiencing six of the cane twice at school. It wasn't that I was a bad child, but I was always fooling around making the kids laugh when we should have been working. As Sister Marie Julie did say, "You're very foolish, Priscilla, because you know there's a gun out there, and you are the bullet!" – meaning that the others were egging me on.

'Once I played Julius Caesar and wore a dress which buttoned all down the front. As I reposed in my toga, the whole class burst out laughing, because the buttons had come undone, and there was I showing off "next week's washing". I loved that – I was always glad of any reaction.

'At thirteen I dyed my hair with a Camilla-tone sevenpenny rinse from Woolworths. My Aunt Vera had auburn hair and I wanted to look like her. You were supposed to mix it with a couple of pints of water and then rinse continually over a bowl, but though I hadn't done chemistry it didn't take me long to realise that if I mixed it to a paste and painted it on with a toothbrush I'd get a much stronger colour – I left it on for hours and hours. At school next day word went round that Priscilla Maria Veronica White had gone all of a sudden from pale-blondish-mousy hair to bright red – bright orange, really. It caused an uproar in the class.

'The teacher, Sister Marie Julie, sat me underneath the window where the sun shone in, which was the best thing she could have done to me. I was in the spotlight, you see, and thought it was terrific. Looking back, I must have been a dreadful child. My mother never made a fuss. I was always spoiled and I guess she thought, "Red hair, what the hell?" It had been fair before, a really boring old colour.'

Her take-a-chance mentality – her Gemini instincts, jumping from one pursuit to another, the edge which she has always pulled or been pulled back from – found an outlet on the playing fields,

'I loved all sports. After swimming lessons, they'd herd us out of the pool bashing a long bamboo pole and I'd take my life into my own hands – always the last one out.'

Her swimming skills made her a lifesaver. Her schoolfriend Mrs Colette McLean recalls, 'We all used to go to the swimming baths and once I had my kid sister, Jackie, with me. She was learning to swim and the pool was very crowded. She got out of her depth and Cilla heard her screaming. She jumped in and held up her head. Jackie was very frightened and Cilla was the first to react.'

Her *Blind Date* audience may not conjure her up as a sporting heroine but Cilla insists she was, 'I was assistant shooter in netball and we always beat the opposition and got quite big-headed, until one day we walked into another school and it was awesome. The girls there were like the Harlem Globetrotters – we never got a look-in.

'Right until the age of fifteen our class teacher taught us everything apart from music. We didn't study things like chemistry and we never had any homework. English was my best subject. My compositions were incredible because I had such a vivid imagination, but I always lost marks for grammar because I wrote how I spoke, which was totally wrong. I loved all the Enid Blyton books and I read *Alice in Wonderland* over and over again. The local library was a godsend. At one point I tried to teach myself Spanish but the only thing I remember is *el burro* for donkey.

'We had books at home but they were all propping up the chimneybreast and my dad papered over them. In a way I feel very robbed of education as a child because there were forty-eight in my class, and I know if we'd had smaller classes I'd have been up there with the best – I'd have definitely stood a chance, anyway. I was terribly happy at school, but when I went into the big world I realised how much education I'd missed.'

Her parents had raised her to believe in the Church's protection and charity; they applied its teachings to day-to-day life. For a young Cilla the Church had a more secular effect, especially on her diet, 'Religion was always a big thing. My mother would go to Mass at 7 a.m., then my father and the lads at noon. You weren't allowed to eat before Communion. The smell of eggs and bacon and finnan haddock was so tempting I'd go at 9 a.m. – then I could have breakfast.

'We were forever going to church and I still love all the hymns. But Confession was a frightening thing. When I was eleven I ate a crumbled Oxo cube on half an orange. I know it sounds weird but it was delicious. It was forbidden then to eat any meat on a Friday, and when I confessed to the priest that I'd partaken of this Oxo cube, I lied and said I'd thrown most of it away because I was terrified of what he'd do. Afterwards, I asked a friend's mother what she thought, and she said it was the worst sin I'd ever committed in my life, lying to the priest under Confession. I thought I'd be excommunicated. So

I went back that same night in tears, told him the truth, and had to say the whole rosary as penance. It was very traumatic.'

Her reaction came from her strict, loving and often typical working-class background; you either went off the rails in a major way or stuck straight to them. The backbone of her beliefs – certainly her work ethic – remains from her upbringing. She was comfortable in a male-dominated family, three brothers and a father who took that role seriously. He was the law. Everyone knew it.

So was the Church. Father Tom Williams, the parish priest of St Anthony's Church said, 'The White family were just one of us. Cilla's mother came to us until she wasn't well enough to.'

The Church and family life were the foundations of Cilla's childhood, and had a great influence on her adult life. Her later charity work and fund-raising for hospitals and medical foundations were in-built. The community she grew up in worked on a value system, which began with helping the folk next door and keeping the family as close as possible, 'Every Sunday when I was a kid I used to go round to my nanny and grandad's house. He'd be sitting by the black-leaded fireplace with his pipe. My mother – had six sisters and one brother, and there were millions of us grandchildren. I'd come bounding in and he'd say, "Which one are you?" I'd say, "I'm Little Cilla, Big Cilla's girl." There was always a stockpot on the fire and home-made bread. My nanny was a saint, so placid, she was incredible. I was mad about doing people's hair and she'd always let me do hers.

'When I was growing up it was a totally different era. We really had respect for the older generation. When my brother was in the Army, if he went in the pub and saw my dad he'd walk straight out. I once went to the pictures with my mam, and her mam and dad were there. She was smoking and she said, "Oh, there's Dad," and put her cigarette out. *My* father was a very quiet man but I knew when he was upset. We used to say, "Dad's got a cob on." But he rarely raised his voice and I was never, ever smacked. In the middle of the week we'd always have *scouse*, which is basically Irish stew. When I was about fourteen I got a bit above myself. I said, "*I'm* not eating scouse." For the first time in my life – I was the apple of his eye – my father was annoyed with me. He told my mother, "If she doesn't eat it don't give her anything else." His word was law and that was that. It was his way of slapping me back but it was rare.

'He'd work nights at the docks, sleep during the day and get up in the evening. I got home from school about 4.40 p.m. and, as usual, I'd be singing. He'd ask my mother to get me to pipe down but he never shouted.'

Young Cilla learned a calmness from her father; she observed that you could maintain control by imposing your wishes rather than shouting and screaming. A quiet determination is always more effective than tantrums.

In those early days, Cilla was a showbusiness fanatic. She was and is the fan's fan. She thinks there is nothing greater than a star, 'I was always into music and bought my first record at thirteen – *I'm Not a Juvenile Delinquent* by Frankie Lymon and The Teenagers. I was also mad on collecting autographs. Liverpool was a very big theatre city and we'd go from one theatre to thc next and hang around the stage-door waiting for the stars. Often I'd send my book in to be signed, but I met people like Dickie Valentine and was thrilled out of my mind to meet Frankie Vaughan.

'I just wanted fame like that. That's all I wanted since I was three years old. One night my mam and dad stood me on the kitchen table and I sang *The Good Ship Lollipop*. For the first time in my life I got applause and I was hooked. I wanted the applause. I have done ever since.'

Her father was a regular at a pub called 'Fitzies' which stood like a goodwill beacon on nearby Bostock Street. There, you bought your round and every couple of weeks it was back to your place for a

'Jarsout', a singsong and a 'Judas', a carryout of drinks to lubricate it. Cilla remembers, 'Everybody had to do a turn. They'd bring in pigs' feet and fish and chips. My Dad would get in shandy for my mother and aunties. The most my mam would have would be a shandy; it was not the thing for women to drink. The men would drink Guinness. I was meant to be in bed but from the age of three I'd creep in and nobody was angry. I'd be in my pyjamas singing *My Old Man Said Follow the Van* and loving it.'

Market-trader Vera Davies – mother of Cilla's friend and autograph-hunting partner in the Liverpool clubs, Billy Davies – remembered, 'When we went to her mother's home she would always act and sing and do things to make you laugh. She'd take off Hylda Baker who was a big name then. She'd do anything. Even then she had a powerful voice – but her mam was a better singer.'

Cilla agrees, 'My mother could easily have been in showbusiness. She poured all her ambition into me. She never tired of me, never told me to shut up. Later on, when I started singing in the clubs I'd come in every night saying, "I'm going to be a star." She never put me down. She'd say, "Of course you are!" She always made me feel I could do anything.'

This confidence has never left Cilla. She can deal with an over-eager fan in the tearoom of the Dorchester Hotel, or thoroughly engage a live television talk-show audience – totally charming Michael Parkinson on his return to the format in 1998 – and, it seems, not miss a beat. It all goes back to her solid upbringing and the support and encouragement of her family.

From the moment he met her, Bobby Willis offered that same support. Unlike so many of the other boys hanging around, he was telling Cilla what he had to give, not what he wanted to take. It was an unusual set-up in those early days of macho Liverpool, and Cilla appreciated the feeling of having a steady arm to lean on. Bobby Willis was always sensible and careful, especially with the detail, and retained his total faith in Cilla. It is that family background, boosted by Bobby Willis, that has propelled her over the years, often to heights she could never have envisaged.

Without Willis to take the time to consider offers, to establish Cilla's commitment to a project – it is her nature to want to take on everything at once – there is every chance that Cilla might have overstretched herself. She is a person who finds it difficult to say no, either to a friend or to a spotlight. Performing is, as she says, what she *does*. Bobby, who came from a similar but harsher background, always understood his wife's need to get going, get on – and finally, probably, both to escape the hardships of a working-class childhood.

Another important influence on Cilla, and training ground for her future in showbusiness was her mother's secondhand clothes stand, situated in a coveted spot at St Martin Market. After school, Cilla would help out, supping up the sweet tea, the atmosphere and the banter. She could encourage those a little slow to buy, deflate the too pushy ... it was another classroom. A place where she learned the art of riposte.

'My mam ran a business and she wanted it to be the best. Even before she met my father she had a stall on the market and she was ambitious for all of us. She'd buy clothes from private houses and if I wasn't at nursery she used to take me collecting with her. If I smell roses now it takes me back because we'd go over on the Ferry to New Brighton. We'd go to the posh places in Queensferry and Birkenhead. We'd walk down those roads with big houses and lovely big gardens. We only had a back yard. My mother had her regular clients and when Biba came along she went into Thirties' gear. She was known as a dealer.

'Market people are a special breed, very strong, very funny, nothing fazes them.

'My mam had her contacts. She knew Frances Maitland who was a well-known antiques dealer in Roscommon Street. Once I'd made some money she would point out "investments" to me. I've got a Charles II dining table, ten chairs and a sideboard worth a fortune thanks to Frances.'

But as both Cilla and Liverpool were nudging forward into the 1960s it was the New World's offerings rather than antiques which most intrigued the young girl.

In the lively postwar years, Liverpool, where the first direct shipping links with New York had been established, was receiving early imports of American sounds before the rest of Britain because of the US ships docking there. The Merseyside crowd were listening to American records before they reached UK shops: Ella Fitzgerald and Nat King Cole were getting almost as familiar as home-town entertainers like Arthur Askey and Tommy Handley.

Cilla was part of the generation who wanted to be 'with it', to be 'hip', and the time and the place were perfect. The group called The Teenagers, especially lead singer Frankie Lymon, had overtaken Shirley Temple in Cilla's musical tastes. And she and her friends were all wearing jeans, just like The Teenagers, and dancing romantically to The Platters, whenever they could afford it, at the Locarno or Grafton dance halls. Cilla is still remembered for dancing faster than anyone. She also bought dresses from C&A but was so desperate to be noticed that she would wear them back to front in a look-at-me style.

While the local strict-tempo dancing palais were still popular, the youngsters of Liverpool – and elsewhere – were struggling to find their own music. Trad jazz had its fans but was being overtaken by skiffle and the Lonnie Donegan sound. Meanwhile, doctor's son Alan Sytner was about to transform the music scene in Liverpool and, in turn, the world. He ran jazz nights at the Temple restaurant in Liverpool, but didn't enjoy the ambience. Having found exactly what he wanted at a club called 'Le Caveau' by the Seine in Paris, he decided to recreate it in the basement of 10 Mathew Street near Liverpool city centre and call it the Cavern Club.

What had been a wartime air-raid shelter and then a wine cellar was in 1956 being used to store electrical equipment. Mathew Street, home to tall, crumbly Victorian warehouses and fruit and vegetable lorries, was in for a shock. A loud one. On 16 January 1957, The Cavern opened to the sound of the Merseysippi Jazz Band. The club was jammed with 600 people; about another 1,500 lined up but failed to get in. This was at a time when the British music business was nothing more than a branch office for American companies: their purpose was to make US records available in the record shops. They had no structure to deal with a British artiste or act which became popular and actually sold records!

Lonnie Donegan and skiffle were selling – and playing at The Cavern. The doorway of the club was lit by one bare bulb; eighteen stone steps went down into the black-painted cellar which was split into three areas by archways. It was a bubble of smoke, sweat, bad lavatories and good dancing – with the kind of music that everyone wanted to hear. It was a template for British clubs of the Sixties – hell-holes that fans fought and paid to get into. *And loved.*

The Cavern, which was turned into a car park in the 1980s by a Liverpool City Council ignorant of the value of nostalgia, was primitive but already legendary by the time Priscilla White was just about to leave school. She began hanging around the clubs, splitting her time between the Iron Door and The Cavern. The BBC supremo John Birt remembers queuing up to get into The Cavern while Cilla was taking the coats. So does former MP Edwina Currie, 'I'd sneak off from school for the lunchtime music sessions and Cilla was there working – and listening to the music.'

Her schoolfriend Jean Prendergast, who recalls being punished at St Anthony's for kicking Cilla ('she wouldn't do my sums for me'), later became her friend, 'She used to take a crowd of us regularly to the Cavern Club. She'd get us in free because she knew the doorman. I remember her singing there. She looked the part, wearing a feathered headband. We had no money then even for the bus. The crowd of us would usually walk home. We loved it.'

In those innocent days when children still played on the streets and teenagers could wander around at night without threat, Cilla would also be allowed by her parents to stay for the all-night jam sessions at The Cavern. After all, Priscilla and John White were music lovers themselves, with a home piano bought from the North End Music Store (NEMS) in Walton Road, Everton, which was owned by Brian Epstein's parents Harry and Queenie. Paul McCartney's family also bought their piano there.

Cilla explains, 'Liverpool was like a village in those days. And I was so career-minded: it was more opportunity to sing, to perform. Everyone knew everyone. I remember Ringo saying to me one night, "Hey, those two old girls over there can really dance." I looked and it was my mam and her friend Vera Davies having a jive.

Although she had left, Cilla was still a schoolgirl at heart. 'A best moment in school was winning *Aesop's Fables* for "extremely good attendance" – just being there – which shows how poor attendance was for everybody else. But I really loved school and never missed a day.

'It was terrible leaving. If I could have chained myself to the railings like a suffragette, I would have done so. I went straight up to my bedroom when I got home and cried till teatime. It could even be part of my epitaph one day, "Here lies Cilla Black – her schooldays were the happiest days of her life."'

English was her best subject, and her final, rather uninspired and now yellowing report from St Anthony's reads*: Priscilla is suitable for office work*.

Not quite. Shortly after that was written, Jimmy Tarbuck told her to 'piss off' and Cliff Richard did a runner on her and John Lennon gave her a chance. A little later Omar Sharif, then regarded as the sexiest man in the world, tried to tempt her into bed and take her virginity.

## *Chapter Two*

# LOVE ME DO

*'He asked me if I'd mind singing with The Beatles.'*
– CILLA ON MEETING BRIAN EPSTEIN

An electric atmosphere swamped Liverpool clubland as Cilla set about finding herself a job. She never aspired to being a superstar secretary but took her school's advice and spent a year at Anfield Commercial College. Although she was more interested in music and the musicmakers than typing, she nevertheless thumped the keys at college, got her shorthand up to 80 wpm and as a stage-struck 16-year-old found herself employed as a filing clerk for British Insulated Calendar Cables, a company not even as exciting as it sounds. When she was typing she sat by a small sliding window in the Stanley Street offices where she could glance out at her world and dream. Sometimes friends would 'visit' at the window.

At lunchtime Cilla would go to The Cavern with Pat Davies, a new friend she had made – and was to keep. They were as inseparable as twins. Pat Davies was good at needlework and a wizard on the sewing machine, and with material they bought together from John Lewis she created their fashions. 'I'd make

Cilla a green frock with orange accessories and I'd have an orange frock with green accessories,' says Pat, who in the 1990s was living in New York.

She says of those early days, 'We didn't do drugs or drink. We were just happy with clothes and music. We'd meet at The Cavern at lunchtime and plan what we were going to do that night.'

Cilla worked at The Cavern every lunch-hour. She got 'five bob', the equivalent of twenty-five pence, and a snack consisting of bread and medicinal-smelling tomato soup, for washing-up and waitressing, earning extra tips for hanging up the coats. Later, American magazines would describe her as a 'hatcheck girl at The Cavern.' 'It was ever so funny – people in Liverpool would only wear hats when they went to church and certainly not at The Cavern.' Sometimes in the evenings Cilla would work at the Zodiac Club, an all-night coffee bar and resting spot for those who couldn't or wouldn't sleep, where groups returning from out-of-town gigs would sit around and discuss their performances.

There was lots of jiving and rocking 'n' rolling going on. And not just at the clubs. At the cinema there was Bill Haley in *Rock Around the Clock* and Elvis in Jailhouse Rock. On Radio Luxembourg the disc jockeys like Pete Murray and Jack Jackson were playing Little Richard and Chuck Berry. On television, programmes like *Cool for Cats*, *The 6.5 Special* and *Oh, Boy* were delighting younger viewers. American acts touring Britain included hitmakers like Bill Haley and The Comets and, in a landmark for the Merseyside sound, a great boost to the aspiring musicmakers there, Buddy Holly performed at the Liverpool Philharmonic on 20 March 1958, around the time Cilla was leaving school.

Billy Fury was in the swivel-hip business and so were Johnny Kidd and The Pirates, their *Please Don't Touch* in the summer of 1959 a major development. Nine months earlier Cliff Richard had won a hit and a giant audience with *Move It*. Cliff Richard is two years older than Cilla. She says that in those days you either went for Cliff or Elvis, not both. Ever practical, she fancied Cliff ('an older man') over Elvis, who she believed would never visit Britain (she was right).

She was also still the most ardent of fans. It was her own sometimes thwarted attempts at face-to-face hero worship that have made her a strong supporter of her own fan club; she is always willing to make personal appearances at their meetings. It goes back to events like her first night out with Cliff Richard – or, more accurately, her star-struck attempt at an evening with the number one British heart-throb of the day. She's reported that after Cliff appeared at the Liverpool Philharmonic, she and a friend followed a taxi she thought he was in. It resulted in acute adolescent disappointment: in the cab were Cliff's group The Shadows and a little Liverpool comedian called Jimmy Tarbuck.

Cliff had already arrived at Tarbuck's parents' home. Her friend Patti Abraham says she recalls exactly what happened that night: 'Cliff drove off in a bottle-green sports car and – you won't believe this – we jumped into a taxi and told the driver, "Follow that car!" Cilla was still at college – the cab fare was going to cost me a week's wages. But I didn't care, we were both too excited. We finished up miles away at what turned out to be Jimmy Tarbuck's parents' home. Cliff had gone inside by the time we pulled up in the taxi.

'We waited outside and then The Shadows arrived – Hank Marvin got out first – and they were really nice and gave us their autographs. When the door opened to let them in we saw Cliff in the hall. But then Jimmy came out and told us where to go …

'We went, but it didn't put us off autograph hunting. Cilla was desperate to meet Frankie Lymon and The Teenagers. We tried to get into their hotel. We thought we'd go and maybe get a coffee and see them but the commissionaire wouldn't let us in. We hung about and managed to see them off to the station when they left. I carried one of their bags. We thought it was marvellous. And, of course, we got their autographs. It was a lot of fun – we did have fun then.

'We went out one night with two lads. I was staying at Cilla's and they took us home. She was standing at the corner of the street with one lad and I was standing in the passageway of her home with the other lad.

'Suddenly, Cilla's mam came out. "Get in here," she said to me. "And where's the other one?" She spotted Cilla with her boy. With that Cilla came along in a big white stick-out skirt. Her mum could have murdered us. And all Cilla could say was, "Mam, they're altar boys." Her mother got us up for Mass next morning.'

For every youngster but especially one so ambitious to be a star, these were tremendous times. Being a Liverpudlian meant, by definition, being trendy. Everything and everyone from Merseyside was exciting, and Cilla found herself running around what was becoming the hippest place on earth. There were more than 300 Merseyside rock groups; the Merseybeat was everywhere. One such group was led by Teddy 'Kingsize' Taylor, a butcher's boy who was 6 feet 5 inches tall and weighed in at 22 stone. Cilla adored him. She sang with Kingsize Taylor and the advertising cards – now collectors' items – read:

*Presenting …*

KINGSIZE TAYLOR
AND THE DOMINOES
WITH SWINGING CILLA

She became known as Taylor's girl. It was a teen romance she's long forgotten, but those with fond memories of the time recall Cilla and Kingsize being literally a 'heavy' item. The group, incidentally, were one of the first Merseyside groups to record in 1957–8.

The Beatles, with Pete Best on drums, were often playing as The

Quarry Men down at the Casbah Club, which was also a haunt of The Searchers, The Undertakers, The Merseybeats, Faron's Flamingos and The Swinging Blue Jeans, who had metamorphosed from the skiffle group The Swinging Bluegenes – which was run by Best's mother, Mona. Ringo Starr was playing with Rory Storm and The Hurricanes. Gerry and The Pacemakers were the leading group in town, The Searchers a close second to them.

It seemed that these days, to make it in Liverpool, you had to be in a band. Cilla found herself not so much *in* one, but singing with lots of them. No one had much money; it was all pretty much hand-to-mouth stuff: groups would load their instruments and equipment on to a number 10 or number 17 bus to get around the city!

Ringo Starr, whose stage uniform then was a hand-me-down red suit, laughs at this but Cilla says she was 'very shy' and would never ask a group if she could sing with them. It was her friends who did it for her. She says, 'the groups would look at you as if you'd gone berserk if you asked to sing with them. Why should they let some daft bird come on stage? But all my mates knew I could sing and they would chant, "Let Cilla have a go."'

Chief cheerleader was Pauline Behan (then girlfriend of George Harrison, later wife of Gerry Marsden of Gerry and The Pacemakers) who, being friendly with Harrison, had more influence than most.

Cilla's chance came out of a lucky moment, when Rory Storm and The Hurricanes agreed to let her sing. At the Iron Door club, bass guitarist and Buddy Holly lookalike Wally Johnson handed her the microphone, 'He was laughing – they all were – but I belted out Peggy Lee's *Fever* and they were quite impressed and asked me to sing again. It was a bit of light relief and let Rory and Wally have a rest.

'Ringo thinks I was a bit flash and that I really wanted to sing. I *did*, but honestly, I had to be persuaded. I never rehearsed and used to say "What do you know?" or, "I'll do what you know in your key."

That was difficult in Rory's band because they could only play in one key – and it certainly wasn't mine!'

The club circuit joke was that Cilla would sing in 'Yale key' just to get a microphone in her hand.

Ringo Starr had his own concerns. Rory Storm, whose real name was Alan Caldwell, was a true Merseyside character, a publicity-hungry, gold-booted Rod Stewart of his time; his group could command £25 a week playing at Butlins Holiday Camp at Skegness. Rory, had given Ringo a precious slot titled 'Ringo Starr-time' and Ringo was anxious about the threat of another vocalist in the group – especially when she wanted to perform *his* song *Boys*.

Cilla remembers, 'Ringo and I used to have fights about doing *Boys*. It was a girl's song. We did it as a duet and even then he didn't concede anything. He used a microphone over his drums and I used to have to sing it bent over his drumkit.'

Rory Storm would encourage her, but he was one of the tragic figures of the era. His sister Iris, who married pop star Shane Fenton (later renamed Alvin Stardust), says that Rory was happy being 'the King of Liverpool' but he died shortly after his father in 1972. He was found dead with his mother who, the inquest established, had taken pills after finding her son's body which was full of alcohol and enough drugs to have caused his death. Nearly three decades later, friends and family have come to terms with it as an accidental tragedy.

When Cilla sang with him, Rory Storm had everything to live for, 'I used to travel to the different clubs in the van with the boys and all the equipment. I'd be dressed in a tight skirt and a cardigan buttoned up. It was all about rock 'n' roll bands – not Ruby Murray and Alma Cogan. At first The Cavern was better known for traditional jazz – when I first went on a Thursday night it was all modern jazz. The Cavern wasn't the first club where all the rock 'n' roll began. It really started in places like the Iron Door.'

The Iron Door, a crowded coffee-and-music cellar in Temple Street, a short walk away from The Cavern was *the* important, magical place for Cilla, where it all began ...

The club crowd remember Cilla affectionately as 'a bit of a card' and 'always wanting to be noticed'. She knew who to keep in with. She started 'doing' Ringo Starr's mother's hair for free. With three brothers she was comfortable around men, one of the lads. Cilla got on with most people. She wasn't a sexual threat – to either sex, in any way. Being a 'good girl' – especially a Catholic one – meant you relied on willpower. The Pill was still a twinkle in the eye of everyday science. Contraception meant Durex or rhythm. In those days it was better being safe than sorry. Cilla may be a figure of the 'Swinging Sixties' and King's Road anything-goes-London but she matured in the 1950s when nice girls – unlike those effervescent girls on *Blind Date* who appear ready for anything – didn't do it. And if they did they prayed they would never be sorry for it. Cilla and her friends talked about it. Gossiped about it. But, like *Blind Date*, there was often more innuendo than action.

'Swinging' Cilla was popular with the girls; she was, in turn, their cheerleader among all the male groups. Any talk of girl groups or anything approaching The Spice Girls would have had emergency calls for the men in white suits and a one-way ticket to Rainhill, the mental home in Liverpool. Cilla was one of only a few female 'personalities' on the scene, and because of that, she got what she wanted – attention.

Dance ensembles like The Shimmy-Shimmy Queens and attractions like Dot Rhone who sat quietly on a stool while The Beatles played were no distraction from Cilla.

There were other girl singers but she had her special following with the bands. In a way, she turned professional with The Big

Three, roughneck rockers who had emerged from a 1950s group called Cass and The Casanovas. She appeared regularly with them at the Zodiac Club in Duke Street. John Lennon heard Cilla sing with them many times; they were his favourite group. And Cilla's since they paid her to sing. But not always. Once she went across the Mersey with The Big Three to appear at the Birkenhead YMCA. Dances there were organised by Charles Tranter who recalled:

'Cilla turned up with The Big Three who were very popular at the club, but unfortunately I had only enough club funds to pay the group. After giving a rousing performance with them as guest singer I decided that Cilla deserved some reward. I quickly dashed out of the place and made my way back to my house which wasn't far away. I picked a bunch of sweet peas from the garden and ran back to the hall. Cilla was very grateful – it was probably the most unusual payment of her career.'

The Cavern had all-night sessions, with groups playing at other clubs and then appearing at midnight or 2 a.m. or 4 a.m. or the breakfast spot to perform their set. It was chaotic. Cilla was in demand and, like these nights, all over the place.

Cilla's singing was definitely becoming more than a lark. She was being accepted on the gig circuit as a legitimate attraction, a bonus for the club. With hindsight she said in 1991, 'I know I would always have been a star anyway. I always wanted to be a star. My father adored me, I was the apple of his eye, and I thought: If I'm the apple of his eye, why can't I be the apple of everybody's eye? It was no great shock to me that I had number 1 records. I became a big pop star overnight.'

Well, it was over several nights that she changed from typist Cilla White to pop sensation Cilla Black. One evening, Cilla was with her usual crowd of big-skirted, big-haired cronies at the Iron Door. With its licensed bar and *No beatniks or tough guys by request* signs, the club was known as the headquarters of The Searchers group and the main competition for The Cavern. By now Cilla was a popular performer there; some groups didn't even have to be asked to hand her the microphone.

On this particular evening, her crowd of girl supporters were urging The Beatles, 'Let Cilla sing.' And John Lennon who, like Paul and George and Pete Best, was dressed in a black leather jacket, black polo, black leather trousers and high black boots with Cuban heels, assumed a lopsided, silly grin. Leaning forward, he shouted back, 'OK, Cyril. Just to shut your mates up.'

Cilla sang her version of Sam Cooke's record of *Summertime*, and from then on her livin' really did become easy. The Beatles, especially John Lennon, were on her side. She had at that moment won the most important friends in her career – the ones who would help her into the hit parade.

Time muddles history so there are always debates, but most Merseybeat followers count this as the moment when Cilla's name started being linked with The Beatles'.

'There was so much going on then that no one knew what song or moment or group was important. People say they remember when they realised The Beatles were going to make it, or Cilla or any of the others, but they didn't. We never knew. Everybody else knew – *after* it happened,' says Ringo Starr.

It was at the Zodiac Club, however, that Cilla had another, equally important encounter – with baker's boy, Bobby Willis. She was eighteen, he nineteen.

'He was ever so brown the first time I saw him in the Zodiac Club,' Cilla recalls dreamily. 'He had white-blond hair set off by the tan because he'd been on holiday to Lloret de Mar, which cost £48 all in for a fortnight. Liverpool being a port I thought he was Swedish, off one of the ships. He was with his mate and I said to my friend that "they look as though they could buy us a coffee and a bacon butty." I was working as a waitress at the Zodiac and my friend and I went over to talk to them in my break. I've always had this weird sense of humour, but he could top me every time.'

After 'clicking' with Cilla at the Zodiac, it seemed Bobby Willis was always going around the clubs, following his girl, 'I was very selfish. If Bobby wanted to be with me, he had to come along while I sang.'

He did. He was always there to hang on to, good-naturedly ferrying Cilla around Liverpool on a thirty-ton Crawfords Biscuits truck.

In the Merseybeat days, Bobby was a talented singer and songwriter himself who contributed seven 'B' sides to Cilla's record successes. He might have become a performer in his own right had things been different. However, Cilla always yearns to be 'on' while her husband seemed content in his managerial role. At a glance it seemed that he was the one who pulls the strings, but Cilla has never been a puppet: she always has to have her say. The constant in her life and career is that she's a Daddy's Girl who always wants to be up there – be it on the stage or the kitchen table – with the spotlight on *her*.

Even in those early days, Bobby Willis had a careworn look in his eyes, but he proved himself a determined, dedicated man. In the Merseybeat incarnation he was also full of teenage flannel. To impress the girls, especially Cilla, he added a couple of years to his age and made out that he was a chap with prospects and a car, and a dad who owned a shop; a lad of substance. As Cilla would find out, he was nineteen not twenty-two, his father didn't own a bakery, his car was hired and he worked at Woolworths in the bakery and confectionery department! But none of that prevented Cilla from becoming, and remaining, 'Bobby's Girl'.

Brian Epstein was another familiar figure on the Liverpool club scene. He was so keen the groups used to call him 'Eppydemic'. Indeed, at one point it seemed that way as this dapper, usually pinstriped, character took over the management of act after act. He, for one, never had any doubts about the destiny of his protetege, whom he listed in the following order of importance: 'The Boys, Cilla and My Other Artistes'.

Born on 19 September 1934, Epstein was an 'older' man to Cilla and The Beatles. And a sophisticated one. He had left school – a fee-paying one chosen by his parents, who were a high-profile couple in the Jewish community – at sixteen and joined the family business as a furniture salesman. Two years later it was National Service, but that lasted only ten months. He hated it and the Army didn't care for him. He was discharged as mentally and emotionally unfit, which in 1952 was the code for, among other things, saying he was homosexual.

And Epstein was actively so, although homosexuality was illegal until 1967 – the year of his untimely death. While stationed at barracks in London's Regent's Park he cruised the Piccadilly clubs, but that landed him in trouble with Service authorities. After getting out of his 'hideous' uniform he briefly went to the Royal Academy of Dramatic Art (RADA), but an incident involving an attempt to pick up an undercover policeman in a public toilet ended his thespian ambitions. He rejoined the family business – this time selling records.

It was in 1957 when he started, a time when the British music industry was a comb and toilet-paper affair, often a mismanagement of some trombones and washboards. Almost everyone working in the UK record business was doing so as a sub-agent for an American or possibly German company, their job to move the overseas 'product'. To start a British group, be it jazz or country or rock, was one thing – but to even imagine recording and selling records by them was heresy. British stars like Marty Wilde and Craig Douglas made 'covers' of American hits, as Cilla would do later. The American songs were clever and commercial. No one in

Britain was writing good pop songs, and those who had, like Lionel Bart, whose *Big Time* was recorded by Adam Faith, had moved on to theatre, to musicals like Bart's *Oliver!* Britain was a market rather than a creative place for music.

That was where Brian Epstein's genius proved so pivotal, in introducing the songwriting skills of Lennon and McCartney into the industry vacuum of the early 1960s.

Epstein, who saw himself as the impeccable Englishman from his shiny toe-caps to his bowler hat, who privately favoured Bach and Sibelius, insisted, 'I am not a commercial person. Really, I am a frustrated actor.'

But he *was* a wonderful salesman. At the family furniture and music outlets – with his help there were finally nine comprising the grandest music retailer in the North-West of England – he sold records in their thousands. One customer often had to be asked to leave: Cilla. She would go into the 'listening booths' and hear the records, scribbling down the lyrics in her college shorthand, but never buy them. It was a typical move. David Williams of Dale Roberts and The Jaywalkers remembers, 'We would sometimes buy a record as soon as it came out, learn the words and music that day and play it on stage the following night. There was a lot of prestige involved in being the first group to play a new song on stage. Members of the groups would sit in coffee bars that had jukeboxes and write down the lyrics as the records played. That was a lot cheaper than buying the records itself.'

Cilla couldn't wait for jukebox plays. Her magic word has always been *now*. Meanwhile, scores of other Epstein customers kept asking for songs by this group called The Beatles. And Epstein's shop assistants were raving about them. Some customers wanted a Beatles record called *My Bonnie*. Hunter Davies in his authorised biography of The Beatles is definite about an important moment in pop music history. He says it was exactly 3 p.m. on 28 October 1961 when Raymond Jones, wearing a black leather jacket, went into Epstein's record store in Whitechapel, Liverpool, and first asked for *My Bonnie*. Epstein had served him, with apologies. He had never heard of the song or the group.

The meticulous Epstein finally discovered it was a German recording by Tony Sheridan and The Beat Brothers, who were indeed The Beatles. In Hamburg, 'Beatles' sounded much too like 'peedles' – German slang for penis. Epstein saw the joke. For once, he ignored the lure of 'peedles' and went in search of The Beatles.

His journey took him to The Cavern, the Fab Four and almost immediately afterward, to Cilla. 'It was John Lennon who told Brian about me. I fancied Brian like mad. He was gorgeous. He was incredible! He had the Cary Grant type of charisma, incredibly charming and shy. I always like that about guys. He always wore a navy-blue cashmere overcoat and a navy spotted cravat. I know now it was a Hermès, but then I still knew it was expensive. Brian had "expensive" written all over him.'

Lots of the Liverpool groups including The Beatles who, with Pete Best as drummer, clocked up 800 hours on stage there, had been tempted away to the German clubs in Hamburg. Rory Storm and The Hurricanes had gone, and part of their contract called for a girl vocalist. Ringo Starr tried to persuade Cilla to go with them but she was just seventeen, under age then for foreign travel, and her father John White would not sign the appropriate paperwork. The trip might have proved very useful for Cilla, as the gigs in Hamburg called for six sessions a night – every night.

Fortunately, Cilla doesn't see it as a mistake, a missed opportunity 'My mam wouldn't let me. My mam and dad said "No", but I wouldn't have gone anyway; I didn't have the bottle. Even when I did travel abroad I was homesick. If I got homesick in the Plaza Hotel in New York, what would I have been like in Hamburg in an attic?'

'I remember Ringo coming to the office and saying he was going to Hamburg and needed a girl singer so could I come? He didn't say he liked my voice – just that they needed a girl to sing. We all looked like beatniks – well, I didn't at work but by night it was gothic, everything black. And there's Ringo at the office looking like Gene Vincent with all the hair and all in black.'

Along with many people she found Ringo – Richard Starkey – irritating with his seen-it-all attitude. Ringo also liked a drink and he always had that self-assurance an extra drink provided. Cilla still wonders what would have happened had she gone to Germany, but recalls, 'Ringo was honest. We had a love/hate relationship. We'd go to the pictures if I had an afternoon off from work, and I used to do his mam's hair. I was really good at it – or so I thought. Thirty years later, Harry her husband told me I used to make a right bloody mess of it. But they'd said nothing. Ringo and I were very good mates. We made each other laugh.

'But going to Hamburg was business. "Why do you want me? "I asked. He was frank, "We don't really want you but it says we have to bring a girl singer".'

Cilla opted out and stuck to the typing and her lunchtime stints at The Cavern and evenings at the Zodiac Club, waitressing and singing. When Brian Epstein signed The Beatles to a management contract on 24 January 1962, the most popular group on Merseyside were currently The Big Three. John Lennon was their greatest fan and those, like Cilla, in the know about politics involving The Beatles, were aware of rumours that drummer Pete Best was about to be sacked. Everyone was sure that he would be replaced by Johnny Hutchinson of The Big Three. Although she was not officially part of the group, Cilla sang with The Big Three often enough to have the inside track on gossip.

'He was first choice,' she recalled. 'Johnny Hutch was renowned as the drummer with the band in Liverpool. But he must have thought that because The Beatles were going to be big he didn't want to be part of them as he already had The Big Three.'

Instead, for £25 a week, it was Ringo, one of the century's luckiest entertainers, who replaced Pete Best in August, 1962. He had dithered about joining Kingsize Taylor and The Dominoes, but they were offering £5 a week less. That fiver changed his life. Just as another, still inexplicable, decision cheated Pete Best of his proper place in music history. Neither Epstein nor The Beatles ever gave an adequate reason for forcing Best out of the group.

Best – good-looking, charismatic, the only Beatle to be on the telephone and have a van for the equipment – was regarded by the Merseybeat crowd as the group's greatest *asset*. Possibly, it was his attractiveness which made him too much for the other three, and also for Epstein who wanted to promote a group, not an individual. The gossips suggested everything – Best wouldn't smile, wouldn't change his hairstyle – to explain his ousting. Epstein also had management problems with The Big Three, who quickly vanished from the scene they had so dominated. Just as fast, Ringo appeared with John, Paul and George. He was in. So was Cilla. She had a longtime friend in The Beatles camp. But it was John Lennon who did the honours with Epstein:

'Brian, this is Cyril.'

'He asked me if I'd mind singing with The Beatles. John Lennon had told him he should sign me and I did an audition at the Majestic in Birkenhead with The Beatles backing me. I must have been dreadful because I was very, very nervous. The Beatles were on the brink of stardom. I sang *Summertime* from *Porgy and Bess* but it wasn't in my key and Brian was not impressed. He didn't say anything at all and I didn't like to ask him what he thought. I had just got up in the middle of The Beatles' act – I had no rehearsal – and I knew I'd blown it.'

Epstein was concentrating on The Beatles, on getting them

recorded by George Martin who ran the Parlophone label for Electrical Musical Industries (EMI). Martin was the smart sage who at that time was looking for some chart success. The Beatles' with Ringo, were the group in Liverpool, but generally unknown outside the city. Finally, after much work and contact-making, Epstein and The Boys' went to London and on 11 September 1962, recorded *Love Me Do* and, on the flipside, *PS I Love You* with George Martin at his Abbey Road studios. It was released four weeks later, and on the strength of it, The Beatles won concert dates and a spot on young singing sensation Helen Shapiro's tour. It is easy to see it now, the attraction of the witty young Liverpudlian lads, but even then in the North of England, many people including Cilla were convinced that The Beatles were going to make it big.

*Love Me Do* eventually reached number 17 in the charts. *Please Please Me*, which they had recorded in November 1962, was not released until January 1963, when the group were touring with Helen Shapiro. By then they were as popular with audiences as the star of the show. Cilla had to sit back and watch as The Beatles took off and *Please Please Me* went to the top. By March 1963, *How Do You Do It?* by Gerry and The Pacemakers – more clients of Epstein – was also a number 1 hit.

The 'Liverpool Sound' was being heard all over Britain. Lennon and McCartney's Do You Want To Know A Secret?, recorded by Billy Jo Kramer and The Dakotas, was yet another success for the Epstein stable. In April 1963, The Beatles released *From Me To You* which went straight to the top of the charts.

Cilla's unfortunate audition at the Majestic made her miss this initial Merseyside musical charge into the Top Twenty. It was eight months before she put it all together again at the Blue Angel Club, where she had won a spot singing with pianist John Rubin's modern jazz group. Her songs included *Bye Bye Birdie* and *You Made Me*

*Love You*, and she admits, 'I didn't know Brian was in the audience. I was totally relaxed and I wasn't singing rock 'n' roll. Later he said to me, "Why didn't you sing like that before?" He didn't mince his words. He was the most honest man. He was like a film star to me – I thought anybody in a suit had to have money.'

In fact, this particular man in a suit – usually a charcoal-grey pinstriped one worn with a white shirt and dark blue tie – was going to make her a millionaire at twenty-five, eventually one of the richest women in Britain and one of the nation's most successful TV presenters ever! Brian had predicted she would be 'the Edith Piaf of the future' but sabotaged his own vision by winning 'my lovely Cilla', as he always called her, her first television contract in 1967 – the last deal he did for her before his death.

Almost everyone who encountered Epstein in the 1960s recalls him as a kind, tolerant man. There are scores of recorded examples of his benevolence to others; he often helped out with cash to singers or acts who had stumbled at the myriad of rock 'n' roll hurdles. For all Cilla's insistence that she would have made it anyway, there was validation of the Epstein role from Bobby Willis three decades later when in conversation he pointed out to his wife, 'Well, Cilla, Brian did help.'

He did more than that. Not only did he put her on the road, he built it in yellow brick. Epstein was uncannily prescient. Out of all the scores of groups on the Liverpool scene, he was the one who signed and marketed The Beatles. By 1967 he had seventeen major acts and composers in his stable, from Henry Mancini to Gerry and The Pacemakers, folk singer Donovan and crooner Matt Monro to The Fourmost and Billy J. Kramer and The Dakotas. Along the way he also represented the first British bullfighter Henry Higgins, who fought under the name Enrique Canadas.

He was so convinced that Cilla White would be a star: apart from The Beatles she had more hit records than anyone else in the heyday of the Liverpool sound. She was almost hysterical with excitement when Brian offered her a contract. Others couldn't see it, including Cavern disc jockey Bob Wooler – already a Liverpool legend and a man with an expert's reputation on Merseyside music talent. He had been with Brian in the audience at the Blue Angel as Cilla sang with John Rubin's group.

Wooler counselled Epstein about Cilla in her hearing. In the parlance of the place and day, he said she was a 'hopeless wonder', a curiosity who was going nowhere. Cilla thought: Please don't say that! I failed the first audition – I don't want to blow it a second time.

She need not have worried.

Epstein asked her round to his offices. Among other dealings, he wanted to make exotic leather clothes for her. Her image needed improving. With her protuberant teeth and bumpy nose – and, according to rival singer Sandie Shaw, her 'funny arms' – the image presented by the young enthusiastic singer was more than an ocean away from her American counterparts. In America, image went hand in hand with talent. It was as much how you looked as how you performed. For instance, John F. Kennedy was the first US President to have won the White House with the help of television appearances. It was the start of 'sound bite' politics and the Andy Warhol concept of 'fifteen minutes of fame'.

Cilla was still in her parochial world, in which the future of The Big Three was more important than local, never mind international or sexual, politics. She was young – and naive. What is more, her awareness of alternative sexual orientations was nil.

In Liverpool, as in the rest of Britain, there was no such thing as 'gay' gossip. Homosexuals were 'queers' and the law supported that general verbal verdict. To The Beatles and British 'beats' in those very early Sixties, 'being queer' was a bit of a joke. They had no understanding of the anguish that Epstein and others suffered because of the law and public opinion. Even the supposedly 'with it' and turned-on Beatles were not truly aware of the homosexual world. Paul McCartney says that the four first heard about 'gayness' from a poet visiting Liverpool in the pre-Beatlemania days: 'It was all shagging sailors, I think.' What shook them up was that the poet, Royston Ellis, told them that one in four men was homosexual. That made them think.'

Epstein had a policy of not talking about his sexuality with Cilla. 'I really didn't know what a homosexual was. Even in the very rough area I was bought up in, they used to say, "Oh, he's not married, you know . . . he stayed with his mother." I only found out that Brian was gay from a friend. Showbusiness is one business in which we don't care what people are: there is no prejudice towards homosexuals, lesbians or colour. We are as one.

'We were very protected by him, probably to a fault. Brian was a man, a perfect gentleman, and I can't think of him in any other way. I can't think of him being homosexual. He never talked with me – I don't think he talked about it with The Beatles or anyone else – and from that he made his own loneliness.'

Merseyside musician Rod Pont said, 'Anybody who was gay kept it to themselves, especially in a town like Liverpool where if a heterosexual thought a man was homosexual he was likely to kick his head in. It was looked on as filthy, disgusting. So homosexuals didn't flaunt themselves as they do today.'

'You might think they would have been more aware, all these brash young singers and music-makers, but they weren't. They weren't stupid: it was just a subject that did not get mentioned – it just wasn't a public topic,' said pop historian David Gibsone, adding, 'There was a lack of knowledge so, therefore, to many people it was a great mystery.'

This sort of ignorance led Cilla into an embarrassing exchange with Epstein when he offered her a management contract following her appearance at the Blue Angel. In response to his offer, she said,

'I don't know if I should because the word's going around that you buy mohair suits for boys.'

Luckily the remark ('I just didn't understand what I was saying') was lost in the moment, in Epstein's pleasure in signing up his 'girl singer'.

*He*, however, still had to audition for Cilla's father at 380 Scotland Road.

And she had to make her first concert appearance at the Odeon, Southport, Lancashire, on 30 August 1963. With The Beatles. It was a lucky chance for she replaced another Epstein act, The Fourmost, who had been offered a big exposure TV spot.

Brian's proteges were doing wonderfully well, and Epstein displayed his fondness for Cilla and his belief in her future by taking his own parents to witness her professional debut. At the end of the show, Harry Epstein patted his son on the back, telling him, 'She'll be the next Gracie Fields.'

## *Chapter Three*

# BRIAN'S GIRL

*'Brian had the sense to see in Cilla something that I hadn't originally seen. I thought she was just this dolly rocker from Liverpool...'*
– Sir George Martin

Brian Epstein had been anointed a starmaker by the music industry. From the beginning of 1963 he had been associated with a dozen number 1 records – itself a record in the history of pop music – but privately he was annoyed with himself for allowing Cilla to get away and was keen to make up for lost time.

What is remarkable is that in all the excitement, the constant flurry of telephone calls and deals, contracts and memos, he did not make more mistakes, lapses in judgement. Epstein was good at essential business disciplines, but not only was the music scene in Britain changing, the 'natural order' of almost everything was being turned upside down.

'The Establishment' were being pushed out of the spotlight by an eclectic bunch of talented newcomers. Painter David Hockney had emerged from Bradford, the Cockney photographers David Bailey and Terry Donovan were focusing on models like Jean Shrimpton, Sean Connery was James Bond and Michael Caine the working-class

Harry Palmer in Len Deighton's *The Ipcress Files.* The team from *Beyond The Fringe* were thriving and George Martin, who had put *The Goons* on record, was busy recording the comedy albums of 'Fringe' founders Peter Cook, Dudley Moore, Alan Bennett and Jonathan Miller.

And then along came The Beatles and the 'Liverpool Sound'. And Cilla with her Mary Quant fashions and accent and fresh outlook, and Brian Epstein.

'I cannot believe what is happening around me,' Brian Epstein confessed. 'I do not think of myself as anyone's boss. I am a friend. I feel very close to all the artistes I manage.'

For all the torment over his sexual orientation, and the private drinking and drug-taking, Epstein was never publicly anything other than the courteous young man who used to sell furniture at his family's shops. His use of 'rent boys', the drinking and reliance on 'uppers' and 'downers' as well as his intake of cocaine, would all increase with the pressure of phenomenal success. It has been argued that Cilla and the groups, especially, of course, The Beatles, kept him alive longer because his involvement with them helped guard him from his dangerous depression and drug binges. To Cilla and everyone else, he was simply a brilliant and successful young businessman.

That was the key to convincing John White to sign away his daughter Cilla into the management and care of Epstein and his NEMS group. John White had bought the family piano from the Epstein. It was a good one; it played the tunes he liked. His memories connected with it were good, rosy ones, seen through the bottom of a Guinness glass – of 'Jarsout' and 'Little Cilla' singing with 'Big Cilla' and bringing the house down.

With the boom of the Liverpool music scene, every other person in the city seemed to be a manager or an agent. Cilla and therefore her family had already been approached by literally dozens of them.

Each one had to pass the Sunday tea test. The tea consisted of leftover slices of meat from the Sunday dinner, with Dad's home-baked tea loaf to follow. The aspirant controllers of his daughter's life would munch as he monitored them. They all failed until Epstein, who John White believed could, like the piano, be relied on and trusted.

On 6 September 1963, Cilla and her father signed her contract with Brian Epstein, who had picked that day, his parents' thirtieth wedding anniversary, as a special one to finalise the deal. Epstein confidently lined up his new signing with George Martin and Parlophone Records who, with the success of Epstein's other acts, were not about to refuse him.

Unknowingly, at the same time, Cilla also signed her contract for life with Bobby Willis. And changed her name to Cilla Black. there are a bunch of variations of the White to Black story. Cilla says it was Epstein's inspiration: that White was too white-bread, as it were; that Black was strong and sexy. The other real and more downbeat reason is that a local music paper got her name wrong, and that mistake was transcribed into the contracts by Epstein's secretary.

Whatever the circumstances, Cilla became two people. And Bobby Willis became more besotted. The Beatles had toured with Roy Orbison, put out LPs, and by October 1963, Beatlemania was official. Worldwide. Everything associated with them was of global interest. There has not been a phenomenon like it since. There have been 'manias' but they were infatuations compared to the media revolution thae Epstein's boys' created. Everyone in the stable was winning. Gerry and The Pacemakers had enjoyed a hat-trick of number 1 records and Cilla was going to London as another bright star in the Epstein galaxy. She was on her way.

As were most of Epstein's business operations. So much was happening that Brian soon realised he would have to move home and offices to London. With him went The Beatles. Eight months later, Cilla joined them there.

The Big Smoke didn't seem to bother Cilla. Epstein's assurances and his track record of success gave her easy confidence. What is more, she knew inside, as she always had done, that she was a winner. It was as if the winning Lottery jackpot numbers were printed on her birth certificate.

It was, as ever, Bobby Willis who was nervous. And careful. He sipped a brandy in a Soho pub when he went with Cilla to London to meet up with Epstein, and waited for her to do a test recording to George Martin. By then Bobby had become Cilla's semi-official road manager, but he was also the writer of *Shy of Love* – a song she was to record for George Martin, the man fast becoming known worldwide as 'The Fifth Beatle'. Paul McCartney's song *Love of the Loved* was to be her first 'A' side single, Bobby's *Shy of Love* the 'B' side.

The carefully orchestrated publicity machine, a trademark of her career, began with the untrue 'revelation' that Lennon and McCartney had penned *Love of the Loved* especially for Cilla. And yet The Beatles had been bashing it out at The Cavern long before; Cilla herself had danced to it. She wanted to do a group arrangement of the song but when she arrived at the Abbey Road studios there was an orchestra ('brass and everything'). The record was duly released, introducing through much PR hype 'the gal with the jet-black voice, the bird-in-a-beat-boy's-world.'

It was a middling hit, reaching number 35 in the pop charts; anyone else would have considered it a great start, a brilliant break. Not so Cilla. She was very disappointed. She had said a tearful farewell to her friends at Calendar Cables and now she was constantly nagging Brian Epstein. She was his 'girl' and she wanted a hit record.

'Epstein really did believe Cilla was the best thing to happen to him,' said David Gibsone, adding, 'For all the time he looked after her, he only rarely regretted working with her – and that was usually when he was confused and disturbed in his own life. She was so demanding that when he had other demands on his time – private or professional – she could be too much. She had every excuse. She was away from home and still really very young, given her background. But she was, at times, too much. Even for him. And he adored her. Absolutely adored her.'

Cilla would say, 'Brian really thought the sun shone out of my eyes.'

She had been featured in the first issue of Bill Harry's publication Mersey Beat – the front-page 'splash' was Gene Vincent's appearance in Liverpool – and the embryonic music newspaper, now an encyclopaedia of the Liverpool era, had detailed her growing promise from her appearances with Rory Storm and The Big Three. Epstein had decided to turn that promise into his 'creation'. Cilla was not to be 'discovered' like Gerry and The Pacemakers and The Beatles. This rather awkward-looking girl was to be Epstein's first designer pop star.

Cilla brought out Epstein's strong female side. George Martin's first impression that she was a 'dolly rocker' and a 'Cavern screamer' was swiftly dismissed by Brian. He gave Cilla some spin doctoring: she had, he decided, a penchant for wearing men's jeans and she talked the language of the clubs. He filled her public vocabulary – and her carefully monitored press releases – with 'fab' and 'endsville' and 'gear'. Weeks and weeks went by as he tutored Cilla, putting all the parts of his star together like Dr Frankenstein. His Cilla creation was a marvellous mirror of what was regarded as 'cool'and 'hip' for the times. Cilla became a thoroughly convincing part of the scene, dovetailing perfectly with Beatlemania.

She and Epstein enjoyed a short but extraordinary relationship. Epstein was, at first, a father figure to her; she was the pliant 'daughter', always happy to curl him around any available finger. Cilla has always instinctively encouraged a protective arm, and in the early days Epstein was quick to provide it. She was his 'girl'.

And he could get quite vicious about any threat to Cilla's progress. He had made that clear in dealing with her career launch record, *Love of the Loved*. He had stolen that for 'his Cilla'.

The song that would be a minor hit on release but decades later turn into one of the most collectible recordings of the era had been marked down for Beryl Marsden (no relation to Gerry), who had made her recording debut as a 16-year-old. Small with a giant voice, she was a British Brenda Lee. John Lennon was happy for her to have *Love of the Loved*, but Epstein jumped in, 'I want that for Cilla,' he told Lennon who, although chagrined at not being able to give his song to who he wanted, simply shrugged his acceptance of the situation.

'It wasn't worth arguing about,' he told his clubland cronies who were gossiping about the 'feud' between Cilla and Beryl Marsden. Cilla herself insists she has never been concerned about rivals or rivalries. Others see her scratching her way to the top, claws out. There was a girl-power boom in tandem with the groups. Dusty Springfield went solo, breaking away from her family group The Springfields, who had dwarfed The Beatles in popularity polls in 1962; from Glasgow Lulu joined Sandie Shaw, Petula Clark and the much-admired, big-voiced Helen Shapiro who were recording in London.

'The only competition I had when I started was Helen Shapiro, though when I say "only" I still think she has a great voice. Then all of a sudden when the Liverpool thing happened there were the others. Dusty was always there. There were no hang-ups with me. I'm a very confident lady. I don't think I'm bigheaded. I'm the first to say I can't do a song better than someone else.'

And the first to say she can.

She insists that even in those early days she knew what she did and did not want. For instance, she was sent the fledgling Elton John's *Your Song* by Epstein partner and music publisher Dick James, but turned it down. Even though, 'I thought it was brilliant. I told him, "It's perfect. It'll be a big hit." Dick himself said, "It'll never be a hit. This guy Reg Dwight (later Elton John) is not very good-looking; he's quite fat and wears glasses."

'I've never worried about my contemporaries. I have enough problems worrying about myself. I was totally confident in what I did. There was a big thrill when Cliff (Richard) did *All My Love*. I thought it was just another Italian song and not good enough for a single. I thought, he's got one of my cast-offs and had a hit with it – and good luck to him. I never knock success. I never regret anything. I was equally thrilled when *Your Song* was a big hit for Elton. I'm thrilled when people are successful. I'm thrilled for myself. I've never been the girl at the wedding, shouting, "It should have been me!" Never.'

But it could have been Beryl Marsden. She had performed in Hamburg (under-age, she was granted a special licence by London's Bow Street Magistrates Court) and would work with bands alongside performers like Rod Stewart and Mick Fleetwood. On Merseyside she was often in the same sentence as Cilla. But Beryl argues, 'We are totally different types of singers with a completely different approach to music. Cilla is a family entertainer – always has been – while I'm more of a singer. People asked me why I didn't make it and why Cilla did, but such questions are ridiculous. Making it isn't about making a million pounds but about being happy with what you do.'

Cilla was happy. She was on the bill of *The Beatles Christmas Show*, in North London in 1963, and appeared a seasoned trouper. She received a fantastic reception which, considering the height of Beatlemania and the squeals for the individual Beatles, was a real achievement. In her 1993 recollections of her career she wrote: 'Everybody else seemed dead nervous and they all wondered why I seemed so confident. I'll tell you what it was – a glass of champagne for courage. And it's worked for me ever since.'

Any tonic helped, for these were competitive times. The British music business of the early 1960s often involved two or three singers or acts fighting each other for success with the same few songs. The first battle was to win the rights to the material. On hearing Dionne Warwick's sophisticated ballad *Anyone Who Had A Heart*, written by Burt Bacharach and Hal David and arranged by Bacharach for Warwick, Cilla wanted it immediately. Epstein had thought the same when he heard the record in America.

George Martin, however, considered it perfect for Shirley Bassey. The latter had enjoyed twenty hit singles including two numbers ls since her recording debut in 1957, and was then considered Britain's greatest female singing star. Both Cilla and Bassey, who awed people in a grand manner and always received first-class attention, were livid. Epstein was beside himself and his protective arm went around Cilla as he grabbed the song for her. It became a number 1 hit in February 1964, thus proving the Cilla and Epstein case.

Upset at missing the British hit parade and knock-on continental glory, Dionne Warwick castigated Cilla and her version of *Anyone Who Had A Heart*. She said that if she had coughed in the arrangement, Cilla would have coughed in exactly the same place; it was not so much a 'cover' version but a copy. And Cilla's voice was 'dreadful'.

'It seems such a long time ago now,' said Dionne Warwick with some understatement more than three decades later. 'But I remember being angry at the time. I thought this little English upstart had stolen my thunder. Even worse, she had turned it into a hit record! I suppose I'm more mellow about it – and a lot of other things – now. But remember, we were all vixens then. It was a cutthroat business. We all had to look after ourselves.'

Even in 1997 Cilla was still defending her recording. 'I thought my version was 100 per cent better than Dionne Warwick's. We did a better arrangement. Bacharach wasn't the be-all and end-all of everything. I just felt there was a little bit of magic on our record, and that was proved when it came out. Dionne's record was released and it got nowhere. Three weeks later, mine went to number 1 and was selling nearly 100,000 copies a day. So, it had a touch of magic.'

Always practical, Cilla points out, 'I desperately wanted to do the song. The kids thought I was wonderful and they hadn't a clue who Burt Bacharach and Dionne Warwick were. And we made it more commercial. I got the number 1, and I deserved it.'

It was hits, financially if not critically, with all the Rolls-Royce trappings, from then on. Cilla Black celebrated her twenty-first birthday with a number one hit *You're My World*. This translation of an Italian song was her only entry ever in the American Top Forty, and also made her Britain's first female singer to have two successive numbers ls. Much fuss ensued. Photographer George Elam took some of the Fleet Street pictures 'I'd never met such a confident girl. We'd ask her to pose this way or that, but she always knew better. But she was fun with it. She was just a girl from Liverpool with a couple of hit records. As far as I was concerned, she was a one-off. But there must have been something, for I did take a couple of extra rolls of pictures of her. I still don't know why. There was just something about her.'

Epstein saw in Cilla a Judy Garland-style entertainer, and part of this early career packaging would be a significant concert – the opening act at the London Palladium in June 1964. The 'startime' variety show was headlined by Frankie Vaughan and Tommy Cooper. Strange company for pop singers: What – Frankie Vaughan and The Beatles? Tommy Cooper and The Rolling Stones? Such combinations were unthinkable. But for miniskirted Cilla it seemed right. When she had appeared on TV's *Juke Box Jury*, critics had said, 'This one can speak,' or, 'She can be funny,' or, 'She should be on TV regularly.'

Crossover careers were only just beginning. The transition of performers from radio to television was sometimes disastrous, with artists unable to make the move. Cilla was one of the first pop stars to be doing theatre, and television was still an infant medium. Cilla was to grow with it, and even then her multiple career (records, television and theatre) was unusual. At the Palladium, where the planned two-week run turned into six months, she learned stagecraft with seasoned professionals. With Cilla no experience was ever wasted: she learned and used the timings and the delivery she studied night after night after night.

'Brian had the sense to see in Cilla something that I hadn't originally seen,' George Martin admits now. 'I thought she was just this dolly rocker from Liverpool, good and different but not in any way a ballad singer. She was a mini-skirted little girl with a brassy voice. He opened my eyes to Cilla's dramatic potential. He had a great sense of vision in the artistes he handled.'

One of the landmark events in Cilla's relationship with Brian Epstein occurred during this time. The smooth, controlled Epstein took John Lyndon, who was to be his production direction, to see Cilla on stage in Coventry. After her performance a hugely happy Epstein asked Lyndon his verdict. 'Well, you know, I'm sure she'll make lots and lots of money out of recording, but whether there'll be much else . . .'

Epstein's nasty streak burst out all over Lyndon 'She's going to be one of the biggest stars in this country for thirty or forty years and you are going to help create it.'

And create it they all did. The Sixties were a blur. They say if you can remember the 1960s you weren't there. Cilla herself says that throughout her career people have always quizzed her about the Swinging Sixties. She doesn't remember some things – but because of concert tours rather than LSD trips.

The record books testify to her workload. They spell out how she worked almost every day, appearing in two shows per day. In her first thirty-two weeks with Epstein she appeared in concert four hundred times. Ahead, there were singles and albums to record – and movies to make. She was in a high-flying business. But the higher you are . . .

## *Chapter Four*

# HAPPY DAYS

*'She's one to watch – in every way.'*
– John Lennon on Cilla, 1964

For all her fabulous success as a Sixties singer, it was always apparent that Cilla was more of a middle of-the-road entertainer than some wild thing of the rock scene. She was renamed, reinvented but never revisionist: the Scouse spots would not rub off completely. Although fiercely proud of her background it has, she feels, held her back professionally, stopped her from becoming a world star, of achieving lasting success in America.

With her mother she had gone to the cinema two or three times a week – favourites were anything with Doris Day or Natalie Wood – and the fantasy American Dream image was implanted then. Cilla lived in a confined space with an outside lavatory: at the movies it was acres of greenery or the palms and luxury of Beverly Hills. With the humble prospect of a bag of chips afterwards, Cilla would sit watching the films and feel deeply envious, 'I wanted it, I wanted to be famous. I wanted it badly.'

When she did become famous it went to her head. It was

champagne and dinner at the best places, like Beauchamp Place in Knightsbridge, and dresses and shoes and lots and lots of pairs of knee-length boots. She splashed out on mink coats and diamonds. She was set off on the spree, she says, when she realised the 'chaperone' provided by Epstein was wearing a mink while she herself was in her Mary Quant plastic mac. She bought a Jaguar. Then she wondered why Brian Epstein – the manager getting 25 per cent of her earnings – was driving a Bentley.

She had only had the Jaguar for twenty-four hours when she went out and got a Bentley, and it has been Rolls-Royces ever since. Even then she was unwittingly rehearsing for her role as the Queen Mum.

By the mid-Sixties, Cilla was singing and dancing in panto as 'Little Red Riding Hood' and appearing in the West End, with that other British institution, the late Frankie Howerd. She was more at home there than in the charts with *You've Lost That Lovin' Feelin'*, her version went to number 2 but it was The Righteous Brothers who went all the way, 'Theirs was 100 per cent better, if only for the reason that it is not a solo record. It's a song for two people, and you need two voices for that great answering thing. The very deep and very high voices of The Righteous Brothers complemented each other very well. I had to do both myself, and although I have a very big range it wasn't quite right.'

It was all so hectic. There were appearances in America cabaret and spots on major TV shows like those hosted by Ed Sullivan and Johnny Carson – but Brian Epstein did not use all his Beatles' clout to push Cilla in the States the way he could have. Decades later, that mismanagement still annoys her.

Legendary British agent Tito Burns says that Epstein just did not know how to make 'trade-offs'. Or particularly want to. In agent-speak there is a way of packaging, of selling say The Beatles and Cilla without spelling out 'to get them you have to take her'.

Burns said of Epstein, 'He hadn't read the showbusiness

dictionary. He didn't know true values in the business, what he could ask for, what he should get. It was understandable. He'd had no training. You felt you wanted to help him. What he did was unbelievable, but it could have been a thousand times better had he had the knowledge of the business.'

Nevertheless, his Cilla was everywhere. Her first album collection, *Cilla* – mostly covers of American soul hits – had sold well on release in January 1965, and she made the Top Twenty with the Randy Newman song *I've Been Wrong Before*. In late 1965 she did a series of one-night shows with the Everly Brothers. It was her last package tour of any sort. Television became a comfortable vehicle for her: she appeared several times with Eamonn Andrews – the Parkinson/Wogan of his day – and on Peter Cook and Dudley Moore's *Not Only But Also*. One appearance she made on *Juke Box Jury*, where as a pannellist she had to judge a selection of that week's record releases, upset Epstein: Cilla, trying to be cool and sophisticated, smoked a cigarette. 'I'd never smoked or bought a cigarette in my life. I did it for effect. Brian told me off. He was it was not ladylike. I didn't even like cigarettes, though I wanted to smoke like Lauren Bacall in those movies.'

She's admitted to trying marijuana. Her story has varied about how many times, but it seems to have been very few. One occasion was, amusingly, during the *Little Red Riding Hood* panto; Cilla says she was sick after the 'What big joints you have, Grandma' experience. On another occasion she was in Epstein's flat one evening with Bobby Willis, when . . .

'We were in Brian's flat with The Beatles and some other people. They were passing around this thing on a pin. It was quite long but by the time it got to me it was quite short because of all the gobs it had been in. I thought, 'Oh no, it's not nice. It's not hygienic.'

There was another time, as she explained on television in 1991, 'We were having a dinner party and a friend said, "Why don't you try it?"

It was the most foolish and silly thing I ever did because I didn't smoke anyway. And I certainly wouldn't advocate smoking or taking drugs. I went into the bathroom to "turn on". I didn't like it – it made me feel sick. Such a confession! It's a bit like Mary Poppins swearing.'

In the 1960s and 1970s drugs were readily available; at some parties they were handed around with the peanuts and potato crisps. Cilla recalled, 'I was offered drugs in those days, very much so. But smoking a joint was bad for a singer's throat so I didn't get heavily into it.'

She was upset by The Beatles' advocacy of drugs while remaining innocent about Brian Epstein's use of narcotics. He was developing into a habitual user of cocaine and, more pervasively as it would turn out, of increasingly stronger tranquillisers.

Appearing with Frankie Howerd in 1966 in *Way Out In Piccadilly*, a revue created by *Hancock and Steptoe* writers Ray Galton and Alan Simpson, along with the comic genius Eric Sykes, Cilla established herself on stage and in a lifetime friendship with Howerd. He adored her. He once said, 'I heard Cilla before I saw her. I was rehearsing a sketch on stage and Miss Black was due to arrive at any minute. Suddenly, there was this shrieking noise from the back of the stalls and I thought: Anyone who can laugh at me can't be all bad, we're going to get along. Then soon after the show opened, her mother and her Auntie Nellie came from Southport to see it. I could hear them shrieking in the stalls and it was exactly the same sort of noise Cilla makes. Obviously, it runs in the family. I suppose it's the family curse.

'Naturally I was wondering how professional she was going to be in her first flush of success. The pop scene wasn't something I was particularly into – much too old for it – although I had known The Beatles. She was strangely innocent, but that might just have been for me.'

Until his death he was as likely as not to turn up at her home, demanding lunch or dinner and plenty of gin and water. Tap water.

Howerd, the long, sad-faced clown, was a disturbed man and a testing dinner companion. He would sit over the dinner table – it was best to sit to the side of him if he was speed eating pasta – and put you on the couch. There would be question after question. Most about sex. He would become an uncle figure to Cilla's kids, but even then he would go on about her sex life.

Sex was a subject that fascinated him. When he was filming *Sergeant Pepper's Lonely Hearts Club Band* in Hollywood in 1978 with the Bee Gees and Peter Frampton, Howerd would spend hours with friends by the swimming pool or over dinner discussing world affairs. And sex. He was 57 years old then and, in Britain, a national institution: a veteran of *Carry On* films, *Up Pompeii* on stage, film and television, *That Was The Week That Was* with David Frost, and a master of sexual innuendo. His own confusion in the matter of sex made it his hobby horse. Given the movie he was making, the conversation often centred on The Beatles – and Cilla. Although Cilla has always said that she did not believe in sex before marriage, the mischievous Howerd commented, 'I never believed she was a virgin when she got married. I think she thought she was. She *wanted* to be a virgin – and when she wants something, she gets it. All her life she was educated in the concept of being the virgin bride in white. Well, you tell me what two healthy young people like she and Bobby got up to before they were married . . .'

Throughout their relationship Howerd would go on about it and other related subjects. But much as he could irritate her at times, he was a genuine friend and that closeness was evident in her upset at his death. There have never been many close friends outside her larger family circle.

She and Bobby Willis were a double act. They went everywhere together. He was always around when she was paid attentions that she may or may not have wanted. Like the night in a hotel in Birmingham when Omar Sharif took a fancy to her. She puts herself down, saying he must have been 'a bit bored' but was pleased that such a major movie star should play court to her. It was in 1966 and she recalled Sharif's usual seduction technique, 'It was just after Dr Zhivago and we were staying in the same hotel. He sent me this bouquet of flowers and asked me to tea in his room.

'Bobby wouldn't let me go. He said I wouldn't come out the same person.'

Years later Sharif had difficulty remembering the occasion, but admitted, 'It was in the days of free love so I'm sure that's what was on my mind. It was, most of the time . . .'

Bobby Willis was most certainly the man on Cilla's mind along with Brian Epstein. For it was Epstein who paid her daily attention. He took her to the London premiere of *Lawrence of Arabia* which starred Sharif and Peter O'Toole in his breakthrough performance in the title role. At one point, Cilla turned to Epstein and told him how much she loved the perfume worn by a glamorous blonde in the audience. The following morning, a full range of the 'absolutely fabulous' perfume which Epstein had found out was one of Christian Dior's was delivered to Cilla's Savoy Hotel suite on her breakfast tray. This was a delightful surprise – and altogether easier to deal with than Omar Sharif's advances!

While Peter O'Toole was establishing an important career with *Lawrence of Arabia*, another British actor was doing the same with *Alfie*. Michael Caine was the amoral Alfie, the Cockney gigolo with a heart of titanium, whose on-screen sexual adventures with co-stars like Millicent Martin, Shelley Winters, Jane Asher (then Paul McCartney's girlfrient) and Vivien Merchant (then Mrs Harold Pinter) are halted by tragedy.

Cilla's recording of Alfie is not part of the movie soundtrack. It was written by Burt Bacharach and Hal David after they saw the film. Cilla recorded it first – Dionne Warwick got her revenge with the American cover version which soared up the US music charts.

Bacharach arranged and played piano on Cilla's version; but the record was produced by George Martin whose magic touch with The Beatles did not always work with a solo Cilla.

'I used to think I was very soulful and sang in an American accent. George Martin would say not to sing the word "there" in my way because it sounded so Liverpudlian. I'd say, "You're right, George, I'll go back and do it again." I'd start singing the song and I'd totally forget. If you listen to my early records you'll notice that "were" and "there" are two words I should lose my accent on. I thought I had totally perfect vocal and accent conversion on Alfie, but I hadn't.'

And she had no control over the movie critics. Her own attempt at being a film star foundered, but the temptation to have a go was there. The Beatles had found success with *A Hard Day's Night* and it seemed she could too through Brian Epstein's packaging. In the Swinging Sixties of British entertainment, barely a Soho lunch went by without some singing idol deciding to become a movie star. Cliff Richard did well with *The Young Ones* and *Summer Holiday* – his title song from that film had knocked The Beatles' *Please Please Me* off the number 1 chart position in March 1963. Others tried to emulate him: Dave Clark of The Dave Clark Five (*Catch Us If You Can*), Paul Jones from Manfred Mann (*Priviledge*), and Mick Jagger (*Performance*). Eric Burdon of The Animals failed a screen-test to co-star with Rod Steiger in a movie version of Evelyn Waugh's *The Loved One*.

Cilla's film reviews have long been 'lost' from her CV and are now buried in the British Film Institute archives. It has always been a naive assumption that by putting popular young stars into a movie you will automatically have a box-office and critical success. It is entertainment-world thinking which persists – look at Madonna in the late 1980s and 1990s who only with the musical *Evita* won kudos. The experiment rarely works. It certainly failed with Cilla, but it was in this British showbusiness environment that she was turning herself into a household name – and a millionairess.' With the dust brushed away, her long-forgotten film reviews read exactly like this:

*DAILY CINEMA*, DECEMBER 1964
*FERRY CROSS THE MERSEY*
UNITED ARTISTS. BRITISH. 7,650 Fr. (85 MIN.) 'U'.
REL: 13 DEC
**STARS**: Gerry and The Pacemakers, Cilla Black, Julie Samuel.
**PROD.**: Michael Holden. DIR.: Jeremy Summers.
**ORIGINAL IDEA**: Tony Warren.
**Type of Production**: Musical.

**Story Outline**: Happy-go-lucky art student Gerry lives across the water from Liverpool with his Aunt Lil and her boarders, undertaker Lumsden and Miss Kneave. He forms a beat group with fellow students and they play regularly at Liverpool's Cavern. Gerry's wealthy girlfriend Dodie persuades impresario Hanson to hear them. Impressed, he agrees to manage them. Gerry and the boys enter a beat competition. After a crisis over their instruments which are taken by mistake to the airport, they are triumphantly cheered on stage and win the contest.
**Rating**: Dizzy, driving tribute to the Mersey beat, centred on the exuberant personalities of Gerry and The Pacemakers. style artless, pace hectic, comedy broad and pop song programme packed. Inevitable teenage box-office winner in the modern idiom.
**Critic's View**: Any similarity between this film and *A Hard Day's Night* cannot possibly be coincidental! Gerry and The Pacemakers are managed by the same man, Brian Epstein, come from the same city and 'arrived' on the same new soundwave as The Beatles. Added to which, the Director of photography on the Beatles' film, Gilbert Taylor, does the same kind of dazzling job on the Liverpool backgrounds here.

Admittedly the celebrated spontaneous high spirits of the Northern pop boys and girls tend to look like carefully nurtured cuteness. Admittedly, the idea of screen-filming close-ups of sweaty pop singers in full cry sounds more attractive in theory than it looks in practice. But they've obviously got what the youngsters love – and this film has the screams to prove it!

The plot exuberantly mixes fact and fiction. And the driving, almost documentary approach to the everyday life of Gerry is interspersed with the music-hall type humour (of George A. Cooper as the undertaker-lodger and Mona Washbourne as Aunt Lil) and speeded-up foolery which harks to Mack Sennett and the Keystone Cops. The music is marvellous, if you like it, and there's masses of it here to like. (Every number, inevitably, a winner.) Gerry and The Pacemakers are an agreeable bunch of boys, with a characteristic intolerance towards anything remotely un-with-it.

Cilla Black, The Fourmost and a big bill of pop artists wade in enthusiastically. though the reverence accorded Cilla Black might more suitably be lavished on Garbo, Dietrich and all three Beverley Sisters combined. Julie Samuel is an appealingly pretty Dodie. It's got the beat, the style, the stars and it's infallibly aimed at the teenage trade. It can't miss.

*VARIETY*, 9 DECEMBER 1964
*FERRY CROSS THE MERSEY*
Dateline: London

Another routine musical which will satisfy pop youngsters. Fair support to topliner pic with certain audiences.

The Mersey Sound which put pop music on the map in this country gets a fair belting in this modest, routine picture designed to exploit Gerry and The Pacemakers, one of Britain's top pop groups. It will have useful support in UK but though the group is known in America for its disks and a fairly successful tour is *Ferry Across The Mersey* unlikely to have much export appeal. It is noisy, corny and full of clichés but Jeremy Summers has directed with zest and some vitality and the pic goes at a reasonable lick. The Liverpool scene shows up well with some adroitly picked-up location work, and two or three unoriginal, but sprightly 'Keystone Cop' sequences add considerably to its comedy content.

As so often, however, this kind of pic falls down because of the laxness over the script, which is used mainly as a framework for putting over pop numbers. It is based on an idea by Tony Warren but the loose screenplay is uncredited, which is significant. Opening shows Gerry and The Pacemakers returning from a US trip. In flashback it shows how the group was formed, helped by a local chick who introduces the boys to a go-getting manager, and despite a last-minute mishap when they nearly lose their instruments and costumes, the lads win the European Beat Group Contest. Undoubtedly stronger material is needed if this type of film is ever to get out of a well-ploughed rut.

The thick local accent and idiom do not help for general consumption and there is a kind of noisy, frenetic, pumped-up hysteria and lack of discipline about the proceedings which palls, even with its modest limits of 88 minutes. Gerry Marsden, as well as writing the songs, leads his group with ebullience but shows little sign of being an actor. As his rich girlfriend Julie Samuel makes her debut. She is pretty, young, blonde, but her inexperience also shows up starkly. Jimmy Saville, a zany disk jockey, appears as himself, as does Cilla Black, a top British thrush, who sings one song and utters a few lines with a pallid personality and dubious success. T.P. McKenna scores as the manager and Mona Washbourne, Eric Baker, Deryck Guyler, Patricia Lawrence and George A. Cooper bring a little of their professional expertise to bear on unrewarding roles.

Most of the humour is naive in the extreme but director Summers gives the events as much pep as possible and has extracted some good fun from the frantic car chase sequences. Gilbert Taylor's lensing is vivid and effective and sound mixer Kevin Sutton has done a valiant, if not altogether successful job in trying to discipline the sound when The Pacemakers and other groups are on a no holds barred beat wingrading.

It was four years before Cilla appeared on film again – and then it was a landmark in her life. No Oscar followed – just a new nose. The American showbusiness bible'did the review honours:

*VARIETY*, 12 June 1968
WORK IS A 4-LETTER WORD

Wayout comedy-fantasy that will need shrewd exploitation to woo masses. Though often funny, entry is over-clever-clever and spotty.

Rank release of Universal-Cavalcade (Thomas Clyde) production. Stars David Warner, Cilla Black, features Zia Mohyeddin, David Walter, Elizabeth Spriggs. Direction by Peter Hall. Screenplay, Jeremy Summers, based on Heng Livings' play, *"Eh?"*. Camera (Technicolor), Gil Taylor; art director, Philip Harrison; editor, Keith Green; music, Guy Woolfenden; title song lyric, Don Black, music, Woolfenden, sung by Miss Black. Reviewed at Carlton Theatre, London. London, 6 June, 1968. Running Time, 93 MINS.

At least Peter Hall has not relied on his eminence as a legit director to get away with an 'easy' chore in his first film. *Work Is*

*A 4-Letter Word* is based on Henry Livings' unconventional and not wholly satisfactory play, *"Eh?"*. A difficult theme for a film, it serves to show that as a film director Hall has plenty to learn.

*Work* is a wayout comedy fantasy. Hall has said on television that it represents for him a 'personal statement'. Just what that statement is, is not easy to decipher and the average cinema-goer will probably be content to extract what fun and entertainment he can from some surrealistic verbal humour, an excess of mechanical gadgets and physical situations arising out of sales used in many other different, diverse types of film.

The picture will need hefty and careful exploitation, for though producer Thomas Clyde and director Hall have not been guilty of over-trickiness, they have certainly not set out to woo the masses. There is an irritating air of improvisation about much of the picture which shows up particularly in the editing. Reith Green clearly having difficulty in keeping Jeremy Summers' wayward screenplay within coherent bounds.

The thin storyline, set three years hence, visualises man struggling against automaton, something of a harkback to Chaplin's Modern Times. Overwhelmed by the DICE organisation which makes such horrors as plastic daffodils and whose skyscraper offices and factories are automated to a point of frenzy, one young man holds out against the system.

With an eccentric logic that springs from the lack of logic around him, Al Brass (David Warner) has decided that the cultivation of giant Mexican mushrooms is his calling in life. To marry a local girl he needs a steady job. To him it is logical to become night watchman in the DICE factory and use it to harness the steam needed by him to cultivate his mushrooms. He moves in with his bride (Cilla Black) and from then on the film becomes a chaotic frenzy as Warner causes destruction by interfering with monster machines that take on an identity and

> will of their own. Film winds with him creating a flock of monster mushrooms shaped like phallic symbols, which create a glorious euphoria in all who sample them.
>
> The plot and 'message' are merely hooks for a series of off-beat situations, some very funny and others over-reminiscent and overstressed. Hall often hangs on to a point just long enough to blunt it.
>
> Had he cast the film with expert farce players it might have turned out very different; not quite on the lines intended by Clyde, Hall and Summers, but almost certainly more amusing and popular. Yet the pic has produced some excellent performances. Warner's performance is vaguely similar to that he gave in Morgan. Unlike any other young British actor, his voice, features and attitude are all completely original. His zany behaviour becomes supremely logical in the face of the surrounding idiocies. It is doubtful, however, whether he yet has marquee pull and Clyde has taken an interesting gamble giving pop singer Cilla Black her first romp in films as b.o. bait.
>
> Her young admirers will regret that Miss Black does not sing, except for handling the Don Black-Guy Woolfenden title song. As a thesp she gets little chance to show her paces and seems rigid bewildered by the crazy proceedings around her. Her personality is likable, but unstriking, and the role could have been played by any other young starlet with equal impact.

These were not the sort of notices Cilla wanted, or had been used to. In 1993 she was still denying that *Variety* had even commented on her performance opposite David Warner. What was more devastating was seeing her nose in close-up. 'I didn't like it so I did something about it.' She makes a joke out of her looks and her attempts to enhance them – remarks like, 'I was surprised when I looked in the mirror as a young girl because l thought I looked like Jean Shrimpton.' Her nose 'bob' at the Queen Victoria Hospital at East Grinstead, Sussex, on her twenty-fifth birthday, also sorted out a longstanding problem. As a child, Cilla had been playing a game of chainy-chain (a long line of children holding hands and swinging each other around) when she had gone smack to the ground on her face. Her nose was fractured and never set properly. There was a bump and she could never say 'plum jam'. Her overcrowded teeth were also damaged in a childhood fall from a school wall.

But it was her profile – that nose – which got the instant attention after *Work Is A 4-Letter Word*. Her mother, one of the old school, derided it as a terrible decision. The practical Bobby Willis thought it was a good career move for someone who was planning to spend a lot of time in front of TV cameras. The couple were very conscious of each other's weak points.

'I did have quite nice teeth until I fell off the wall in our yard when I was a girl. I really had too many teeth as I got older, they all bunched up rather. Ohhhh – I don't like my teeth!

'I still like to think I look like Brigitte Bardot and Jean Shrimpton, as they were in the Sixties. I got the shock of my life when I first saw myself on telly and in photos. "I look like Brigitte Bardot," I thought, "I can't look like that!" TV is terrible on me because I have a round face, and now I'm at that age where I don't want to lose too much weight. I'd rather look like an old cherub than a scrag end.'

But it was television rather than film that was seen as the platform for Cilla. There were plenty of film offers but the only one that interested her – the classic 1969 caper movie *The Italian Job* with Michael Caine and Noel Coward – fell through her hands when contract talks failed. She was shrewd enough to see that pop singers and their celluloid vehicles do not easily win Academy Awards.

In the years between *Ferry Cross the Mersey* and *Work Is A 4-Letter Word* she had established the all round entertainment persona which would take her on through the decades. It was an important time and her contacts were immaculate. In his authorised biography *Many Years From Now*, published in 1997, Paul McCartney talks of creating *It's For You* for her, 'I wrote it for Cilla. It's not a bad little song. I remember when we first went to America, plugging it to all these DJs we used to meet. "Look," we'd say, "there's this girl singer in our stable and you should listen out for this song". It didn't do so very well. I ended up writing a few songs for Cilla.'

With The Beatles on her team, the Sixties should have promised sunshine all the way for Cilla. But there are stresses and tensions with such huge and immediate success. The battle is to stay at the top of the hill and not go screeching down it. And, of course, there are many sharks around, trying to feed off you. Fortunately, Cilla had the ever-loyal Bobby Willis by her side to keep her safe and settled.

But Cilla has always been anxious to keep going. She had appeared on endless television shows, topped the bill at the London Palladium, played cabaret and released hit singles, LPs and EPs. Other solo female singers like Dusty Springfteld and Sandie Shaw were popular, but Cilla was everywhere . . . from London to New York and Sydney, from Blackpool to the West End. She had been one of the first of the Beatlemania-era singers to tour in Australia (her original tour in 1965 was with Freddie and The Dreamers), and her cheeky brand of humour had appealed to Down Under audiences. They liked her casual 'g'day' sort of attitude. They also enjoyed her leggy mini-skirted look – she was the mascot of the Swinging Sixties. Her drive was never diluted by success; the more she got, the more she craved it. Her confidence apparently overwhelmed any obstacle.

It was all so different for Brian Epstein. As his artists soared, his own life crumbled. He was washing down amphetamines, drinking and not sleeping, and in the process losing the plot. His attention wandered, and because he had lavished it so much on Cilla, that was where it was most missed.

She was hurt. She talked endlessly to Bobby Willis about it. Had she upset Epstein? Had Bobby? Had both of them? Did Epstein not like her any more?

During the run of *Way Out In Piccadilly* with Frankie Howerd, the usually meticulous Epstein seemed to be ignoring his star. After the opening performance he rarely attended the show which ran for nine months.

Cilla complained to Bobby. She was as important as The Beatles. She was a star. She was insulted. She was also very young, and although always able to disguise it with her apparently never ending confidence, insecure beneath the champagne smiles.

She tried to arrange meetings with her mentor but his office, it seemed to her, just gave her the runaround. The Liverpool 'family' had disassembled; London was now the centre of Epstein operations. It was all going terribly wrong. Cilla and Bobby Willis decided to leave the control of Epstein management. The news devastated Brian, whose depressions— fuelled by drink and drugs – were getting deeper and longer. He knew he had not nurtured Cilla as he always had in the past. But she was being difficult.

Cilla, in turn, had no inkling of his torment. He was like a god to her. Later she was upset on learning about his depressions, 'In those days I was full of "What's happening to *me*?" I was so very young . . . we all thought Brian was a Superman. Suddenly we discovered he was vulnerable. It was quite a shock.'

Epstein called a crisis meeting at his home in Chapel Street in London's Belgravia. He provided lunch for Cilla and Bobby Willis on the roof garden and poured out his problems – and tears. Cilla and Bobby Willis were also crying as Epstein begged them not to desert him: 'There are only five people in the world I care about other than my family: The Beatles and you. Please don't leave me, Cilla . . .'

In turn, she mothered him. She held Epstein to her and there was no embarrassment for any of them. If there is one moment when Priscilla White really became Cilla Black, that is it.

She went from being controlled to being in control. Bobby Willis would always be there, but from then on, Cilla called the shots.

And because of that, she could control her anger. Before that meeting she had been wildly upset when entrepreneur Robert Stigwood had telephoned her to discuss a business deal. She only talked business with Brian Epstein, she screamed. What the hell was going on?

Simply, Epstein was cracking up.

He had felt she was not truly understanding his position, his problems. Cilla was so self-obsessed she had no idea he had any problems. Now that she did, she had decided not to leave him. The decision did not make her any less demanding. Epstein had, as ever, charmed himself out of the trouble his adoration of Cilla had landed him in. Until his own problems began to overwhelm her he had been totally attentive to her.

He strove to get their relationship back to where it had been, but Cilla was being difficult. She turned down his plan that she should represent Britain in the Eurovision Song Contest. Sandie Shaw had just won it with *Puppet on a String* and being practical, Cilla was certain the UK would not get the winning votes two years running. She was just correct. Cliff Richard carried the flag for the UK with *Congratulations* which, although a number one hit, came second in the Eurovision Contest to Massiel of Spain with *La La La*.

She was still 'my Cilla' to Epstein. He was friendly with Beatles' rivals The Rolling Stones and their Svengali Andrew Oldham, who was also looking after Marianne Faithfull. The sultry singer had a hit with the Stones' *As Tears Go By* and was Mick Jagger's lover. Epstein often had dinner with Jagger and Faithfull – true figureheads of the decade's sex, drugs and rock 'n' roll scene. However, despite several invitations, he would not manage the wayward Faithfull – the antithesis of girl-next-door Cilla – who, in clouds of illegal smoke and erotic innuendo, would become one of the lasting images of Sixties' decadence.

There was no conflict of interest between Cilla and Marianne then, although Epstein said there could be, and years later in 1997 Cilla did throw a legal wobbly over British TV Channel 4 documentaries involving them both. It's possible that Epstein just wanted to have Cilla as his only female star. He was as 'in love' with her as he could be; he was at his best when she was around him. He was always ready to make her happy. When John Lyndon was at rehearsals for a series of concerts starring Gerry and The Pacemakers in Great Yarmouth, he was called by Epstein who had been told that Cilla was miserable in Blackpool. 'You must go to Cilla in Blackpool tomorrow. Cilla is unhappy.'

A private plane had been arranged for Lyndon, who at first said he was too busy to go. Epstein insisted. Lyndon flew to Blackpool, made Cilla happy and in turn did the same for his boss. 'Moments like that are to be cherished,' said Lyndon. 'If Cilla was unhappy, or any of his artists, then out of his own pocket he would have taken the last ten quid to make sure that they weren't. This is what was so lovely about him.'

'Everyone you talk to who was around Epstein and The Beatles knew that Epstein really had a concern and care for Cilla Black,' said David Gibsone. 'That's what made it so tough for him when Cilla acted up.'

Tito Burns, who was the manager of Dusty Springfield and The Searchers, tells the story of how he once bumped into Epstei coming out of Cilla's dressing room at an awards show at Wembley Stadium. Epstein looked 'white as a sheet'.

'He said he was having a hard time. He said, "I'll do a swap with you. You give me Dusty and I'll give you Cilla." I said, "Thank you, Brian, but I like the way Dusty sings."'

Epstein's upsets with Cilla did not last long; for all their ups and downs, Epstein loved his Cilla. He had been hammering away at getting her a television series. She, cleverly had seen the power and future of television: it was here to stay while pop singers appeared from nowhere and often returned there rapidly. She was desperate for her own show.

On 25 August 1967, a Bank Holiday weekend Friday, Epstein received a call from the BBC. Cilla was to get her own TV series! He began work on the contracts. Forty-eight hours later, he was discovered dead at his home in Belgravia.

Rumours and theories appeared beneath big headline news of Epstein's early death, dwarfing reports of the Arab Nationalists' violence against British troops in Aden. Exactly three weeks before his thirty-third birthday, Epstein had fallen victim of the rough homosexual sex he favoured; a lover had murdered him, some said. Or was it a burglary, gone wrong? Or had he committed suicide? Something he had attempted before.

The speculation was mixed in with facts. Epstein's father Harry, until 1966 a warden at the Greenbank Drive Synagogue in Liverpool, had died-only five weeks earlier. Epstein had sat *shiva* (traditional Jewish mourning) for his father and was terribly concerned for his mother Queenie's welfare – and for his own health, having just left a private clinic. The Beatles' contracts were about to be renegotiated at the end of September. Epstein had much on his wandering, often drug-befuddled mind.

But at his death, in his arms were Cilla's television contracts. She is convinced that was evidence enough that he did not kill himself. How could he, when her career was literally in his hands? Nevertheless, there were empty pill bottles around. Epstein's life was over but, bizarrely, Cilla's new one was beginning.

Cilla's early career is pedantically written off as an adjunct to that of The Beatles, but she never played a subsidiary role in the enigmatic Epstein's life or thinking. Indeed, she was instrumental in keeping his life together and, in so doing, also keeping the Beatles united. Brian was the fifth Beatle. 'He was one of us,' said John Lennon.

We only know it now, but it was the demands of managing The Beatles and watching over Cilla's career that helped Epstein survive as he drifted along in his own perilous ocean of drink and drugs, delusion and disillusion. Shortly before his death, Epstein was using heavier doses of drugs to get to sleep. And when he did close his eyes and fall into a final uneasy rest, he would often sleep-walk. Then, he would snap awake and work on his papers, on contracts and schedules for his growing roster of acts. His need to do well by the stars he had helped create, especially Cilla, motivated him. Associates said decades later that he would have done anything to hang on to Cilla's respect.

'When you study the times and the people involved it's awfully clear that Cilla was the schoolmarm in all of it. Epstein and The Beatles and the others may have had power and popularity but they were still "frightened" of her,' said Merseybeat expert David Gibsone, adding: 'It was something to do with the times, of a respect for a woman's place. Women could be intimidating to these lads and they would not push their luck. John Lennon would be cheeky with her but he would only go so far: cheeky not naughty.

'It's the same all these years later on *Blind Date*. The "Blinders" only get to go so far – if they go over the line they are in trouble.

'Brian Epstein was fearful of Cilla's anger, of upsetting her. There's no question he held it together for as long as he did as much for Cilla as self-preservation.'

Without Epstein, the Fab Four, albeit arrogant and cheeky and full of marijuana and meditation and Maharashi Mahesh Yogi teachings, were never again to be as united. Or to stay very long together in their New Age manifestation. Flower power dissipated them. After Epstein's death they, like Cilla, had to grow up. Another world and decade wasn't far away.

*Chapter Five*

# SAD TIMES

*'I don't think I would have lasted five minutes without Bobby.'*
– CILLA BLACK ON HUSBAND BOBBY WILLIS

He may have been a fledgling overseas operator but Brian Epstein's charisma was international. He was a dominant personality – meeting royalty and presidents along with the Fab Four. His death was global front-page news. The obituary pages of newspapers in cities like London, New York and Los Angeles ran columns on his achievements. 'Meditation turns to mourning for Beatles,' shouted the *Liverpool Daily Post* on that bleak Monday morning of 28 August 1967. Cilla was on holiday in Portugal. She and Bobby Willis were at a nightclub with Welsh singer Tom Jones (he had got his break on a show with Cilla, replacing the controversial, trouser-splitting P.J. Proby) when she was given the news.

A waiter, something of a Fawlty Towers Manuel, had bluntly announced at her table, 'Your manager is dead.' Bobby Willis thought it was some sort of prank. He was furious, his soft Liverpudlian tones driven into high-pitched shouts. Tom Jones, who was not so closely involved with Epstein, took charge of the situation. He telephoned a local English-language newspaper which confirmed the waiter's tragic information.

Epstein, that strange, confused and complex man, had won his way into the hearts of scores of people in what was and is a tough and often superficial business. Of all his artistes – The Beatles, Gerry and The Pacemakers, Billy T. Kramer and The Dakotas, The Fourmost, Donovan, Matt Monro – it was Cilla to whom he had felt and been closest.

'It's true. Brian's dead,' Tom Jones told her quietly.

Cilla had never lost anyone before. She didn't know where to look or what to say. Bobby Willis held her arm. Tom Jones, just a young man himself, was also trying to find something to say.

Of course, in such situations, there isn't anything that can be said. The shock and the desolation of the death of someone close are so loud inside that little else can be heard. 'I was stuck for words,' recalled Tom Jones in 1997 at his home in America. 'Cilla and Bobby looked lost. They were shaking their heads we didn't have any details, we didn't know what had happened. Cilla just kept asking questions we couldn't answer.'

She said of the moment 'When I heard the news of Brian's death I just felt utterly alone. I'd never lost anyone so close or been to a funeral before Brian's. Anyone who was really close to him loved him.

'I was a coward. I didn't want to go on. But that's not what Brian would have wanted. He was so much more than a manager to me . . .'

Later, John Lennon explained his totally honest reaction to the news when he told *Rolling Stone* magazine, 'I thought "We've fucking had it," I knew we were in trouble then. I didn't have any misconceptions about our ability to do anything other than play music. I was scared.'

So was Cilla. She flew back to Britain twenty-four hours after hearing the news in Portugal. Fleet Street and the radio were providing some of the answers. The Beatles had been in retreat with their Himalayan guru in Bangor, Wales, when they got the news. George Harrison's initial reaction revealed where the group's collective mind was: 'You can't pay a tribute in words to Brian. There is no such thing as death, only death in the physical sense. Life goes on.'

Elvis Presley sent a message of condolence. Cilla, distraught and desolate, read the newspapers with tears pouring from her eyes. Crowds, many in Oriental robes and decorated in flowers, roamed around London's West End where a concert by Jimi Hendrix (Cilla's three sons are all Hendrix fans and thirty years later still had posters of him in their bedrooms) had been postponed at the Saville Theatre which Epstein financially controlled.

As Harrison and the others talked on Sunday, 28 August 1967 – Epstein had been scheduled to join them that day to be initiated as a member of the International Meditation Society – their manager's other acts like Gerry and The Pacemakers and Billy J. Kramer cancelled concerts or paid respects. Hitmakers Gerry Marsden (on holiday in a caravan in Wales) and Cilla (on holiday in Portugal) as well as The Beatles were told by the Maharishi to have pleasant thoughts of Epstein as they would reach him wherever he was.

Scotland Yard were investigating the death but detectives put the decision, and incredible press and public pressure, on the Coroner to decide if the circumstances merited an inquest. They did. Medical evidence said Epstein had taken half a dozen Carbrital sleeping pills to get the rest he craved. His insomnia, turned inside out and back again by his increasing use of narcotics, had driven him to the edge. The verdict was an accidental overdose which had tipped Epstein's immune system over the edge.

Epstein's body had just given up. No testing for an AIDS type of virus was done, but given his promiscuous homosexual lifestyle and drug use, experts say there is evidence he died of an AIDS related condition; his continuing bouts of glandular fever and high temperatures before his death point to a gestation of the disease. 'He was certainly involved in the big elements of the AIDS time bomb,' said an official at the AIDS Healthcare Foundation in Santa Monica, California. He added, 'AIDS takes some years to gestate and we are still discovering more and more about its beginnings – and its victims. Brian Epstein could have been a casualty.'

The sudden death of their manager certainly warned The Beatles away from drugs. 'You cannot go on taking drugs for ever,' said Paul McCartney, and even Ringo Starr who was to spend decades in an alcoholic haze offered, 'I hope the fans will take up meditation instead of drugs.'

The inquest and the necessity for a post mortem had confused the funeral arrangements at the synagogue where his father had worked and been buried in July. Under Jewish law, a body should be buried within forty-eight hours of death.

Cilla laughed at the ceremony. It was a nervous release of all her emotions which had been building that day. Epstein was a terrible timekeeper and his business associate Peter Brown – waiting for the ceremony to begin as heavy motorway traffic had delayed Epstein's corpse on the trip from London to Liverpool – whispered to her, 'He can't even make it to his own funeral on time.' Cilla couldn't control her laughter. She was in such a state – compounded by the Jewish law that women cannot attend the actual burial – that Epstein's mother had to take her into the synagogue and give her a sedative. The Valium calmed her.

Epstein's body was taken to the Jewish Cemetery at Long Lane, Aintree, and buried in Section A, Grave H12, near his father. Cilla wasn't present to hear Rabbi Dr Norman Solomon upset the mourners by trying to bury Epstein's reputation with him, calling him part of the decadence of the Sixties. It was astonishing stuff. The Beatles had stayed away to stop it turning into a circus. But, through

George Harrison, they were in some way present. Jewish law does not allow flowers at funerals but at Harrison's request a white chrysanthemum, wrapped in a newspaper headline about the funeral arrangements, found its way atop the coffin. Elsewhere, a distraught Cilla was comforting and being comforted by Queenie Epstein and other female family members. Later, The Beatles tried to entice her into an attempt to contact Brian in the spirit world. The thought left her tongue-tied, bumpy with goose pimples: she did not accept.

The stories have persisted that Epstein killed himself but Cilla has never, never believed them. In 1997 she insisted, 'He was very up. He'd just seen us off to Portugal on holiday. His auntie was moving down to London and he'd bought her and his mum a flat. In Grosvenor Square, opposite the hairdresser.'

Her memory for detail is very good although sometimes there are gaps and it is left to others to fill them in. With Epstein went his Judy Garland dream. In its place he had left a note for his secretary to contact Cilla in Portugal asking her to get in touch as soon as possible on 'an urgent matter'.

That 'matter' was *Cilla*, her BBC TV series which ran for nine weeks from the end of January 1968, finding an average weekly audience of thirteen million. With it she established the foundations of a format and personality which, in essence, have not changed in thirty years. Bobby Willis says, 'Cilla's the star.' She insists, 'He's my talisman, my security blanket. 'Together they were united in their devotion to succeed.

'Cilla always lights up at the idea of going on stage,' said Frankie Howerd. 'I have always been awed by it but she jumps in. There is no fear other than not being asked to do it again. That's what keeps her going. She's afraid only of saying "no" and not being asked again. It's silly and irrational but it's there. It's part of the work ethic of her background: you get nothing for nothing, and if you think you have got more than you deserve, then you're always terrified someone is going to come in one night and take it away from you.'

She herself uses an old joke to try and disguise her obsession, 'We've got a big fridge in our house and when I open the door the light comes on and I start smiling.'

It did not appear in 1968 that anybody or anything could spoil Cilla's party. Showbusiness friends like Cliff Richard, Ringo Starr and Lulu made guest appearances on her show *Cilla* and the theme tune, Paul McCartney's *Step Inside Love* ('it was cabaret, it suited her voice,' said McCartney) became another successful single record release.

Again, she was everywhere. It was the year *Work Is A 4-Letter Word* was released and, posthumously, Epstein got the blame for her involvement in the flawed enterprise. It was Brian, people said, who had been swayed by the snob theatrical appeal of Peter Hall, and not serious considerations of his protegee's career.

Cilla said in 1997 'I wasn't desperate to get into the movies let alone play a terrible, dowdy part. Not only was I the only non-actress in the film, I was also the only one who had never worked on Shakespeare. I enjoyed it. It was time-consuming but it was money for old rope.' Even in the early years, thin-skinned but unsinkable Cilla had bounced back from much worse than high falutin' film critics. She headlined her own show on stage up and down Britain and did a second tour of Australia where they adored 'the funny sheila in a mini-skirt'.

Gracie Fields had sent her a telegram on the first night of the *Cilla* series. In turn Cilla had been given a nice trip to Capri, paid for by *TV Times*, to 'interview' the other 'lassie from Lancashire'.

The idea was to show two entertainers comfortable in themselves, the Queen and the Pretender, as it were. But unfortunately, Gracie Fields couldn't stand Cilla. Maybe it was vanity on her part or a misread threat, but Gracie found her far 'too pushy' and told a photographer at one of their encounters, 'She wants to be me – even before I'm in my grave. She's awful. What a dreadful person she is. She obviously doesn't care about anybody but herself. Look at the way she treats people.'

Fields, whose career spanned seven decades, was so adamant about Cilla that in her authorised biography *Gracie Fields*, written by David Bret, she talked about living to see a good film biography made of her early days in Rochdale – but definitely without Cilla in the title role. That was something that had been suggested and Fields was strongly against the idea. 'Cilla isn't an actress. I'd rather be done by Maggie Smith.'

She talked about others who might play her in a film. If not Maggie Smith she favoured the attractive, dark-haired singer Susan Maughan (her big hit was *Bobby's Girl*) or Patricia Routledge, who found her own television fame in the 1990s as Hyacinth Bouquet in *Keeping Up Appearances*. Patricia Routledge had talks with the BBC about the role but the programme was never made.

What is extraordinary is that Gracie Fields and Cilla were so similar; one might not have come along without the other. 'It is no joke to be an uncrowned and unguarded queen,' J.B. Priestley, who had written the scripts of two of Fields' films, said in 1947. Priestley believed that Fields' appeal was due to her ability to dominate audiences by alternating sentiment and broad comedy. Some of the same could be said of the Cilla of the 1990s because of the parallel of audience and appeal. Priestley wrote about one but it could, in part, have fitted the other, 'She was a mill girl immensely enlarged and intensified by talent and art.'

Cilla was oblivious to all this. As she was to anybody, with the exception of Bobby Willis. It was understood by those around them that they would marry – when it was right for her fans.

Having moved on to television from the rock scene with its 'sex sells' marketing it was reasonable for Cilla to no longer be 'available'. Being single helped sell records, but marriage was seen as a plus for armchair audiences. Even in the late – and still 'swinging', somewhere – Sixties, the evening 'family entertainment' slots were pulling in the highest ratings. And those who were watching television at those times were the people with money to spend. On the topic of spending, there is a story that, from the day she started at London Weekend Television with *Surprise, Surprise*! and *Blind Date*, Cilla wore the same pink towelling bathrobe, a special offer in *Woman's Journal*, for more than thirteen years. She herself says it was done for luck, but behind the scenes at LWT there were unlikely stories that she was just too mean to spend her own money.

Cilla was a prime-time commodity and has remained one; Bobby Willis was the always likeble buffer, the antithesis of a showbusiness Mr Fixit. All his life, it seems, Bobby looked after Cilla and his budgies. He usually had twenty or thirty budgies at home and a dozen cockatiels. The man who could have been a Top Ten singer or songwriter spent his life looking after his birds – Cilla and the budgies. Together they made it work through that most corrupting of terrors – time.

One visitor to Cilla's rooms backstage recalled being met by a happy, smiling Bobby Willis. 'I'll go and tell Cilla you're here,' he said, and wandered into the dressing room. Much crashing and banging and shouting followed – 'enough to waken the dead'. Then Bobby Willis emerged, saying, 'She'll just be a moment.'

And so she was, bright and shining, just as if nothing untoward had occurred. Bobby Willis just beamed; he was a man who cultivated a resilience like the Rock of Gibraltar. He was supposed to be the Al Capone of the relationship – the hard nut in contract negotiations including a landmark 1991 deal for one million pounds, which not only made Cilla one of TV's top earners but helped London Weekend Television regain its franchise – but it was his wife who packed the machine gun in their house. The image of Cilla as the 'little woman' being coddled and content to perform at the click of a camera, flick of a switch, shine of a spotlight, was just not the whole story. She's never been a puppet.

Mr and Mrs Robert Willis beat all the statistics against marital longevity – an admirable achievement as showbusiness unions especially are prone to temptation, and separations are more prevalent than in the nine-to-five life. They lived their lives like Siamese Twins: they both swear they have never spent a night apart, other than for the births of their three sons since their wedding on 25 January 1969.

It was Frankie Howerd who convinced Cilla to officially become Bobby's Girl. She and Bobby Willis had a tremendous falling-out in the Sixties – neither of them will say why – but Howerd played matchmaker and got them together again – it was something they couldn't resist – for a holiday in the South of France.

After their wedding he became a close family friend. He remembered her children growing up, 'They don't call me Uncle. They call me Frankie Howerd. They say, "Come here, Frankie Howerd!" They treat me a bit like one of The Muppets. I go to Cilla's for lunch and I never give her any notice, in my usual unselfish way. I just ring her to say I'm coming. I like being at Cilla's. We give each other advice and talk about our problems. They have a very nice log fire and I like standing in front of it like a County Squire. As you get older, you tend to feel more vulnerable. I do, anyway, and you tend to cling to the people you know already. It can be a lonely life. People go on about actors gushing over themselves with their "darling" this and "darling" that, but I'd rather people be insincerely polite than sincerely rude.'

It was a double celebration that 25 January at Marylebone Register Office in London, it was Bobby Willis' twenty-seventh birthday. As the groom was a Protestant ('a lovely boy, he'd make a good Catholic,' said Cilla's mother after meeting him for the first time), Cilla had to get special permission for their second marriage ceremony on 6 March at St Mary's Parish Church in Woolton, Liverpool.

She says they didn't want a fuss at either ceremony, but Robert Willis marrying Priscilla White was clue enough even without an information 'leak' to Fleet Street picture desks, and at Marylebone, photographers snapped Cilla in a £10 scarlet mini-dress (she took up the hem herself) bought in the King's Road in Chelsea, and Bobby Willis in a dark suit and blue and white spotted tie. The best man was their friend, the men's fashion designer Tommy Nutter. Cilla's everlasting pal Pat Davies and entertainer Michael Crawford's then wife Gabrielle were there, along with Peter Brown, who only a few months earlier had made her laugh at Brian Epstein's funeral.

This was an occasion to laugh for joy. With the cropped hair and the dress bought from the shop Granny Takes A Trip, displaying the endless legs, it was a freeze-framed dolly-bird Sixties image. In contrast, her new husband was toned-down, with a more traditional image, rather like Brian Epstein.

Six weeks later at Woolton, the church blessing of their wedding had a more family than King's Road feeling around it.

Her father gave her away and Cilla was still the centre of attraction with a fashionably short ostrich feather-trimmed white jersey dress and glistening white grin and knee-length boots. The dress had been a gift from the Jean Varon designer company in London, and she had chosen her wedding ring (an Asian 'lucky' ban) herself in Hong Kong.

The family were full value: Kenny Willis was his brother's best man and Cilla's mother had on a Mrs Shilling-style hat – a family wedding tradition which her daughter kept up on her Blind Date weddings—and George Martin and Tony Barrow were present representing the business side of the 'family'. Cilla's three brothers and her brother-in-law Bertie Willis were happy to be present. Brian Epstein's brother Clive was also there as a reminder of the triumphs of the decade that was ending.

There were laughs and 'jars' and songs from the relatives – not quite the *Liverpool Lullaby* but as well meant and sentimental. It was a wonderful family affair. But for all her anchored roots, Cilla, just 26 years old, had already written her place in the entertainment almanacs. Her place was clear later that year at the Royal Variety Performance at the Palladium. It was also a top hats and tails occasion, with Cilla appearing with Ginger Rogers. With the Sixties nearly over, she had become an indelible part of British showbusiness, like her favourite *Coronation Street*.

As with her relationship with Bobby Willis, Cilla had begun a remarkable romance with the British public. Both have endured because of her efforts, and her refusal to use her success as a platform to turn herself into something she is not. This has also kept her close and loyal to her friends. 'Cilla treats everyone as a friend,' said Jimmy Tarbuck. 'Just because someone has not made it the way she has, is not a reason for her to ignore them. She's a good girl – she'll always look after you.'

Cilla and Pat Davies, who is now Pat Pansor, have always looked after each other. As teenagers they met at the Jacaranda Club in Liverpool. Cilla sang successfully; Pat Davies sang flat and went into public relations. She says she helped bring up Cilla's children before marrying Californian radio executive Geoffrey Pansor and moving to Los Angeles in 1980.

But like many 1960s' friendships it has remained solid. 'We were real products of the Sixties, you see,' said Pat. 'We have been friends since the age of fifteen. We lived near each other and even travelled on the same number 3 bus. Cilla used to live in Scotland Road and I was in Spellow Lane. We lived around the corner from each other. She was brilliant in the clubs. I used to serve in the coffee bars and she was always getting up and belting out songs. She had so much life. She always has had. It was a really fascinating time to live.

'The music was everything. In those days we didn't need drink or drugs. Everything happened in the coffee bars. God knows, we drank so much coffee my mother used to warn us we'd never sleep. It was a completely different world then from now. Cilla was doing a song called *Boys* and Ringo Starr was doing the same song at the same time. Our friendship was a gradual thing but the same crowd used to hang out at the same clubs and we got to know each other. I'm tone deaf, the worst singer you've ever heard.

'I remember I did beat her to the top of the bill one time – when our mothers put on a show in what was known as the "Mothers' Club". It was the one and only time in my life that I took billing ahead of Cilla. Throughout our friendship I have watched Cilla turn from being a teenage hopeful in Liverpool to a superstar, and I can tell you she deserves everything she has got. She has worked so hard for it. She just keeps going.

'But throughout she has always been just a normal person to me, not a bit showbizzy like you might expect. Just an ordinary friend with her feet on the ground. I don't envy her a thing because I know she has worked so hard for what she has got. I have seen her on the way up and she never gives up.

'Now I live in Los Angeles and if we don't happen to speak to each other for a while we can just pick up the phone and start talking from where we left off. We go on for hours – you should hear us. Of course, we will argue sometimes but we never hold grudges. I know she will always be there for me. When I lived in England I had my own key to her house; I was part of the family.

'Cilla has her own way of doing things. People don't always agree with her, but she knows her mind. She knows what she wants . . .'

*Chapter Six*

# ON THE COUCH

*'I wanted to be a nun for a while. I liked the outfit and they had such incredible complexions and were so serene.'*

– CILLA BLACK, 1997

When Bobby Willis died, Cilla had been married for more than thirty years. She and Bobby had three sons – Robert, Ben and Jack. Sadly, they lost a daughter Helen, who was born prematurely in 1975 and lived for only two hours.

Their stories through the years give an oral history of their times, their marriage and family, of the triumphs and tragedies. And, always, of Cilla's attempts to stay, or at least appear, 'normal' in her transition from working-class girl to media millionairess, from gyrating Sixties dolly to more matronly television queen of the *double entendre*.

This is Cilla and Bobby Willis talking, usually to promote a stage show or a record, or a TV series or a charity function, and they reveal – sometimes unintentionally – not just the secrets of a showbusiness marriage but also the mundane side of matrimony – the places most married couples have been sometime in their relationships. As she says, money does not buy happiness, 'but it bloody well helps.'

'I knew as a little girl I was going to be a star, all right. I just didn't know I was going to last . . . I was always dressing up and showing off. And every time I go on stage it's the same. Show me an audience and I can't wait to go out there. I think I was born under a lucky star. When I began singing, it all came so easy really.

'One minute I'm living with me mam and dad in Liverpool, and the next I was a star. It was storybook stuff.

'It all took a bit of getting used to. But once again, I was lucky. In the beginning there was Brian Epstein, who managed me, The Beatles and all the other Liverpool lads. We were always appearing places together and we were a gang. It was like youth-club outings.

'Then I met Bobby and he was always with me. After I got married I thought that would be that. I'd had six good years at the top and I'd give it all up and have babies. But I carried on singing and the success kept coming. The furthest I went away from home was Blackpool. I remember being shocked later when I did a concert at Sheffield and discovered they had a Woolworths and a C&A. I had naively believed that only Liverpool had shops like that! I once thought of spending only half a year in Britain filming and the rest at my home in Spain. After six weeks in Spain I was bored to tears! I realised I was too British to spend six months there every year. I'm British through and through.

'I've got everything I want now – and I'm not bothered with jewellery any more since we had a robbery at our house in 1984. We never got any of it back. Now all I want is to see the children do well.

'I think about retiring but . . . I've seen what the future can be like. I saw Gracie Fields in Capri before she died. I went to talk to her at 11 a.m. with the sun blazing down – and she was singing the words to her song, '*Sally, Sallyyyyyy*' I turned to Bobby and begged him, "Don't ever let me get like that." But I know that's how I'll be . . . Bobby will understand.'

Some years ago, Cilla remarked, 'We're more in love now than when we first married. If anything were to happen to Bobby, I just couldn't go on. I'd really have to retire from the business. I wouldn't like the idea of giving everything up, abandoning what we've worked for, but I'd have no choice. I daren't think about what would happen if Bobby wasn't here to share things with. He's the reason for me being here. He's my taste, I'm dead common with none of my own.

'Heaven knows what rubbish I'd have accepted in the past if Bobby hadn't put the dampeners on. I wouldn't have lasted in this business five minutes without someone like him beside me. It's a very lonely life. I became a professional singer in 1963 and had to be on the road and constantly "on" as we called it. After two shows at a theatre or club, I'd come back so hyped up it would take time to wind down. What I wanted was a nice glass of wine and a chip buttie – or whatever the hotel could lay on at that unearthly hour. And it was nice to share that with somebody. Somebody like Bobby.

'Now, when I'm trying to come down after recording *Blind Date* or whatever, Bobby's there. He paves the way for me to get on with my job, which is basically enjoying myself. All I have to worry about is getting the false eyelashes on straight, then going out and doing it. If there's ever a fracas behind the scenes, Bobby protects me from it.

'Who'd protect me, tell me what's right and wrong, or say I was being too flash, if he wasn't around? The woman they call Cilla Black is all down to him. I'm his product, his package deal. But at home with the kids and friends, I'm plain Cilla Willis . . . Bobby's girl. Almost from the moment we first met, when I was working as a typist during the day and singing in clubs at night, I've been used to seeing him around. He's been my talisman, my security blanket.

'He always stands at the back of the studio when I'm recording for London Weekend Television and we have secret signals, like a tennis player and her coach. If I'm going on too much or someone's said enough, he'll make a throat-slitting gesture that means, "Get him off."

'He knows because he's been with me since the beginning when we first went to London to meet George Martin. It was only the second time I'd been to London. He was with me when I worked with Frankie Vaughan. I was fascinated by Frankie. I used to stand in the wings and watch him work an audience. He had them in the palm of his hand in five minutes. I picked up all my stagecraft at the Palladium fram Frankie, all the tricks of the trade. I watched, I listened, and I learned.

'Saturday night after the last show I'd do the six-hour drive back to Liverpool to be home for Sunday dinner. I hated being in London. I had a telephone by my bed in the hotel, but I didn't know anybody in Liverpool who had a phone.

'When it got too much I'd always take it out on Bobby. Once after a show in Monte Carlo – I'd had to learn French and sing in front of royalty – my nerves were so stretched we had a huge row and he stormed off to Liverpool. We were always splitting up, with Bobby driving back up North through the night.

'But he was always there when it mattered. We've always had the philosophy that this business has to work for us. Bobby banned important people from the dressing room because he didn't like the way they behaved. His attitude was, "Nobody's going to put a gun to our heads." Bobby prefers to be the one to fire the bullets and that's why our partnership has worked. He thinks I should worry only about putting the false eyelashes on and going out there and doing it. I'm very well protected; if there has been a row, it's never with me. I don't know how he can do business after losing his temper, because it would eat away at me for days. But people *do* take advantage, and if he ever feels I've been walked over, he'll really flip.

'I'm anything for a quiet life, though I told Ringo off once when we were on holiday in the South of France. He was asked for his autograph and he refused. He said, "I'm on me holiday." But we were on the beach and, my God, if you don't want people coming up for your autograph, then don't go to the beach. It took him longer to refuse to sign than actually doing it.

'He said, "Don't you understand, I don't want to sign autographs on me holiday?" I said, "Look, just sign it, or let's go." I don't see the point in making such a big issue out of not signing. I've been in a restaurant and I've literally had the fork halfway to my mouth. People have come up, got hold of my arm, put my hand down and put food back on the plate. But that's what I regard showbusiness as being about.

'Bobby could easily have been overawed in the early days, but when it came to the crunch, his tough upbringing stood him in good stead. His mother died, leaving four sons and Bobby, the youngest, was only eleven. He was still at school, but he had to clean, shop and cook for his three brothers and father, who worked at the flour mill.'

Bobby said, 'My mam always had a weak heart. When she had an attack, the old fella used to jump on her and give her the kiss of life. Wherever she went, she carried a little bottle of brandy and a sugar lump. She'd been ill over Christmas and my dad had sent her to her parents to be looked after. The day after Boxing Day, one of my brothers came home and he just said, "Our mam's dead." Eight months after that, my brother Ronnie died of cancer.

'I learned to put on a front, to disguise my feelings. I've got a terribly unconfident side to me. Our Ben takes after me. He'll become aggressive sometimes and I know deep down his stomach is full of butterflies.

'When we came to London, I bought Cilla her first two dresses. Being a Northern male, I didn't like it when the roles were reversed and she was the one with the money. My mother was a moneylender in Liverpool before she became ill – I've always been keen on the good things in life. I'm the cook of the family. That's the one time there's trouble— when she complains about my cooking.'

It was then, apparently, a rare show of annoyance. Bobby Willis played golf and looked after his budgies and Cilla. They said they did get bored and irritated with each other sometimes. But they were an ongoing double act. She said, 'I just can't bear to think of Bobby not being here. It upsets me, makes me depressed. We're a team, two pieces of a jigsaw. Being married to someone in the business with an ego as big as mine, would have been impossible.

'When we met it was Bobby who had a voice that sounded like Johnny Mathis and he was the one being offered record deals but he turned them all down.'

He says 'I didn't have the guts, the balls. Either that or I did it for love. I've always been bowled over by Cilla's talent and I don't think I could ever have achieved what she has. It was like songwriting. I saw what Paul McCartney and John Lennon were doing and I gave up writing songs for I knew I could never be as good as that.

'We were on *This Is Your Life* when they honoured Jimmy Tarbuck and I had one line to say. My leg was shaking like a pneumatic drill. I lost a lot of sleep over it. And then I stood there and forgot to say it. Cilla's the star, I'm better in the background. I can deal with everything behind-the-scenes. I'm not Cilla's husband then – I'm the manager. She's a product and it's up to me to get the best for her. My philosophy is to give everybody the chance to earn a living. So we operate on a kitty when we're doing a TV show. Cilla gets a fair fee, but there's enough left to make the show sparkle. If it didn't she wouldn't have been on the telly five minutes.'

From the outside their relationship can seem strange. In person, Bobby is nervous, almost stammering. On camera, as he says, he is and looks lost. It is in sharp contrast to Cilla. But they clicked from the very start:

'He was my first serious boyfriend – the only one I ever took home to meet my family. I didn't believe in sex before marriage, that was unheard of in my day. I was a good Catholic girl. Anyway,

I wouldn't tell you if I had. That's between Bobby, me and the bedpost. He was a bit of a Don Juan in those days.'

He says he had his standards, 'If I was going out with a girl, I never two-timed her. For one thing, I couldn't afford to. I'd see other girls and look for the door. Whereas with Cilla, I'd think, "Great." We'd sit in a coffee bar over one drink and be laughing all night. Often I'd go to the clubs where she was working and she'd charge me to come into her club. Pre-marital sex wasn't an issue. Where could you go? Your family were always in the house and you certainly couldn't afford a hotel.'

Cilla's view was more practical than moral, 'The great fear of having a baby was enough to put you off. And I had more important things on my mind than sex. I wanted to be a star.

'I love Bobby more than ever but it has to be said that romance is not his strong point. He didn't even ask me to marry him! We'd been together seven years and were in a TV production meeting when our friend Peter asked why we didn't tie the knot. Instead of asking me, Bobby turned to Peter and said, "If you sort it all out we'll get married." At the next meeting a week later Peter said:

"Right, I've done it. Come with me, we're going to put up the banns." And that's how we ended up getting married. When I tease Bobby about it now he says, "What I said to Peter was my proposal." It never occurred to him that I might say no.

'The most romantic thing Bobby has ever done for me is giving up his own career so I could pursue mine. He has a great singing voice and when we met he was the one being offered the record deals.

'There was no question about me giving up my career – Bobby has always been cleverer than me and there was no way I could handle the business side. I'm just a girl who can't say no. If it wasn't for Bobby, I would end up working every hour of every day. I also have an enormous ego and I'm terribly selfish. Our marriage would never have survived if both of us had tried to stay in the business.'

Their few close friends always said that in private their roles were reversed. Bobby Willis said, 'Cilla hates walking into a crowded room if it's full of stars.' She agrees, 'I'd rather be with normal people. *Blind Date* works because it's just me and the public. When I go out to dinner, everyone expects me to do an act, but it's Bobby who is the raconteur. I'm quiet. On the box, I'm Cilla Black, but away from it I'm Mrs Bobby Willis.'

They had definite views on marriage. He said, 'If a relationship is worthwhile, you have to work at it. Married life is a compromise. What I want to do may not be what Cilla wants, but she'll come along with me, and vice versa.'

She said, 'Professionally, it's very different. Bobby tells me what to do and I do it. But in terms of our marriage, I can't be doing with this seven-year-itch thing. If you've been given the responsibility to bring up children, then that's what you must do. Nothing in this world would make me hurt our kids. Even though I'm a total embarrassment to them every time I'm on TV. When I come on, they switch stations.'

He said, 'Cilla was a star before they were born. They've known nothing else but Mum being on telly. They must have had some stick at school from it, but they've never said anything about it. We kicked out right from the start with the notion that this business has to work for us. So it's never a threat. No one can threaten us.'

Cilla said, 'Bobby's the one who has to be hard. I always warn new directors not to shout at me or I'll dissolve. You don't get the best out of me if you're nasty. Neither of us can put hand on heart and say that we don't get on each others nerves sometimes. We do, and we row, but it's not often and it's nothing major.

'I know I irritate him when it comes to films. He's very much a film person and I can only take so many films on TV. I'll say, "I've seen this." And he'll say, "Oh, you've seen everything!" So I just move to another room.'

'I'm like the kids,' said her husband. 'They must take after me. They'll watch a favourite video over and over again, and I can watch my favourite films over and over again.'

'What really irritates me about Bobby is that he tells me the same stories all the time. I know all the names of his friends Jimmy Kirby, Sylvia Oldby – people from his childhood. I mean, that's really irritating.'

Bobby Willis confessed, 'If anything annoys me, it's when I'm talking and I say, "Well, last Wednesday we went to so and so," and she'll say, "No it wasn't, it was Tuesday." As if knowing the exact day affects the story! She's too much of a stickler for detail.'

'I have to nag him sometimes just to get something done,' said Cilla. 'We still argue, but Bobby's so easygoing. I'm a harper, always going on about things. If I ask him to move some furniture, I can guarantee he'll say, "I'll do it later." Why not now?'

Her husband responded, "What's really hard to live with is Cilla's obsession for constantly wanting to change the paintwork and the wallpaper in the house. I'm happy with it. It looks great. But Cilla gets fed up with the decor after five minutes.'

She used to say he was more a softie than a shouter, 'He's a right big crybaby when he's watching sad films on the telly. *Surprise, Surprise!* really makes him blubber. That's why he stands at the back – so no one can see him crying. LWT do actually provide Kleenex for Bobby every time he's there.'

Unsuspectingly hinting at the difficulties she was later to face, Cilla remarked, 'Now I'm conscious of time slipping away but Bobby's got a great philosophy. He always says, "Tomorrow's the unknown something to look forward to." But if he left me to make the ultimate deal Up There, I know I couldn't go on. What would it all be about if he wasn't here?

'I'd be totally lost without him. I couldn't have existed without Bobby. I'm very shy underneath. Also, you're talking about my wage ticket. Money embarrasses me. I don't even know what I'm paid for *Blind Date*. I'm totally the artiste, the performer. Get me the eyelashes, get me on there, and I'll do it.'

Many of her fans still believe she lives in Liverpool, but Mr and Mrs Willis – as they insisted on being called to local tradespeople – moved into their home in seventeen Buckinghamshire acres once owned by Sir Malcolm Sargent in the autumn of 1970. She still makes much of her beginnings but the woman with a docker father didn't care much for Harold Wilson, and soon embraced Thatcherism. To Cilla, like many Northerners of her age group, anywhere south of Watford is 'London'.

The big family home followed five years in London, at a 'cottage' in Regent's Park and then a flat near Broadcasting House, and she understands the notion that the geography stretched her loyalties, 'I've lived longer in London than I ever did in Liverpool, so maybe the people who say I've forgotten my roots are right, but Bobby and I are the only two defectors. All our families are still in Liverpool. You've got to understand that we are still very clannish. All our cousins, nieces, nephews are in Liverpool, and it's still like a village there. Most of my friends are still in Liverpool and nothing goes on there without me knowing about it. We may not live there any more, but our family, is there. Our history is there.'

And in 1997 she hinted that she might have stayed there if the road transport system had been better, 'If we had had the motorways we have today when Bobby and I first bought our house, there is no way I'd be living in London. It used to take us about five and a half hours to drive down through the fog to the TV studios, and I couldn't bear it any more. We had to live near to London.'

They bought the ten-bedroom house in Buckinghamshire, in the commuter belt town of Denham, for £40,000 and inflation made it worth something close to thirty times that in 1998. They both talked about the conservatory they added in 1993 like a suburban couple who have added on a bedroom extension to their semi-detached.

She said at the time, 'We've worked hard for the family life we have, but I have to say it's got a lot to do with money. It does help. We brought our kids up to know the value of money and made them do odd jobs to earn it. We learned at a very early age that the only thing we could give them at the time was an education. I think unemployment has a lot to do with the demise of family life. There's only so much love you can give your family, and if they're unhappy or haven't got things to do, I think that's the problem. We are lucky in the respect that we both have a close family and they have all done well. Call me old-fashioned but I actually do think that the violence we see in movies has a lot to do with it.

'I don't like to get angry. I never lose my temper in front of others – if I get upset then Bobby deals with it. I can't upset myself. I can't be doing with that. I can't have a go at anyone because I'd be even more upset if I did. I only ever lose my temper with Bobby. If I can't let off to my husband, or my loved ones, then something's wrong. Bobby will put it all in perspective for me. He says life's too short. He's incredible. He's a total optimist. If you were right-handed and you'd lost your right arm, he'd give you twenty great reasons why you didn't need that arm. He's fantastic.

'So when I am a bit down . . . I mean, people think I'm up all the time like I am on telly. If I was like that all the time, I'd be awful. I'm not up twenty-four hours a day. I do have my down moments. I'm terribly selfish.

'I don't like to upset others – so I take it out on Bobby instead. I'm very selfish in that way. I'll pick, pick, pick until I get him to react so I can justify having a go. It can't be easy for Bobby to live with that. But I'm too selfish to change.

'Even though I have a big ego, Bobby is the boss at home. I'm not like Cilla Black who you see on the telly. In real life I'm just plain Cilla Willis, Bobby's wife and mother of our three boys.

'I can never forget or forgive and I will go on for days and days endlessly saying to Bobby, "I can't believe they said that." I dissect and analyse the situation over and over again until Bobby eventually says, "Tomorrow is another day, love. Just try to forget it." He is very easy-going like that and brings me back down to earth. He is also a great hugger. When I'm upset, going on at him, he'll put his arms around me and give me a big bear hug. Mind you, he even hugs grown men, so I don't think that's got anything to do with romance!

'Bobby always says nothing in the world can replace a hug. He is very much my security blanket, the rock I cling to. Even though he's not Mr Romance, he is a softie at heart. He pays me compliments all the time, boosting my confidence. I am my own worst critic and if I'm feeling low I'll sit and run myself down.

'Bobby says, "Don't be silly, love. You just don't realise how good you are." Even though I've heard it a million times, it always makes me feel better. I totally believe in Bobby. If he told me to go and climb Everest, I would, no questions asked. I trust him completely. Like everyone, we do have our rows. But it's never the big things – we always talk about those – it's the little ones. He squeezes the toothpaste tube from the middle and leaves the loo seat up, which makes me livid.

'Bobby is Mr Tough for me. He is overprotective and will always try his best to make sure I'm not upset. But at home I'm the one who has to be strict with the kids.

'But even after all the years of marriage we still sit on the sofa, holding hands, watching the telly and having a hug. There's still nothing better for me at the end of a long day than cuddling up to Bobby. We have never spent a night apart since we got married. I can't bear being away from him.

'Even if he goes to play golf, I miss him terribly. I get very anxious if he's five minutes late and he goes bonkers if I don't get home at exactly the time I've said.

'I always want his approval. If I go to buy a new outfit, I'll always wonder "Would Bobby like it?" before handing over the cash.

'Bobby's not the lovey-dovey type in a sentimental sense. I remember when I was pregnant with our son Jack and went into hospital to be induced. They gave me something like an Exocet missile, and twenty minutes later I was in labour. I wanted Bobby to be there to hold my hand while I did all the hard work. He was sitting there reading the papers and I shouted at him, "Get the flaming nurse!"

'He dashed off and came back with a nurse in tow. He was standing next to her when she looked under the bedclothes – and he nearly fainted. He went as white as a sheet and ran out of the room. Jack was already halfway out and two minutes later he was born. Bobby did come back eventually, looking very sheepish.

'He has a memory like a sieve and if I don't remind him he even forgets his own birthday. But he did remember to be romantic once, it was Mother's Day and we were in Australia, where I was working. I thought it would be nice, just for once, if he could remember, and he did. At dawn, he woke me with a huge bouquet of flowers and then brought me a breakfast of Buck's Fizz – champagne and orange juice.'

Together they always had high hopes – and the expectations to go with them.

He said, 'I suppose I did fancy her the first time I saw her, but it was her personality I loved. Without meaning to be rude or anything, there were much better-looking girls around in them days, but they bored me and Cilla made me laugh. It's funny that she thought I had money because I had a suntan then that's why she fancied me, but it was all down to a cheapo holiday from Thomas Cook.

'We had our dreams in the beginning. We aimed for the top. When we first came down from Liverpool and arrived at Euston Station, it was the scariest moment in our lives. I think that's when work and our relationship became one. We made a bond that's lasted all through our lives. What we did was a big adventure but we don't analyse anything. That's because that's kept us together. We always had our feet firmly on the ground because our family always put us in our place.

'It was weird. Cilla would be the top bill at the Palladium and then we'd go straight home afterwards and the family would shout at her for sitting in her dad's chair. We'd have a lot of silly arguments in those days. I'd drop her off at the theatre and we'd have a row and then I'd go, "Right then, I'm off." I'd drive 200 miles up the motorway to Liverpool but then I'd turn the car around and go back to London.

'But those were just teething problems – we got all our squabbles out the way when we were kids. I suppose we have changed. We can sit with the Queen and the Duke of Edinburgh and still feel comfortable. Cilla's becoming quite good at cooking now. If she cooks something horrible no one eats it.

'She's got a bit of commonsense – it's only taken thirty years to learn! She makes a good Sunday lunch. I prepare it and she cooks it.

'We had a big argument years ago when she thought she knew best. I cooked this leg of pork with all that lovely crackling. Cilla was getting on my nerves. She kept saying, "Me mother never cooked it like that she stuffed it" I said, "How can you stuff something that's got a bone in the middle of it?" So I lost my temper and threw it straight out of the window. There's this tramp walking around the street with a beautiful leg of pork and we had to eat Spam. We even fought over that – there was only one can and we were starving.

'She knows exactly when to say sorry, whereas I don't. When I say sorry the timing is always wrong. But she knows me like a bad penny – she can suss me out. She knows me better than I know her. We're not demonstrative people. Cilla is very untidy but she's never had to wash one of my socks or iron my shirts. I do all of my stuff myself.

As my mother died when I was a lad I've always looked after myself. You wouldn't catch me doing the washing-up, though.

'I'm terrible when it comes to crying. I even cry in Coronation Street. When they film *Suprise, Surprise!* she holds it together like a tower of strength. I have to stand at the back so no one can see me blubbing like a bloody lemon.

'The most romantic thing was when we were in Cannes in the South of France. We were at the Majestic Hotel and Sacha Distel came over to see us for a champagne breakfast. The waiters were falling all over us and I was thinking how nice it was to be in one of the best hotels in the world. I thought: I'll have a bit more of this – and I have. We've had loads more champagne breakfasts.

'I could have been a success with my songwriting. They used to say that stuff about me having a voice like Johnny Mathis. But I repeat – I didn't have the balls. I'm best at not worrying and looking after Cilla. We've stayed together because I still fancy her. I'm not really a jealous person but I would still smack anybody in the face who tried to come on to my wife.

'I've done it once and I'll do it again. This guy came up to Cilla and started touching her up in a club back in the Sixties. He started being rude, so I gave him one. Cilla didn't see the first smack but she saw the second.

'We come from similar backgrounds and we're honest with cach other. When a friend heard us arguing he said, "You sound like a married couple – you should get married." We had a final row on the Wednesday, got married on the Saturday and had one night's honeymoon at the Ritz . . .'

*Chapter Seven*

# HEARTACHE

*'My daughter lived for only two hours ...*
*not a day goes by when I don't think of her.'*
– CILLA BLACK IN HER FIRST INTERVIEW ABOUT THE DEATH OF HER DAUGHTER.

Cilla's life was expanding. It was 1970, she was pregnant with her first child and she had become a brand name on British television, the star host *and* guest who could pull in the audiences if not the favour of the critics. Cilla plunged on regardless.

Her *Cilla* television show had literally bridged the 1960s and 1970s with the third series running through the 1969–70 Christmas and New Year season, and still pulling in a vast audience of more than ten million viewers a week. Her single *Surround Yourself With Sorrow* was released in early 1969 and reached number 3 in the charts. Then came *Conversations* in July, which reached number 7. She closed the year with the recording *If I Thought You'd Ever Change Your Mind* and it sneaked into the Top Twenty at number 20. Her early 1970 concert commitments were like little dots on a map of Europe, stretching from Holland up to Denmark and Sweden and down and over to Madrid before crisscrossing to Germany and France.

There would be new homes in Spain and the English stockbroker belt, and variety concerts from Scarborough to Malaysia, and pantomime, and TV series on both BBC and ITV, including a situation comedy run called *Cilla's Comedy Six*. She would be working with familiar UK faces like Alfred Marks, Bernard Cribbins, Ronnie Corbett and Jimmy Tarbuck, or America's 'Nutty Professor', Jerry Lewis and Bob Hope. There were single records like *Baby We Can't Go Wrong*, released at a time when it appeared nothing could, which remained towards the bottom of the pop charts in 1974, and albums which made little impact.

She had moved on. The public's perception of Cilla was changing, as was her audience. She wasn't the only one getting older. She still saw herself as the pop star who was doing television, but it was clear to others who were more detached about her career – even hands-on Bobby Willis – that Cilla was a natural 'entertainer'.

That was her talent and the essential secret of her longevity. Sexuality and sexual situations were becoming more a part of television, but Cilla had no craving for excess. She had also grown out of the 'fun' of danger – and that equated with her audience. The 'swingers' had their following, Cilla her much greater one.

The essential, professional Cilla was always game for anything. She was pitching herself in the Seventies as a television entertainer of the dimension of Lucille Ball, but even in Hollywood where the situation comedy is heavily invested in and highly prestigious, the likes of *'I Love Lucy'* and its immediate satellites are intensely celebrated because they are so rare.

The critical Seventies weren't ready for a too-different Cilla but she was always tuned into the bottom line – the number of viewers, the bums on seats. She used early incarnations of the *Sun* newspaper (because of its mass circulation it has regularly been the Fleet Street shoulder she's cried on) to attack her critics in 1976, 'Anything that's popular the critics hate. I know when I do a good show or a bad one. I think that my variety series earlier this year was good ...'

She then makes her populist point, 'It averaged thirteen million viewers and was among the BBC's biggest audience programmes with seventeen million viewers. You can only knock success.'

Cilla was growing up personally as well as professionally. Bobby Willis had always taken care of the business side of her career, but Cilla gradually became more interested in the statistics of her success, realising that her fame had become a target for the doomwatchers, those just waiting to see her topple. She herself wanted to be seen to be succeeding.

Privately, away from the spotlight and the fantasies, she was about to face an awful reality and to have the religious faith which had been the backbone of her own upbringing seriously challenged. She had seen how the showbusiness machinery worked and was shrewd enough to know it was better to be driving the engine than just be a train passenger. This was even more important as she would soon have to synchronise family and professional activities.

The birth of her son Robert on 26 July 1970 was the first big family event of the decade. Cilla's business sense was torn about the tens of thousands of pounds pregnancy would cost through lost work, but her maternal senses won: 'At twenty-five, I thought, God, I've been a pop singer for six years. It was quite a long time and I wanted to have children. Desperately.

'All my girlfriends had two kids so I thought I'd better do something about it. All these years ago if you got married and had children that was the end of your career as a pop singer but I said, "To hell with this! I'm going to get married and I'm going to have children." When I had Robert the career just went from strength to strength because they said, "Hey, God, she can sing and she can actually have kids as well. She's normal."'

Cilla and Bobby Willis already had a pair of French sheepdogs (Sophie and Ada were the first of nearly a dozen over the years) and they craved more room than was afforded by their apartment near

Broadcasting House, the BBC headquarters at Portland Square, London. They wanted a home which would be a reasonable commute from the capital but also offering the space which they could now easily afford. Sir Malcolm Sargent's former estate in Buckinghamshire went on the list not, at first, because of its ambience but its location near to Denham Golf Course. Bobby also saw the transport advantages of having a local airfield.

Cilla herself wanted a 'nest', and with what was on offer behind the gates in Tilehouse Lane, she thought she'd found another golden doorstep into a world where nothing could ever go wrong. But no one of us is immune to the tragic events that can occur at any time.

Her life after the birth of Bobby Junior was something like *Monday to Sunday Night at the London Palladium*; if it wasn't *Holiday Star-Time* somewhere it was *Christmas Special* somewhere else. She was – and is – The Performer, appearing with legends like Ethel Merman and Henry Mancini, The Dudley Moore Trio or Cliff Richard, or comedy acting with Roy Castle or Richard Wilson many years before he appeared in *One Foot in the Grave*. Her professional association with Beatles musical mastermind George Martin had ended because of his ensemble recording and corporate commitments, but she still had a recording deal with EMI.

It was during this change of pace in her life that her dedication became most obvious. Some who have watched her over the years, like producer Johnny Hamp who knew her in her very early days promoting records at Granada Television in Manchester, would point out how quick she was to pick up on things, to *learn*. 'Cilla has never been too proud to ask for advice and, more importantly, to take it,' said Hamp.

Others, less generous than Hamp, have pointed to Cilla's determination and called it obsessiveness. It is important to understand that at this point in Cilla's life and career – and you can rarely see that line that separates them – it could have all gone pear-shaped. Fashions and the demands of television had somersaulted and were rolling in different directions. It was Cilla's feet-on-the-ground mentality and toughness of character which allowed her to roll with it, to stay in business.

The work, the change, takes its toll in many different ways. Cilla, like other great professionals, makes it seem that the first notes of her TV duet partner Ethel Merman's anthem – *There's No Business Like Showbusiness* – have only to sound and the smile goes on with the sequins. Clearly, it is much harder than that. And the longer you are doing it, the more difficult it gets.

Cilla makes much of her capacity to be 'on'. But associates – and Bobby Willis in some of his very rare candid moments – have talked about her similar capacity to be 'down'. She can switch off – and that means *off* in every sense. Those close to her admit that it is difficult, a challenge, being Cilla Black for twelve, never mind twenty-four, hours a day. After public appearances or promotional sessions she will shrug her image off with her high heels.

Stretching back on a sofa with a glass of champagne she will then 'dish the dirt', giving her true opinions of what she has done or seen, who she has won over or failed to charm. Someone who has worked closely with her said, 'You have to tread carefully. It's part of her personality that she's not keen for other people to shine too much. She wants to be number one in every situation. You just watch her on television through the years and you'll see her elbowing into centre stage ...'

Of course, that's part of getting there. And staying there. Being Mrs Nice isn't going to make it. Look at the wider picture from Streisand to Joan Crawford and back again – especially with female performers who have to battle age as much as fickle public taste – and it is clear that no matter how hard someone acts the part of happy-go-lucky, it will never be convincing. Fame just does not work that way. Ask those still on Merseyside. Or Iowa. The rule is there are no rules; and, equally, no boundaries.

Cilla spent a few weeks being a full-time mother, but with Bobby Willis on the telephone the career campaign was always running. One year, toddler Robert Junior went on his own cruise – with his nanny around the Greek islands while his parents flew aff to Australia and New Zealand for a concert tour. At the same time *Confectionery News* elected her 'Personality Mother of the Year'. She had moved a long way from sex, drugs and rock 'n' roll.

Her parents had never wanted to make a break from Liverpool even after their grandson Bobby Junior was born. There were the other children and grandchildren to be close to too; and Liverpool was home, the friends, the neighbours, the family. John White, who had visibly shrunk in stature, had died suddenly in 1972 from a heart attack. It was a cruel, faith-rocking time for Cilla: 'I've rather fallen out of friends with God,' she said at the time. Docker John White's wife wanted to remain at the family home. She would spend holidays at Denham, but never ever wanted it to be a permanent move: her life had been one of fierce family duty but also, like her daughter, of independence, a confidence in her ability to care for herself which was in itself a genetic gift.

And although the Willises had moved into a home only a five-iron shot away from the first fairway of Denham Golf Club, there were problems in joining the 'snobby' golf club. Prospective club candidates had to be sponsored by two established members who had known them personally for two years. 'Difficult? It is extremely difficult,' said club secretary Brigadier Roger E. Moss, adding, 'I knew who Cilla Black was – you couldn't help knowing – but they hadn't got a hope. We have a hell of a long waiting list. We were sent some very nice people down from the North, but there was nothing we could do for them ...'

In 1973, plans were afoot to build the M25 London circular road

– right through Tilehouse Lane, bulldozing the Willis property and that of Roger Moore, who was then the 'new' James Bond busy filming *The Man With the Golden Gun* with Maud Adams and Christopher Lee.

Another television personality, Raymond Baxter, the then presenter of *Tomorrow's World*, was also affected. It was a little close to home even for the future-thinker who had long advocated a British motorway network. While he blustered, Cilla Black and family enjoyed the Spanish sun with Jimmy Tarbuck and his clan before returning home to sign the petitions and questionnaires. Cilla was all for fighting the planners all the way to the beaches, but thankfully they retreated of their own accord and the M25 moved off, slowly, in another direction.

Walter, Dingle and Leo had joined the French sheepdog collection, making more of a crowd at home. On 30 April 1974, it was the turn of the nursery to get an increase in numbers; Cilla's second son Benjamin was born at Queen Charlotte's Maternity Hospital in Hammersmith, London. At this point, Cilla's Liverpudlian street-trader roots; her hoarding instincts, became apparent: there was no need to buy new baby clothes, she still had all of Bobby Junior's. Many families do this but most rich ones especially working-class 'nouveau riche' ones – would be likely to go on a spree. Not thrifty Cilla.

Ben, like Bobby Junior, was as worry-free as it is possible for children of the famous to be. Cilla was fiercely protective of her private life. She had another image now – that of a mother of two children with which to deflect intruders into her world. She has never played the *Hello!* game at home; she will pose and chatter endlessly in hotel suites or at theatres or television studios. But the early and sacrosanct rule was never to allow the media into her home environment.

Ben's birth had been worked into her schedules; unfortunately, it had meant her missing the important, high-profile *Morcambe and*

*Wise Christmas Show*, of 1973, but by the middle of the 1970s Cilla was on top form again. The UK Writers' Guild had named her 'Top Female Comedy Star' for the first of her *Cilla's Comedy Six* programmes, all of which attracted ratings of around eleven million viewers. Still, the critics were relentless. As far as they were concerned, she had reached thirtynothingdom.

But it was in her real world that true agony lay in wait. She was pregnant for the third time and she and Bobby Willis were hoping for a daughter. In the summer of 1975 she was due to do a summer season in Eastbourne and several concert dates around England and Scotland. She was seven months pregnant and working in Coventry when on a cold Friday evening in October she was taken ill after the second house at Coventry Theatre and was rushed to hospital.

She had walked offstage in a gown specially designed by the BBC's costume wizard Linda Martin to slim her down, but with the audience still applauding, by the time she reached her dressing room she was in labour. Her baby Helen was born in the early hours but did not live past breakfast-time. She says that not a day goes by without her thinking about Helen, the daughter she and Bobby Willis longed to have and in a tragic way do, for they will never forget her or what might have been.

Cilla was delivered of the baby girl she longed for, but her joy was short lived. Doctors had to tell her that Helen, whose lungs had not properly formed, had died – and she says that part of her did too. For a women who lives in a 'can-do' world it was even more devastating. Here was something you could do nothing about. It was over. Ended. Stopped. You couldn't change your mind, make it happen again, but with a different outcome. It was final. And awful.

For once Cilla was powerless. She felt as if her legs had been kicked away. She wouldn't talk about it to anyone. Years later it is still a misery for her: 'Anyone who hasn't lost a child can't try to understand how you feel. If your baby lives, if only for two hours, you can never, ever forget it. Not a day goes by ... my other children are a constant reminder and you thank God you have them.

'I kept asking why? Why me? Though I'd always felt marvellous during pregnancy, and had worked until five months with Robert and seven months with Ben, had I gone on too long with Helen? Had I been too sure of myself? That was the guilt thing.

'After that depression got me. I shut myself in our bedroom and never wanted to come out. I'd be there still if it hadn't been for Jimmy Tarbuck and his wife.'

'Jimmy was wonderful,' recalled Bobby Willis sombrely. 'Someone had to fill in at the theatre that Saturday. I phoned him in Scarborough and he left the golf course, drove straight to Coventry and went on stage in his golfing gear, with a hole in his sweater. A week later he asked what he and his wife Pauline could do to help and I told him that somehow we had to get Cilla out, perhaps to dinner, try to make her laugh.'

A date was fixed up and, because it was the Tarbucks, Cilla went out. She smiled. It was a breakthrough of sorts although nothing would ever be the same again, 'After that I knew if I didn't plunge back into work quickly I'd never sing again. Val Doonican had taken over in Coventry but he wasn't free for long, and the show had to go on. I went back two weeks after ... It was Val Doonican who'd first sung *Liverpool Lullaby* and, generous as always, he urged me to do it, saying it would be ideal for me. It's a traditional melody, with marvellous words, and I'd been singing them that autumn season. In the dressing room I ran through the lines in my head for twenty minutes while I was making-up. When I got to *Lullaby* I managed the mental run-through from "Oh, you are a mucky kid" right until the last two lines: "But there's no one can take your place. Go fast asleep for Mammy".'

The show *would* go on, but as Cilla left her dressing room she asked Bobby Willis to take *Liverpool Lullaby* out of the programme.

It remains one of her most popular hits, but she admits, 'There was a time after losing our Helen when I thought I'd never be able to sing *Lullaby* again. For the first eighteen months after I lost her I saw her in every pram other mothers pushed and I had to turn away. I scarcely read a paper in case there was a story of a baby being left on a step, in a dustbin, for that made me feel really *violent.*

'Then my obstetrician told me that doctors, too, were always asking that same "Why?" Why, in one year, did as many as 10,000 babies in England and Wales die before they were seven days old? He said doctors themselves had started a charity, Birthright, to raise money for extra research into this, and into the cause of babies being born with defects. After that I did a TV appeal for it. When your baby dies you feel you're the only one in the world to know such sorrow; until someone tells you that yours was one of 10,000 to die in a year, though Birthright has helped to get that number down considerably. So it'll always be my special charity.'

'Birthright said to stop being so selfish and they showed me that I could actually prevent people from going through what I had experienced.'

The late actress Diana Dors had also lost a baby in 1975, and she helped Cilla deal with the loss of Helen. 'She was marvellous. I had never met anyone who was in the same position and it was nice to talk. She was a tremendous help to me. I think she coped much better than me. It was just a very black period. Bobby knows me inside out and he knew what was right for me, but I wouldn't listen. We're too close.

'I'm very private in my grief. I don't want to share the down sides. The sadness never goes and in the beginning you get quite selfish about it. You look at everybody, and all you see are babies everywhere. You say, "Why me?" Then Bobby said one day, "Well, why not you? What makes you so special? Why *not* you?" And it all suddenly hit home. I thought: Yes, why *not* me?'

Jack, a surprise redhead, was born on 20 October 1980. The machine which monitored his heart at Queen Charlotte's Hospital had been bought with the help of money raised by Birthright. Jack's birth, just as his personality would develop, was quick and easygoing. But he brought back all the memories:

'I just had a feeling that this baby was going to be all right ... I think that is the way you have got to think. I had lots of check-ups but not because of what happened before – it was my age. I was thirty-seven when I had Jack. They were just very careful with me.

'But being pregnant again brought back what happened so vividly. There was no warning last time that anything was wrong. It was terrible to go through a pregnancy with all the expectation and excitement and then not to have anything at the end of it. I learned to take each day as it comes ... I do that with my career as well. They told me at the time that "every day is a better day". Gradually you learn to live with the pain and go on.

'I think I only managed it because I'd come to accept that I'd been blessed with two sons and a daughter, though I lost her, and should be grateful for the happiness I had. Once I relaxed, our Jack happened.'

The supportive, matter-of-fact side of Bobby Willis had its great strength at such times. When it was serious business, the man who could get tearful at tiddly emotions rather bottled it inside. He confessed, 'You get over it in the sense that you don't burst into tears every time you think about it. It is, "Time heals everything", It has to be.'

They both insisted that Jack was not a replacement for Helen. Cilla said, 'He was the new baby I'd wanted for so long. I always wanted to have six kids, but I settled for four. People say to me, "You had three children" and I don't often correct them and then tell them "*four*". I don't want to embarrass them. People don't really know but I don't want to go into a full explanation of what happened.

'Bobby and I had fabulous childhoods and our kids will never forget what a great family of relatives, and friends, they come from. That's why we wanted a big family of our own. It's what real living is all about. But I've been really lucky in that I've been able to have a family and a career.

'When I had Robert I'd said I was going to give up work for six months. But then, after about four weeks, there I was cleaning the kitchen and hoovering in my sequined dress. Being at home was driving me up the wall. I was going mental to get the gear back on and go out there and perform. Like any mother, if you're not happy, the vibrations go through to the baby. I was back at work within six weeks. When I was at the 2 a.m. feed stage with the boys I'd have Kenny Everett on his late-night radio show saying, "And now here's one for Cilla. She'll be up now Brillo-ing the baby's bum."

'I couldn't bear being away from it all for very long. I needed to get back. But my being their mother has had its problems. Ben was five and we were outside his school when his pal grabbed me round the legs and shouted, "It's Cilla Black." Ben was quite upset. Once, when Robbie was about fifteen, he refused to walk by my side. It was the time Joan Collins started going out with toy boys. Robbie kept lagging behind and I told him to keep up but he wouldn't. Eventually he said, "I don't want people to think I am your toy boy."'

In 1998 she was thinking futuristic, 'I like the idea of being a granny. I think I would make a better grandmother than I did a mother.'

A *glamorous* grandmother. She had a hysterectomy when she was forty-three and is a devotee of Hormone Replacement Therapy (HRT). The operation in 1984 followed emergency surgery after she began haemorrhaging during preparations for the first series of *Surprise, Surprise!* – a programme which certainly did surprise many critics by being such a huge ratings success.

The casualty drama of emergency surgery and a blood transfusion left Cilla and Bobby Willis with much thinking to do. It's a fearful thing, a close-call with mortality. A hysterectomy is a debilitating operation to undergo but, remarkably, they simply cancelled four nights of cabaret and with the promise that she'd be back on stage on schedule, Cilla was booked instead into St George's Hospital in Tooting, London.

'"The show must go on" is probably part of Cilla's genetic working-class make-up,' said a colleague at LWT. 'You don't let anything get to you; you don't let people down, you don't let yourself down and, most important of all, you don't show up the family.'

Her surgery was completed on 15 June 1984, and on 16 July she began a nine-week run – with nine shows per week – of summer season at the Royalty Theatre in Great Yarmouth. On time.

'It's a typical story of Cilla. She always has to prove she can do the impossible, that nothing will faze her, upset her.'

Behavioural experts say Cilla is a textbook case of a 'Daddy's Girl' wanting to prove to him that she is as good as her brothers. This, they say, makes her a dominant personality, and this shows itself in her marriage and business life. The main fear, and it is not just mind experts who talk about this but Cilla and Bobby Willis themselves, is that it could all vanish overnight. Their commonsense tells them it is impossible, but you cannot harness dreams, *nightmares*, the way you can deadlines.

Cilla was to need lots of bravado to help her withstand the stunts – and the critics – on *Surprise, Surprise!* which found her once again enjoying her fabulous popularity of the late Sixties. Number three son Jack was literally still a lad then but she believes television – along with longtime nanny Penny – was her saviour as a mother.

'All the work is done in the evening, so you are there to take them to school and there when they come back. When I do *Blind Date*, I go to the studio, no rehearsal, get my make-up on and I'm home by 9.30. It is the best business of all to be in if you have children.

'I've always been Cilla Black on the telly to the children, so it was never strange for them. When they were younger, Basil Brush used to be on the other side so they'd watch that instead of me.'

*Chapter Eight*

# BUBBLY TIMES

*'There was never any question to me that it was anything but Cilla's show.'*
– BOB CARLGEES OF *SURPRISE SURPRISE!*

Her remarkable self-propulsion had kept Cilla in the spotlight but not as much as she would have liked. Her Sixties contemporaries, Marianne Faithfull, Sandie Shaw and Dusty Springfield, had all vanished into other places or lives, but Cilla's brash, bums-on-seats mentality had assured her own survival. She had moved on from the quirky frocks and crash-helmet hair, but was still raring to go – preferably in the right direction. There's the story of Bob Hope who, when getting on in his career, was advised to relax, to take a cruise. In all seriousness he asked his roomful of agents and joke-writers, 'You want me to try out the one-liners on the fish?'

As a working mother, Cilla had sterling domestic back-up from husband Bobby and nanny Penny, who joined the household in 1972 when Bobby Junior was 21 months old; the entourage of housekeeper Margaret and chauffeur/gardener Tom live in a cottage in the grounds at Denham.

The birth of her third son Jack was a useful camouflage for what

Cilla regarded as a lack of decent television exposure. Variety-style shows had lost popularity and Cilla, like others who had not found an ongoing TV 'vehicle', was feeling the effects. There were plenty of concert bookings and appearances in the Middle and Far East, but not that incredible popularity that comes from being beamed into millions of UK households every week. And Cilla has always needed the home crowd, for her parents, friends – *and* enemies – to see her doing well. Her self-esteem requires regular doses of reassurance. And what better public platform than primetime television? See, a million people love me? Why not five million? Why not ten million? It is, like the Holy Grail, an endless quest.

For someone with Cilla's energy, hanging around for the right TV show to come along was overwhelmingly frustrating. She was facing her fortieth birthday and forty, for every female performer, remains a dangerous age. British TV is much less 'ageist' than American TV, but still there are doubts, and fears that younger and just as bubbly performers are chasing *your* popularity, *your* pay cheques. True, Cilla had earned a lot of money from an early age but she has never been comfortable with it: she has always wanted more.

So at this time, during a minor interruption in her lavish fortunes, she and Bobby Willis decided to learn more about the business they were in, how to better negotiate and deal. Bobby Willis, who was keen to branch out in his showbusiness management – he did so in 1984 with clients including Petula Clark – used the period for further education in the financial machinations of the entertainment world. This certainly got the couple safely through the Thatcher years. Bobby, with his tremendous faith in Cilla's talents and his refusal to sell her short, was brilliant at it.

Whether it is a fear of not getting a fair deal, or paranoia because of witnessing first-hand what a cut-throat climate she works in, those who have negotiated with Cilla and Bobby Willis over the years maintain that what is at first on the table is never enough. Cilla and

Co. can be convinced that it is, but, like The Receiver, they want everything in detail – and in writing. She has never been one of those showbusiness 'Let's shake on it' types. Her performances may be easygoing but her contracts? Never!

Even in 1997, when she was the highest-paid woman in British television, with a lottery-winner lifestyle, Cilla was still observing that old dictum: look after the pennies and the pounds will look after themselves. Only Cilla's version was to look after the thousands and the millions would look after themselves.

In 1997 Channel 4 had planned a series of rather low-budget programmes – to judge by the lack of archive film footage and range of interviews – on women singers of the 1960s. It was titled *Brit Girls*. Cilla, along with Lulu, Sandie Shaw and Marianne Faithfull, was to be featured. Whatever side you take in the following row there was, at least, a misunderstanding. Cilla thought the planned programme involving her was a one-off, a stand-alone documentary.

When she found she was simply one of a quartet of 'Brit girls' she went ballistic, even though her son Bobby Willis Junior was involved in the production. She called in her lawyers, who claimed that she had only taken part in the programme because she believed it was exclusively about her. In the High Court in London they accused Granada Television of 'misrepresentation'. As it turned out, Channel 4 went ahead with the documentary about her, retitling it *Cilla*. They also agreed to delay screenings of the *Brit Girl* series, postponing the advertised Saturday night Marianne Faithfull episode in December 1997.

It is the little things that often tick off newspapers, and when their prized television listings, often planned and printed weeks in advance, are interfered with, they get irritated. Whatever the motives, a ruffled columnist on a downmarket Sunday paper took umbrage at Cilla. She wrote: '*... Mrs Lorra Lorra Ego hit the roof ... Cilla is getting a bit above herself: This isn't how ordinary lasses from Liverpool behave.*'

The comments alluded to Cilla not wanting to share screen space with the other Sixties' singers. At London Weekend Television (owned, as it happens, by Granada) the finger was more on the money – literally, '*She was paid a nominal fee on the basis that it was a stand-alone documentary, but the show had been sold as part of the 'Brit Girl' series. Cilla would have been able to command anything from £50,000 to £70,000 if she knew that was going to happen. That's what she is looking for in damages. This is a matter of principle that she feels very strongly about.*'

Her argument was that Granada, the primary maker of the series, failed to tell her that her interviews would be used for a series. She sued as Cilla Black Ltd, seeking £70,000 damages for alleged breach of contract.

The *Brit Girls* (renamed *Girls on Top* following the legal action) was intended as an 'affectionate celebration and nostalgic tribute' to the Sixties' singers, but it ended up the subject of *two* legal actions an impressive number even for a hard-hitting documentary. Cilla made her upset well-known. During her career, Helen Shapiro – who Cilla had once called her major musical rival – had two number 1 hits and eleven Top 50 songs, but was dismissed in Press material for the series as a 'one-hit wonder' and a singer who 'shone brightly but briefly.' She planned to sue for libel. Her manager and husband John Williams said the alleged libel could affect sales of her 1998 gospel album and nationwide tour.

For Cilla it was clearly a money over ego situation, but it was also one which activated her inbuilt protection mechanism for the longer term: nostalgia pays dividends, and as a participant in such enterprises she was due her going rate. Consider what archives of *Blind Date* will be worth as the cable and digital revolution brings hundreds and hundreds more channels. Yes, Cilla will turn up at the opening of a door – but only when appropriate performance, syndication and residual fees have been established. Bobby Willis' belief in his wife as his best product was total, 'I'm not selling a brush that does not sweep. This is just the tip of what she can do,' was his verdict in 1997.

In the early 1980s, many different deals were being discussed, but it was not only money that was at stake here; Cilla badly needed a sparkling new TV show to present. The BBC had been her home for nearly a decade but the ITV companies appeared more open to ideas, and had the cash to spend on them.

It was a sign of the times – of Thatcherism and Harry Enfield's Loadsamoney. Cilla had her Rolls-Royce and nearly died in it, 'We were driving back to London from Liverpool in our Rolls when we skidded all over the M1 and ended up facing the way we'd come. An AA van coming to our rescue skidded and smashed straight into us. As it reached us I shouted "God!" and threw myself against Bobby. I was convinced I'd end up dead. The van ripped off one side of the Rolls but left us unharmed.'

With hindsight you might wonder how Cilla Black survived on the BBC. She would seem created for the Independent networks, which are aimed at a mass audience.

The search for a new 'Cilla' television series went on ... and on. During those endless marketing and programming conferences at ITV and BBC, it always seemed that Cilla was agreed to be a sensational asset, but ... she needed a suitable backdrop for her personality. Otherwise it was Punch without Judy, a newscaster without the news: it doesn't work.

Cilla meanwhile enjoyed hugely successful tours of Australia and summer seasons and countless concerts, but it was only in January 1983, when she had been out of the spotlight for several years that she made a marvellous impression during an appearance on Terry Wogan's chat show; and this led to her reinstatement on TV.

On the *Wogan* show, in which Cilla sent herself up and was fresh, in every sense, she had her host, his audience and, more importantly for Cilla, his bosses hugely entertained. It was her unknown audition and it proved the point: in the right environment Cilla was a winner.

An ITV executive watching *Wogan* was convinced she was perfect for a new show.

*Surprise, Surprise!* had originated at Channel 4, which in the early 1980s was very much a 'new ideas' sort of place. A series of programmes had been discussed; two episodes were actually filmed and shown, but then the idea was shelved. Over at mainstream London Weekend Television, however, there was a lot of excitement about *Surprise, Surprise!* Alan Boyd was then Chief of LWT's Light Entertainment Division. He – like every other person in the job before and after him – was desperate for a 'family' show which would not only bring in huge ratings but would retain them week after week and establish an ongoing loyalty.

Cilla Black has been part of the British viewing culture for almost as long as everyone has owned a television set. It is in our nature not to give too warm a welcome to a newcomer on the screen; anyone who is not familiar has to prove themselves. Which is why Cilla is such a valuable performer. With her, you're not just paying for today – but yesterday as well. That was one reason Boyd, along with other LWT programmers, regarded Cilla as the magnet, the established star who would bring her own following. But they also needed interaction with the audience and the subjects of the show, plus a source to provide the novelty every week. You can't have a show called *Surprise, Surprise!* without surprises no matter how talented or popular the host!

In 1983, with her fortieth birthday looming, Cilla recorded a test show of *Surprise, Surprise!* To her delight, it marked a new era of popularity for her. She had fan clubs going back to the Sixties, but this new programme transformed her appeal. Masses loved her; some, predictably, loathed her. With Cilla as presenter, the girl-next-door image vanished for ever, and in came Auntie Cilla, with her nudge-nudge, know-what-I-mean, been-there-done-that, I'm-just-one-of-you-really public persona. The show was all 'Cilla-grams' and way-out costumes, absurd but fun stunts in the air, at sea and elsewhere – anything to give the cameras a lively scene to capture.

The programme certainly captured audiences from the start, with its poignant scenes of tearful reunions, songs and dances and, in the beginning, the help of Christopher Biggins. Biggins would later be replaced by the wonderfully talented Bob Carolgees, who appeared with his dog Spot.

Carolgees himself soon became enormously popular with the viewers, 'Doing *Surprise, Surprise!* was one of the great experiences for me. I know I got very popular with folks, but to me it was never anything other than Cilla's show. I had a phenomenal run with it. You just don't get chances like that every year – no, every decade. She is the great professional. She knows what is needed, what she herself wants and is prepared to do, to make it all work. You don't succeed without putting in the hours, doing your homework. She makes it look a doddle and people think that. Of course, that's the trick, that's the talent.' He said admiringly.

For Cilla it was the start of her unique run as the most valuable female in British entertainment. There was not a British actress or singer, and certainly no other female television performer, who could equal her in audience pulling power in the years that followed the launch of *Surprise, Surprise!*

Frankie Howerd was still a regular support at Sunday lunch, always ready at the end of the telephone with encouragement. He was wise about Cilla's needs because they were so like his own: – 'She wants the approval. She knows she can get it from the audiences – that's her job. But she wants the pat on the back from the rest of us, the other people in the business. She's like a schoolgirl who wants to be top of the class. Second place isn't any help at all.'

Cilla herself was delighted with *Surprise, Surprise!* while Bobby Willis raved about it. This was a format – and a longrunning contract with LWT – which could be hung on to and developed. It *was* a winner, and being such high-flying professionals, they knew it.

The metamorphosis from Cilla to Aunt Cilla, incidentally, took just a couple of weeks to effect. Soon she was in benevolent charge, looking after everyone. Unfortunately, the transition also made her Aunt Sally for the critics – a group both Cilla and Bobby Willis have been at great pains to tolerate. Their public reaction was, 'they are only doing their jobs as they see it,' while privately they admitted to disliking it. 'We love success and dislike anyone who knocks it,' said Bobby Willis, further explaining the family creed, 'We've always had a simple philosophy: this business works for us and we don't work for it.'

With any star, any public person, be it politician or religious leader, there are plenty of clay feet marching through the past. With Cilla you are always dealing with a double personality, a Gemini butterfly, a woman christened Priscilla White who won world renown as Cilla Black. A person who by nature hates routine but made her fame, in theatre and on television, by strictly adhering to just that: always meeting her marks and deadlines. A dual personality is something that can disturb the small hours even on a luxury mattress stuffed with fivers.

The pressure, in public, on Cilla is neverending. She copes with it as relentlessly as it imposes itself.

Carolyn Hooper worked on the series as a sound 'boom' operator to get her union 'ticket' by doing the number of hours required by television industry-union rules. Now working as a big screen writer and director, she says she enjoyed her time on *Surprise, Surprise!* – especially the location work, 'We were all over the place, which made it more interesting than being stuck in the studio all the time.

'Cilla was always up for anything to make the show work. One time we were on location in Scotland doing a *Surprise, Surprise!* from Loch Lomond – all kilts and *hoots*, *mon* and that sort of thing. But, as you might expect with West of Scotland weather, the rain interrupted our plans. Again and again.

'Bobby Willis was with Cilla and they retreated to their caravan, one of those luxury Winnebago sort of things they go on location with: it has a kitchen and a loo and somewhere to rest.

'Bobby and Cilla had a case of champagne with them and were quite happy to stay there while the rain pelted down. On the series there seemed to be endless supplies of champagne. It must have cost tons of money, unless it was written into her contract and supplied by LWT. Mind you, it didn't seem to affect her at all.

'When the rain stopped, there was Cilla in an orange jumpsuit and the pancake make-up to match, out there on the banks of Loch Lomond belting out *Ain't No Mountain High Enough*. It was, I must say, quite a sight.'

By her fiftieth birthday celebrations in 1993, Cilla was getting somewhat testy about her so-called consumption. She has said many times that she shares a bottle every evening with Bobby Willis. But offered a glass during promotional work for her thirty years in showbusiness she reacted vocally:

'I don't know where this idea comes from that I'm so fond of champagne. I'm offered it everywhere I go. No, I won't ... I'm going shopping.'

She has a glass of vin rosé instead. Then, just one glass of champagne to wash it down, as it were. She was clearly annoyed, 'I don't take anything for granted. Champagne ... people think we have it all day long. I couldn't go shopping if I'd been guzzling champagne. Think how boring you'd be. Besides, I don't want people to think we're wasting money on champagne. I'd rather give the cash to my children.'

In 1991 Cilla told the London *Evening Standard* that when she was twenty-four, Mick Jagger gave her a glass of his Mateus Rosé. 'It was pink,' she told the newspaper, describing her attraction to the wine. She went on, 'These days I like a drink as much as anybody, but not when I'm working. I had my lesson when I saw Judy Garland in the wings at the Palladium. It was pathetic. I don't know if it was drink or drugs, but her manager had to prise her fingers off the pole she was clinging to, to get her on the stage.'

Four years earlier she had talked about her regular Sunday mornings and making the coffee at 8.30 a.m. and added, 'Then about 11 a.m. I have a glass of Buck's Fizz to jolly me up before I do the hoovering.'

But, as Bobby Willis pointed out, if they are going to drink champagne they prefer Moët and Chandon.

Cilla says she is a remarkable sparkling advertisement for the bubbly – she has only had one hangover. She was asked in March 1998 about her 'first hangover' and explained, 'It's not just the first, it is the only one. It was when I had a car crash. I was going too fast to stop on what I thought was an amber and ploughed into this girl's car. My knee was hurt and I couldn't walk and my chest was bruised. In the evening I was still in a state of shock, so out comes the champagne.

'When it came to going to bed I couldn't walk. Bobby said, "I'll carry you upstairs" and he picked me up and we fell down the stairs. He could have killed me. The next day I had a sore head but I don't know whether it was a hangover or because I'd banged my head.'

Of course, Mr and Mrs Willis usually travelled first class. That was the way Bobby liked it. And Cilla over the years has become accustomed to the Rolls-Royce life and the private planes from Denham airfield for short trips. In 1975 they invested in a Spanish holiday home near Marbella, a golf resort with houses overlooking the ocean.

Then it was sand, swimming pool and kids, and in the 1990s – with the villa extended and named *Casa Roll* – it was still a place for her to paddle and let her hair down after long sessions recording *Blind Date* and *Surprise, Surprise!* What was a surprise – because her 'paparazzi senses' are so acute even abroad or 'off-duty' – was that there, in the land of sangria and sun, Cilla let her publicity guard down. It was there that she was photographed revealing more rolls of fat than swimsuit. The street-trader's daughter, enraged but in control, bounced back, as we said, by telling her Sabbath evening audience, 'I'd like to thank the *Sunday Mirror* for publishing my holiday snaps. It saves me getting mine developed at Boots ...'

She has a triumph over adversity attitude, a willingness to turn every negative – literally in the case of the Spanish snapshots – into a positive.

Cilla confounds the critics. It has been a hallmark of her life and career. What is so bewildering for all those marketing people with their clipboards and consumer surveys is that the public view is often contradictory. In one survey in the 1980s, Cilla was voted as having the most irritating voice in Britain.' At the same time as being monstered by the critics and dismissed by the public, she was hosting two of the most popular shows in the UK, with ratings comparative to the biggest regular television successes worldwide.

As the critics looked down their noses at *Surprise, Surprise!* it was fast becoming a huge hit. Cilla, publicly, laughed off the critics; privately she was hurt.

Away from the cameras she got into increasingly black moods. Not only was she *always* denied commercial and critical success, she never got any respect. Shirley Bassey was treated like royalty; around her the fans bowed and scraped. Cilla ... well, she was always 'Our Cilla'. Some fans still believe her favourite lunch is pie and chips washed down with brown ale. The People's Entertainer would like some adulation from The People other than 'How-ya-doin'-Cilla?' And the only critics who bestowed much of a good Press were the fawning, regular 'safe pens' crowd, always aware where their next glass of champagne was coming from.

Cilla found it all unfair. It seemed a crime to be popular – but then that is the normal Press game – the 'tall poppy' syndrome: as soon as you put your head above the crowd they want to chop it off. The mentality is worldwide but the impact is more brutal in the smaller melting pot of British showbusiness.

But on the surface as the hatchets plunged into *Surprise, Surprise!* she grinned and bore it. First son Robert was thirteen when it got quite nasty and his mother was voted 'Wally of the Week'. For some reason, this, more than all the other criticism, hit a sensitive spot. Cilla braved it, 'You have to remember that I haven't suddenly become famous. I had been in showbiz for six years when Robert was born. A few fellow artistes ask me how the children have taken criticism of *Surprise, Surprise!*, but it's not the first time I've been knocked. It happened years ago. One critic really hated me but I had to laugh because I thought it was a compliment when he said, "She's so bad my daughter likes her".'

Her theory that she was the victor in it all was proved by the scheduling of another series of *Surprise, Surprise!* Her view, 'If the public hated the show it would have been dumped. And the Beeb have thrown everything at us to combat *Surprise, Surprise*! They even chucked in Victoria Principal in TV movies.'

Ms Principal, late of the Ewing family and *Dallas* had, she says, never rated herself as a big gun in the UK TV ratings wars. Cilla did. But the platitudes she spread were like treacle. Were the critics unfair? 'They have a job to do. If they want to say things about me ... well, what can I do about it?' and, 'Actually, I quite enjoy the criticism. It's quite nice being Wally of the Week. You're up there with a lot of stars. I would have taken offence years ago but if I met these critics I wouldn't be bitter.'

'She cut me dead,' said one of that critical community about a reception at the LWT headquarters. She was strangely surprised that Cilla had been hurt by negative comments, and argued, 'We'd all been having a few drinks and she wasn't happy. You would think that after all these years she would be able to take it, but she can't. Publicly, it's "no problem, love."'

Cilla shared some of the criticism with the bulky ebullient Christopher Biggins. It wasn't his TV talent they were cruel about, it was his figure, she argued. 'I do feel sorry for him,' she says. 'And I get upset because I don't like the personal things. When they say he's fat, that's not nice.'

She is still a believer in that showbusiness saying that there is no such thing as bad publicity. With the shallow *Hello!* magazine journalism of the 1990s spreading through newspapers worldwide, it was apparent that anything that attracted attention, from misdemeanour to murder, could be a plus. On American television, the shock value – something predicted by *Blind Date* creator Chuck Barris – was hard to maintain. Brawls on screen as in *Geraldo* were not enough to satisfy viewers; audiences and, even more graspingly, television producers, sought sensation.

Cilla, in 1998, had only had to deal, in comparison, with rather mundane matters. There were the lesbians Linda Smith and Rachel Clarke on *Surprise, Surprise!* who, until she read the newspapers, Cilla was unaware were planning a gay 'wedding'. Cilla and the *Surprise* staff had arranged for Linda's daughter Kimberley to meet her father for the first time. Linda had been separated twenty years earlier from her first husband, American serviceman Bob Lowe, soon after Kimberley was born.

The father-daughter reunion was the super 'Surprise' of the evening, but viewers did not know that Linda – mother to two teenage children by her second husband – was waiting for a divorce so she could 'marry' Rachel. Indeed, later the couple, who lived in Colchester, Essex, exchanged rings and cut a heart-shaped wedding cake, and although they said they had enjoyed affairs with other women, insisted, 'This relationship is special.'

When Cilla was presented with the facts of her lesbian contestants she saw it as 'all the more publicity.'

Linda Smith had no doubts that Cilla knew all about it, 'Cilla obviously knew we were gay because we were holding hands. But she did not bat an eyelid. It did not matter to her at all. I think she thought it would be good for the show, for business.'

Some 'Surprises' do not 'air', often by the sheer impossibility of the requests. One macabre case file remains hidden in the show's archives. It involved the first wife of mass murderer Fred West. West, who killed himself before going on trial for the 'House of Horror' killings at 25 Cromwell Street, Gloucester, was suspected of more than twenty murders. He married his first wife Catherine Costello in 1962 – he was twenty-one, she was eighteen – and they lived in Ledbury, Hereford, and in Worcester. She was last seen alive in 1971. Her 9-year-old daughter Charmaine vanished at the same time, both victims of West's fiendishness.

As the biggest murder enquiry in recent British history was being pursued in 1994, Catherine's three sisters Isabella Prentice, May Lappin and Georgina McCann wrote to *Surprise, Surprise!* asking that details of their sister be broadcast on Cilla's *Searchline Appeal* segment: at the end of every show viewers are asked to help people trace loved ones.

They had no idea that only weeks later detectives would order 'digs' for bodies including that of their sister at Midland Road, Gloucester, where West lived before moving to infamous Cromwell Road. 'When we wrote to Cilla we had no idea what had happened,' said May Lappin, adding, 'No one will ever know what we all went through.'

The letter asking for help was one of thousands received at LWT, whether *Surprise, Surprise!* is being broadcast or not. Almost all the letters are personal requests to Cilla. Many people write saying things like, 'We know she'll care,' or 'We know she'll help,' and regularly, 'Cilla won't let us down.'

It is a great pressure. Such shows are. They attract terrific audiences – like the 'intimate' American intense psycho-talk shows run by the woman Cilla says she would like to be, Oprah Winfrey – but they involve tightrope television. How far can you go? With *Surprise, Surprise!* such a success, it was clearly time to knock it. And 'relationship experts' joined the critics. Some called for the banning of the series as it involved 'emotional roulette'.

A tame psychotherapist was rolled out to pronounce, 'It is like watching a public execution. Millions of viewers who watch the show see tearful relatives in nerve-jangling reunions but when the cameras stop, the guests become forgotten people. They can suffer heartbreak because of guilt and remorse over the "lost years".'

Lieutenant-Colonel Colin Fairclough, who is Director of Family Tracing Services for the Salvation Army, has acted as an adviser to the series. He said that some reunions have ended in disaster: 'They wanted to bring a man on the show and reunite him with his natural mother. I pleaded with them not to do so and fortunately in this case they agreed. The man hadn't told his own wife and children he had been adopted, and was very embarrassed by it. A great number of reunions have sadly gone wrong after the programme is long forgotten.'

Cilla became the centre of the continuing 'victim television' debate. When she shrieks the catchphrase, 'Surprise, Surprise!' people are plucked out of the audience to meet longlost relatives on stage, but instead of being a pleasant surprise it can often be a nasty shock being confronted by Uncle Harry or Auntie Sally whom you had prayed never to meet again. The show had no professional counsellors on the set or follow-up counselling service. It took a long time for this to sink in at LWT. The series had been running for years before the debate threatened the broadcasting of it. Psychotherapist Barbara Thomas said:

'There is all the anticipation of this great emotive point. The camera zooms in on them immediately after the reunion. It is horrible, because it should be a private moment. The audience is whipped up by Cilla Black at what is an incredibly traumatic time for the guests. It is gross that the most emotional time is in front of millions of viewers.

'They are gawping and it is really sick. The programme's makers have never realised what a Pandora's Box they are opening. They offer no counselling for the relatives. It is a "Thank you, you've got our ratings up and now go away".' Mrs Thomas, who counsels patients traumatised by reunions, added, 'The show offers the guest the chance of meeting up with lost relatives and precious little else. Just weeks later they are likely to feel guilt and remorse over the separation and lost years. Yet the show makes no allowances for this. They don't realise they are playing with fire.' The adoption society Norcap, which counsels adults who discover they have been adopted, monitors the series. It offers a counselling service, a helpline, and advice on searching for parents. Children's Society spokeswoman Rachel O'Brien said, 'It traumatises these poor people, just to make so-called "good" television. I have seen programmes where old ladies are picked out of the audience to meet long-lost members of their family without warning. On *Surprise, Surprise!* they are just left to get on with their lives once they have satiated the demands of the audience.'

Alan Burdell, of the welfare group The Post-Adoption Centre, said, 'I certainly wouldn't advocate bringing people together on a programme like *Surprise, Surprise!* These sort of meetings need careful handling. It's dangerous to do it in the context of a TV programme.'

Cilla ('I always like to be in control') hates surprises but argues that it is all for love and fun and vice versa. In 1997 during the fourteenth season she said, 'I do get emotional - it's difficult not to. And you can't help others getting emotional when you are bringing people together who have not met for decades. I think *Surprise,*

*Surprise!* is a very worthwhile show. We *don't* just leave people dangling after the show. We also try and have fun on the show and after all the years I think we have got it down to a fine art. It is a fantastic opportunity to reunite many people who hadn't seen other members of their families for a long time.'

But she does agree such meetings can be emotional. Scottish radio personality Steve Jack says Cilla was very emotional when she appeared 'live' on his radio programme broadcast from Edinburgh. Jack – then a popular broadcaster with Radio Forth and later a weekend interviewer for Scot FM Radio – was at the restaurant he owns in the Scottish capital when he recalled his 'close encounter with Cilla'. Jack, who will be forty-six in 2003, sipped coffee as he spoke, 'She was certainly drunk. I was a wee bit annoyed but I was looking forward to the chat. It was the afternoon show, two till four and we always had a guest slot, and I was looking forward to it – a big star coming into the station. We had a lot of big stars, Sophia Loren and Charlton Heston and these sort of people.

'We sometimes had two guests in one day but this was a live interview and we had promoted it quite heavily that she was coming in. She did. She kind of flopped down in the seat and I was a wee bit surprised. Bobby her husband was next door amongst the controls, watching things.

'She had certainly enjoyed what she had been drinking. That would have been after lunchtime you see, half past two or half past three. She didn't slur her words but I was a wee bit disappointed that she lacked that bit of professionalism to do that, you know. It was a big deal for the station, a big day. Absolutely. You want it to be right. You know, if you're interviewing somebody and it's live on radio and they've had a drink you think to yourself, "Oh, what's going to happen next?"

'It puts you really on edge because you don't know if you are going to lose control or they are going to lose control of themselves and say something....we had a control button for members of the public but we wouldn't have a button for "Our Cilla" at that time.

'Nothing untoward happened but it put me off. And I always remember it when I see her; I always think of that day when she was drunk. Weird, isn't it? I assume she was having lunch with someone here in Edinburgh and one drink led to another and in she comes....I'm not saying she portrays herself as a goody-goody or anything like that but she always has been seen as the girl-next-door, as an example to people.

'I've met many stars over the years and they're just human beings. We shouldn't say things about them that we wouldn't about the guy next door. And we wouldn't say "He turned up drunk" or he took this or that, or did this or that, unless he portrayed himself as something different.

'I wasn't shocked by Cilla. I was disappointed.'

*Chapter Nine*

# BIG BUCKS

*'Everybody needs good neighbours ...*
*with a little understanding ...'*
– THEME SONG TO THE AUSTRALIAN TV
SOAP *NEIGHBOURS*

Although almost everyone would argue that her cheeky Liverpool image has been the making of her, Cilla has always resented it.

This was the 1980s and money seemed to be cascading into Cilla's hands, from TV commercials – for Typhoo tea and Heinz Baked Beans – to increasing cabaret and concert appearances, offers which increased in tandem with her television exposure. Cilla could have been forgiven for wanting to stop the world. And get off.

Yet again and again she wanted reassurance – of her status, her stature, her *position*. It made her picky about deals and about how she lives. She's had a thing about Shirley Bassey from her early days in showbusiness, and will often repeat the same complaint, 'If Shirley Bassey sweeps into a room they go all funny and swoon. If they see me they slap me on the back!'

The disrespect reached Monty Python heights when she delivered a 'Cillagram' for the *Surprise, Surprise!* series to Holyhead. The town had requested that she sang to them all in the High Street. The staff at the local Woolworths all went out the front door to hear her. The robbers went in the back door and had time to loot all the stock. Cilla saw the joke, saying another act had stolen her spotlight.

'Cilla was always the most forward of all the children; she would elbow her way into any situation,' said her Aunt Mary, who still lives in Liverpool. In later life Mrs White could not get many of her thoughts coherently together but she did say her ongoing memory of Cilla was, 'All of us used to say how like her mother she was. Her mother would always stand up for herself and her family, and get what she believed belonged to them … She used her elbows to protect those around her and to get on.'

It was 1997 when a tabloid newspaper discovered Mary White existing in 'pathetic' surroundings. There were no rugs, not even a worn carpet in her home, it was reported, but instead, '*The cold, bare floorboards are stark testimony to the grinding poverty in which Mary White lives out the last years of her life.*

'*Just one more forgotten pensioner in a Britain that doesn't care? But this is a pensioner with a difference, with one of Britain's most famous stars in her family. Mary White's niece is Cilla Black, the cheekily cheerful TV hostess with the smile of a millionaire and the lifestyle that's a world away from the pitiful plight of her destitute aunt. Mary says, "I expect Cilla could afford to buy me a nice cottage in the country."*'

And any readers would, as intended, expect she could.

It was heavyweight, heartrending material accompanied by a photographic portrait of a *shivering* Mary White who lives, she now says, quite happily in a block of flats in Kirkby, Merseyside. After the article appeared Liverpool City Council went on 'public relations alert' in that they did not want any of their 'elderly citizens' to be seen to be living in deprived conditions. Especially one who could find her name in Sunday newspaper headlines. 'Anything Cilla does has to be golden around here,' was the word from the community relations department. 'Cilla's like The Beatles – she brings the tourists in. She doesn't live here and I can't think of the last time we ever had her do a Liverpool event, but she plays up Liverpool and we play her up.

'It's all complete nonsense but we don't complain, she doesn't complain – and the public certainly don't ask questions. It's like Nottingham and Robin Hood – who's going to say it's all a load of bollocks?'

Certainly not Brian Roberts, who wrote the story for the *Sunday Mirror*. Roberts explained: 'She (Cilla's Aunt Mary) really can't gather her words. We just did the best we could with what we had. But I'll tell you – all hell broke loose. The council wanted to know this and that, and there were legal letters flying around.

'I gather Cilla was not at all pleased. It was not the image she wanted and she seemed to get very upset about it.'

In the article, Mary White was quoted in reaction to the possibility of Cilla wanting to help her, '*If she offered, I would tell her I'm happy where I am. I haven't seen her for a long time so I don't expect she knows how I live. She has done well, but I don't want her money.*' The report continued, '*She scrapes by on her £36.60 pension, and says, "I worry about the cost of the heating, but I must keep warm."*'

At her mother's funeral in 1996 Cilla had met Aunt Mary for the first time in years. When she is asked about her now, in light of the article revealing the living conditions of her beloved father's sister, she is matter-of-fact:

'I wouldn't know how to get in touch with her. I'm close to my Aunt Nellie (her longed-for but lost daughter Helen was named after her), because she and my mam were the best of friends, but I know Mam wasn't very close to Aunt Mary. I did see her at the funeral and she looked incredible. Neither she nor her family have ever tried to get in touch with me. I receive letters addressed to *Cilla Black, The World*, so I'm sure they could have got in touch with us if they wanted to.'

Indeed, if her help was needed, a fortune-teller would have told her. Cilla may have disregard for The Beatles' mystic movement days but she is always aware of 'the fates'. One fortune-teller told her that her career would end while she was in her early forties – and she spent the evening in tears. While many would laugh off predictions she says, 'I do believe in the fates, that what and will happen is what is meant to be. I think we all do, which is why horoscopes and fortune-tellers are so popular.'

The emphasis of the story on Cilla's Aunt Mary was the contrast of their circumstances, their fortunes. What made Cilla such an easy target for this particular tabloid treatment was the way she revelled in her baubles at that time. The late Liberace would regale his audiences in Las Vegas with his over-the-top stage outfits and accoutrements and tell them, 'Enjoy them – you paid for them.'

Liberace, the original celebrity laughing-all-the-way-to-the-bank, could get away with it. Cilla, because of her own background, is uncomfortable with the subtle aspects of wealth. It appears on her fingers in walnut-sized diamonds and in the storage fridges reserved for her furs: she has a Russian sable, a red fox, a silver fox, a full-length white mink, a mink jacket, a raccoon coat, and a coat made of monkey fur.

'I started spending money on clothes in the early days because I had to do so many television appearances. I'd go out and buy something expensive for an interview and I wouldn't worry about it, because I was actually wearing it for work. Even if I didn't wear that outfit again, it had served its purpose.

'Then as time went on, things got completely out of hand. I'd go out every week to London's most expensive boutiques and buy things I'd never even wear. I still shudder when I remember a Paris designer dress I bought which I've never had on my back.

'I have two whole wardrobes packed full of clothes, plus an extra rack which I keep in the solarium because there isn't space to put it

Cilla across the years

*Top left*: A girl with ambition in 1963.

*Top right*: A year later tiptoeing to success at the London Palladium.

*Bottom*: At the start of her TV career.

*Top*: Twenty-six years later life's still a laugh – joker in the pack at the 1996 Comedy Awards.

*Bottom*: Everyone's favourite entertainer – chatting to Prince Charles and Eastender Wendy Richardson.

*Top*: Cilla with newborn Bobby Junior in 1970.

*Bottom*: Toasting success with 'Eppy'.

*Top*: Planning the high notes with George Martin.

*Bottom left*: Cilla with friend and mentor Frankie Howerd in their long-running West End show.

*Bottom right*: And going sky high with Bobby.

*Top*: A royal audience for Cilla with Jack and Bobby, as she collects her OBE at Buckingham Palace in 1997.

*Bottom*: Cilla is supported by her sons at Bobby's funeral in 1999.

Smiling at the wedding of Robert to the beautiful Fiona.

Bobby's girl with the love of her life.

anywhere else. Bobby gave me this beautiful pear-shaped diamond. It cost £50,000 and it was then I decided enough was enough. I'd already got diamonds I hadn't worn for years. And I suddenly thought, What's the point in keeping on getting things?'

She called in Pat Davies to help, 'I opened my cupboards and told her, "I've got all these clothes and I want to get rid of a lot of them. I simply don't have the space." Well, Pat was horrified. "Cilla," she said, "these are all new." And I said that I knew they were, but would she please take them away and get rid of them. It was then she said, "Look, in future when you go shopping, I'll come with you." Nowadays, I won't set foot inside a shop without her. I've met a number of people who are born into money and I admire them. I'm still learning to live with it.

'When I'm not working, I find it an effort to dress up. I know I should get all dressed up and go out to a restaurant in the West End. But in my heart of hearts, I'd rather stay at home and watch *Coronation Street*. I've got marvellous friends, but they never get invited to my house. I'm a dreadful cook and I couldn't hire someone to do it – I wouldn't know what to do with a cook. It's just not me. I'd probably end up in the kitchen waiting on the help myself. I'm the same about having a chauffeur, although we've got a super Rolls-Royce, which I love.'

About her home there is a mania. Her attitude mirrors that of other stars who have moved from working-class backgrounds to money. While those who inherit can often live with dust, those who earn it usually have to polish. Cilla is a polisher. She likes everything to sparkle. When her children were growing up she wanted the bathrooms perfect for them; there was also the comfort factor, making the 'nest' warm for everyone. The Denham house is scrubbed, polished and hoovered five days a week by the help. At weekends Cilla will often do it herself. Pat Davies recalled that in their growing-up years in Liverpool their mothers used to springclean the whole house on Sundays after church, moving all the furniture to get the duster or Hoover into the most obscure spots: if you worked for it you looked after it.

Cilla, said Pat Davies, always joked that she had a fear of royalty turning up unexpectedly. The Queen's car might break down and the lady herself might turn up on Cilla's doorstep and catch her out with the place in a mess. So, Cilla is a Hoovermaniac.

Her luxurious home is like a badge of success, 'Daft, isn't it? When you've had nothing like me, you can't believe your good fortune when you can afford to have what you want. When the only time you had a bath was once a week in the public baths and it cost you four (old) pence, you never quite get used to six bathrooms. I use them all in turn.'

At home you will not find the television Cilla. Indeed, her fans will not find her at home at all because of Bobby Willis' adamant conviction that their house ought to be off-limits. Mr and Mrs Willis were never at home to the public. In the past she has turned down thousands of pounds from *Hello!* style magazines for photographic snoops around her home, which has had the lookover of designers from London's Sloane Street. There's a Colefax & Fowler feel about the place, with its quiet pastel shades, mint greens and salmon pinks. There's that Charles II dining table which seats ten – more if you pull the chairs in from next door – and antique wardrobes and sideboards which in the public rooms boast everything from her *1997 Best Comedy Award* to her treasured *Best Presenter Trophy* from the Royal Television Society, and the bedrooms conceal her lavish collection of all-white underwear. She insists on white only, which gossip says goes back to the taboo subject of John Lennon and her knickers …

It was Bobby Willis who was adamant that this was their totally private space. Cilla could put her feet up and watch Coronation Street in peace. They could talk quietly over a glass of champagne. They rarely entertained at home, business meeting were conducted in restaurants and hotels, often at the Dorchester in London, instead. During the working week, staff cleaned the house from top to bottom. At weekends, while Bobby happily pottered around, Cilla got out the Hoover. While those who inherit wealth can often live with the dust, those who earn it usually have to polish. Cilla is a polisher. They bought an apartment on the beach in Barbados and created their own 'nest'. Bobby's plan was to create an escape from the pressures of their hectic schedules – it was like starting a new, fairytale life: Bobby wanted the best for Cilla.

Her 'castle' was invaded in 1984 by robbers who cut their way through her elaborate home security and stole around £100,000-worth of her treasures, including her diamond engagement ring. The family had not been singled out, according to the police, but were rather the victims of ongoing raids on luxury homes in the area. That, strangely, was a comfort. The robbers hadn't been after Cilla Black's belongings in particular – they would have taken anybody's that were worth selling on. Cilla's main regret was for the loss of her diamond engagement ring.

Success has its hurdles. One of them is envy, especially in a neighbourhood like Denham, where there is a certain sense of propriety about the community. Some of the locals have never liked Cilla or Bobby Willis. A drive and wander around town, albeit on a very unscientific survey, brings many stories of 'strangeness' or them being 'standoffish' or 'above themselves'. 'Who do they think they are?' Some residents do not want to offend in public but will dish the dirt anonymously, complaining about late-night noise and 'goings on' and the like, which is all hearsay. Irene Catt, who was a parish counsellor for more than twenty years, is, at least, upfront:

'Just because she prances around on television she thinks she's everyone's friend. She isn't and she never could be.'

Cilla believes all the snobbery is because she was a pop singer when she moved in, but the residents seem to find 'television light entertainer' and certainly *Blind Date* hostess even more difficult to accept. 'We all watch the show, just like everybody else,' said Robert Shriver of the local taxi company, adding, 'But around here they don't like to admit it. But, funny, on a Monday morning they all know what happened.

'They don't like her and it's understandable. She's done nothing for the community. She lives here but she's at great pains to avoid mixing with the locals – it's as though she's frightened to get too close. They call her "Miss Haversham" because no one ever sees her.'

The locals are some carefully protected and cared-for acres away from Casa Cilla but they must have strong telescopes behind their net curtains. They certainly got her into deep water when she began digging up the back yard for a swimming pool. The interested onlookers complained to South Buckinghamshire District Council that she was excavating 'a lake' in her grounds. Without permission. The Council pounced immediately and the bulldozers and the work – having added up already to a hefty sum of £10,000 for digging, £2000 for earth removal and £30,000 for the swimming pool lining (all, of course, plus VAT) – had to stop. The Parish Council finally put an end to the whole project.

'It's quite clear Cilla Black thought she would get away with this because she is a big star,' recalled Irene Catt. 'We have lots of big names in Denham, like Sir John Mills and Paul Daniels, but they don't act like this. In all the years she has lived in Denham, she has never joined in the local activities.

'She is not very popular here. An alert member of the community noticed a load of digging going on at the property. Denham is a small place and because we are in the Green Belt we are very concious of any alterations.

'We made some enquiries and discovered the "lake" was not legal.'

Mrs Edna Townsend, who would be one of Cilla's closest

neighbours, said: 'The field next to Cilla's house used to be so pretty and they turned it into a complete mess. I knew nothing about a lake being built until workmen moved in. I think it was wrong that something on that scale was being built without local people being consulted. My worry was it would smell in the summer.'

Another neighbour, who preferred to remain anonymous, said, 'What she did was a bloody cheek. Stars seem to think there's one rule for them and another for the rest of us.'

Cilla herself publicly feigned absolute disdain about the whole thing – and about those complaining, 'I don't hit back,' she said, 'because I wouldn't know them if I fell over them.'

That, said her critics, proved their point although Rosemary Temple of the Parish Council was, with hindsight, a little more generous, 'Our main concern was that an excavation of that type could upset the water table. Sometimes people don't realise they need planning permission. Maybe that's what happened.'

Nevertheless, it appeared that Cilla would never have much luck even with celebrity neighbours. Her relationship with magician-entertainer Paul Daniels was 'difficult'. They lived close to each other in Denham but Daniels suddenly decided to vanish from Buckinghamshire to Berkshire. Daniels maintained, 'I saw very little of Cilla and never liked her. She only lived three doors away but she never took part in the local community. She's a strange woman.'

Other close residents, who include Mike Oldfield (most famous for *Tubular Bells*), say they have no view on living near Cilla. Why? There's no need, they say. They never meet her.

The neighbours, who she would prefer to get on with but believes are 'snobby' about her, are something Cilla does not like to confront too often. Like her figure.

Cilla's height takes the tape measure to five foot, six and a half inches; the scales – when she's in best shape – hover around nine and a half stone and she's a size 12. She'd put on nearly a stone and a half when those *Sunday Mirror* photographs were taken of her in Spain: it was not some sudden weight gain but, like most people, the insidious result of just not monitoring the diet and allowing the weight to gradually pile on.

For most people, life's too short to worry. For Cilla – and other publicly 'fat' victims like her friend *Richard and Judy* television presenter Judy Finnegan, and international 'fat' star Marlon Brando – it can be part of business. That was all the incentive Cilla ever needed. During the 1997 season of *Blind Date* her look and shape appeared to improve by the week. It was not always so, 'When I look at old pictures of myself I want to cringe. I looked terrible. I have this little voice in my head which screams, "Please don't tell me I looked like that." I went through a phrase when I thought I looked dowdy and frumpy. Years ago I never had to diet, but once I hit forty I noticed the pounds slowly creeping on because my metabolism had changed. Before I knew it, my face was looking chubby and I could pinch a whole lot more than an inch around my waist.'

First she tried the American Scarsdale Diet, which rotates and teams foods and bans alcohol. She then attempted other mainstream diets which included grilled fish, steamed vegetables and salads and allowed some alcoholic drinks. Despite her proven willpower she found such diets hard to keep to.

So hard that when she was on a diet she started putting weight *on* …

'Now I count the calories all the time. I know the calorie content of everything I eat. I've made it my business to know how to balance my diet. If I want some chocolate I will only eat a chunk rather than the whole bar. My ambition is to be eight and a half stone and size 10. I've bought the size 10 clothes ready for that day. My body's in good shape. I've got great legs and I wouldn't know what cellulite is. But the face! It's the face of a fiftysomething woman and I want to look thirty-five. I guess I'm vain. I must be, otherwise I wouldn't put three layers of foundation on before going out to the supermarket.'

She has always considered the possibility of a facelift, according to those around her. She would have had the operation before, but success has stopped her; stringent commitments to *Surprise, Surprise!* and *Blind Date* have not given long enough breaks for the cosmetic surgeons to do their work and her face to heal in time for her to be before the cameras again. She knows about the possibility of laser surgery – it heals more quickly – in Los Angeles.

Vanity is involved, certainly, but it is also a business investment, arguably a tax write-off. She did it with her nose, so why not the eyes, chin, cheeks, giving the Full Monty a lift? Although she will always recall one of the more important reactions to her nose operation, 'Me mam called me up and made a dreadful fuss. She said: "Why put yourself through all that? It's bad enough having an operation when you've got no choice!" '

Her critics, like the neighbours, sneer at her 'prancing about on television' and her contemporaries – usually those who have not done anything like as well – are snide about her career choices.

'I could never do a game show,' said Sandie Shaw, adding, 'It would be awful. I would die of embarrassment. I don't watch those programmes so why should I be involved in them? I'm moving on. Anyone of icon status like me realises that there has to be an interplay of deep unconscious fantasy between you and your audience, and I don't think people like Cilla Black are icons. People like David Bowie and Jimi Hendrix and me, we summon up a whole consciousness. We are not just a moment of time. It is an ongoing thing. We are deeply enmeshed in people's lives. They grow and we are still with them.'

Well, Cilla certainly is. And you can argue that she *is* an icon – in our millennium time. Arguably, there never was a female icon of the Sixties. Marianne Faithfull was the flag-waver for the excesses of the era, but her music never came close to icon status. Similarly, Dusty Springfield, who died of breast cancer in 1999, was the best singer of them all, but she got lost in her own world of problems. Sandie Shaw? She had eleven Top Twenty hits, won the Eurovision Song Contest in 1967 with *Puppet on a String* (a song she thanked you for not mentioning three decades later) and, the lasting memory, *sang in her bare feet*. She is the antithesis of Cilla.

While Cilla got her teeth around the chirpy chipmunk professional life, Sandie Shaw, the equally working-class girl from the Ford motor company home of Dagenham, Essex, has been more introspective. In 1997 she was working at establishing herself as a 'fame counsellor' and pitching a television interview show idea to Granada Television. While Cilla might be considering a facelift, her contemporary seemed to be seeking consciousness-lifting, 'Other people see me as an icon. I am used to people having opinions about me, some of them quite off the wall. I see myself as this woman who looks after her kids and has had a few husbands. People get incredibly upset when they find out I had a bad time and no money, which is really funny. People get so worried. I am really happy and my life is fantastic. People must be told that or they come up to me and say, "Are you all right now, Sand?" '

Cilla's OK. It's time that's the problem. She is aware of it and, unlike the neighbours, she is always ready to face up to it, saying, 'I like the way I look but I just don't want to get any older. Turning fifty was awful. God, you should have seen me, I was so depressed. My hormones were playing havoc with me. The thought of never being able to have babies again was just terrible. I think that's why I prefer the company of men to women. All that women my age talk about is their hysterectomies and, quite frankly, I think there's more to life than talking about your hysterectomy. I've had one so I'm not knocking women who've had the operation. It's just that I find them so boring to talk to. I'd rather be in a group of men telling dirty jokes. I like to think that men still find me attractive, but nowadays it's only the golden oldies who do. When I look at some of the girls who come on to *Blind Date* I can't help thinking that I've got pairs of tights older than they are.

'Unfortunately I've always been seen as the girl next door and although it's been good for me, I hate that image. When I was a pop singer, I wanted to be the femme fatale. Sex is bubbling over within me. There's a burning cauldron there but people just don't see it. I'd love to be like Shirley Bassey.

'I've gone from the girl next door to the granny next door, which is awful because I *really* see myself as Jean Shrimpton. Yet people see me as being inoffensive and no threat to anyone. It's a bit like being a packet of soap powder.

'I'm amazed that people still want to employ me. It can't just be because I'm a nice person, and it's only as I get older that I'm beginning to appreciate that perhaps there is a certain amount of talent there that keeps me going. But I actually don't know what the hell it is that I've got. I'm really looking forward to being a grandmother. I can't wait for my sons to have babies. I love the vulnerability and total reliability of babies, and I know they will adore me because I won't have any of the hang-ups that mothers have. I will do everything right and my daughters-in-law will hate me because I'm so perfect.

'To go from being the girl next door to the granny next door is my ultimate dream. I'm not like Gloria Hunniford who doesn't want to be called Granny. You can call me Granny, Rover or anything just as long as I've got grandchildren.'

## *Chapter Ten*

# BOBBY'S MOTHER

*'We have already spoken to Mr Willis and in view of the way the accident happened we will certainly be questioning him further ...'*

– A POLICE OFFICIAL, FOLLOWING A FATAL ACCIDENT INVOLVING BOBBY WILLIS JUNIOR

Cilla is one of Britain's best-known celebrities and for anyone famous enough to be known by one name, be it Churchill, Sinatra, Mussolini or Lassie, things can become difficult. Cilla aims for privacy by assuming the mantle of Mrs Willis at every opportunity.

In company, her longtime nanny turned house manager Penny still calls her Mrs Willis, as do all the staff at home in Buckinghamshire. In family situations she always wants to play it that way. With contractors and school teachers, doctors and lawyers and all sorts of everyday advice from hedgecutting to ironing services, the security system to the land's water table, she has to get on with her life. As did Bobby Willis. Imagine a plumbing disaster with water spraying everywhere and the workmen are in awe and only wanting an autograph rather than plugging the leak. It's happened – and it keeps happening.

What do you say when you walk in and Cilla's directing you to where the disaster is? She has it planned. 'At home she is very much

Mrs Willis and no one else,' says a friend. 'If she starts it off that way, the people calling at the house have to be very dense not to understand immediately what the situation is. It really is a very simple arrangement which is best for everyone. It's easier and obviously much more efficient.'

Cilla explains one example very close to her: 'It started when the children were small. I remember Ben had a little friend who grabbed me around the knees – he was that small – and said, "I love you, Cilla Black." Ben said, "No, this is my mummy. That's your mummy over there. You should go and love your mummy."

'So, I decided it was wrong for teachers to call me Cilla. Plus, I didn't want to come home and have my own kids calling me Cilla. It's just basic respect.'

In the High Street in Denham she would get that, but it is Penny who does the shopping there, for good quality minced beef for the boys' favourite shepherd's pie.

Cilla has been around a long time, from Biba to Donna Karan, from The Beatles to The Verve, from Hughie Green and *Double Your Money* to Michael Barrymore and *Strike It Rich*; she is certainly not some celebrity pop punctuation like The Spice Girls.

It is mostly that which makes separating her two worlds impossible. Almost everything that happens to Cilla happens to her publicly. That includes tragedy. Which means presenting two faces to it: one for the cameras and one for the small hours of the night when it looks not just bleak but bleaker.

The fatal accident involving her son Robert was like that. It was a horror, in a moment, that came from nowhere. She was returning home in a chauffeured hire car just after 8 p.m. on a Tuesday evening in September 1990, when half a mile from her house the way was blocked by a man stumbling in the road. It was her son, reeling with shock from a traffic accident. Robert Willis' face was covered in tears of dismay as he wandered around the narrow roadway near the family home.

It was happenstance that Cilla almost drove into the accident. Her son had been emerging from a junction on to the A412 in his 1989 Renault 5 when he was in a smash with motorcyclist Richard Potter. As he turned on to the main road, his car collided with Potter's Suzuki 750cc. Potter, twenty-five, and his pillion passenger were flung from their bike and badly injured, but Robert Willis only suffered minor cuts. As Cilla, confused and concerned over her dazed son, was dealing with him, Potter from Virginia Water, Surrey, was being taken to Mount Vernon Hospital, Northwood, where he died. His pillion passenger, Mary Sholto-Douglas, suffered a nasty leg injury. Thames Valley Police cover the area. The official report says: '*The accident happened at about 8.20 p.m. on Tuesday night. Mr Willis was turning out of a side road on to the main road and struck the motorcycle in the nearside lane. The road was blocked for two hours.*'

On the night of the accident they said, 'We are still investigating the circumstances. We have already spoken to Mr Willis and in view of the way the accident happened, we will certainly be questioning him further.'

Cilla's son Robert was breathalysed but the test was negative.

No matter where the blame lay for the head-on crash, the headlines surrounding the accident were due to the Cilla connection. Whatever she did or said was going to be or sound wrong to the grieving extended family of social worker Richard Potter. Even years later when more cruel problems affected them.

The motorcyclist who suffered brain damage and a fractured skull had an 18-month-old daughter Ruby, and his common-law wife Joanna Thurston was three months' pregnant with their son Nathan when he was killed. In 1998 pictures of the two children and of Richard sat on the office desk of his father Roy Potter at his business, Surrey Fasteners, in Ascot, Berkshire.

Mr Potter and his wife Noreen have never fully recovered from the death of their son. In 1997 Mrs Potter was diagnosed with cancer and in early 1998 was undergoing treatment. A family friend said, 'It seems to happen when you are at a low ebb – it's just another tragedy in their lives.' David Lee, the financial director at Surrey Fasteners and a close friend of Mr Potter's, said, 'As you might imagine, it has been a difficult time for them. Roy has had a lot to weather.'

The Potters and Joanna Thurston and her family have always felt that Cilla's side not only got all the attention but the understanding and condolences. While she was expecting her son in March 1990, Joanne Thurston wept as she said: 'I feel terrible. All the sympathy has been for the pain caused to Cilla Black and her family. But I am the one who is left without my husband. I have not heard a word from Cilla Black, her family, or anybody connected with them. I feel bitter about that. My life has been devastated.'

Her mother Gillian said, 'She seems to be the forgotten person in this tragedy.'

The Cilla connection was not forgotten and it resulted in much private grief and public bitterness as the lives of two families were joined in the tragedy. It is the way of showbusiness people to be emotional, but Cilla is a control freak. So, it was a shock when she cried at a Variety Club pre-Christmas lunch and talked about Robert's car accident. Another guest speaker was Frankie Howerd and Cilla looked over at him as she told the celebrity crowded room, 'We do have a lot of problems in our life and Frankie has been a great counsellor, especially over what happened to our son.'

Frankie was asked to explain his role but simply said, 'I just tried to help in any way I could. I've been very concerned for Robert and I did all I could for him. That's what friends are for, after all. And I have been friends of Cilla and the family for years.'

Cilla was presented with a silver heart at the lunch at the London Hilton for her work in showbusiness and charity, but the 'luvvie lunch' did not find approval with Roy Potter, 'To use a celebrity dinner as a platform to talk about her family anguish is sick. It smacks of both self-pity and sympathy seeking. She may have had them in tears but she has not even had the decency to get in touch with us – not one single word. She has not even picked up a phone to offer her condolences. Everyone seems so sorry for her. She should try being in the shoes of my family and then she would know what being upset is all about. We are without a son this Christmas and a lady who was to be his wife is left to bring up her two children on her own. It was a sickening act of self-pity. Cilla Black's living is made using the media and the public eye, and it seems she is taking advantage of this to wrongly gain sympathy.'

The hurt of the Potter family was clear. The dead man, a ten O-level student from Wellington College, a Berkshire county rugby player and an English trialist, could have gone into his father's steel parts distribution company. Instead he decided to travel, met Joanna on an Israeli kibbutz in 1985 and, after hitchhiking round Europe, the two set up home in London. When she became pregnant with Ruby he took a job as a residential worker for the mentally handicapped in Hillingdon, London, and Joanna became a warden in a sheltered-housing scheme. He is very much remembered by his family, and the mother of his children said, 'Richard didn't waste his life. It's almost as though he knew something would happen. Richard was a devoted father. At the end of August, I was pregnant with a second baby and he decided he was going to sell his Suzuki 750cc. He wanted to buy a Campervan so we could go away for holidays together as a family.'

In the months following her partner's death she could not forgive Cilla for her emotional Variety Club outburst. She said in an interview, 'I'd cried a million tears since Richard died, and reading Cilla's words brought back all the pain.

'The way Cilla's talking, you'd think her son was the only one involved and her family were the sole victims. Because Cilla Black's son was driving the car and not a plumber's boy we've had to suffer more. We are not allowed to grieve in peace.

'When you see Cilla Black on television and read the interviews, she seems so nice. I don't want to sound like some jealous whinger but I hoped against hope she would make some effort to contact me. I don't want any admission of guilt, I just want to know she feels sorry for my loss. I don't want to believe that we are only the forgotten victims. Ruby hasn't forgotten. When she sees a motorbike in the street she still shouts, "Daddy, Daddy." '

Cilla, usually one to take the initiative and confront and deal with public concerns – she has always been her own best 'spin doctor' – failed to comment to the newspapers in general about the criticism of her reaction to the tragedy. She was somewhat stuck in a no-win situation. At the time she had a regular column in the *Daily Star* newspaper and used it to offer her feelings:

*'This morning my son Robert is going to Uxbridge Coroner's Court for the inquest into the tragic death of a young motorcyclist who was in collision with his car.*

*'As a loving, caring, concerned mother, my place is at Robert's side, giving him comfort and support.*

*'But I won't be there today, although his father will. And no doubt some people will ask why, if we're such a close family, I can't take a morning off.*

*'The truth is, that I shall be sitting indoors, listening to the ticking of the mantelpiece clock until he comes home. I desperately want to be at the inquest, but if I turn up it could become a circus.*

*'There will be photographers and sightseers, and the grieving family of the poor motorcyclist Richard Potter will have a lot of attention focused upon them at a time that they least want it.*

*'But by staying at home, I hope the way will be clear for the inquest to take place in a calm and dignified manner.*

*'I'd hate to draw attention away from the investigation into the circumstances of Richard's death.*

*'I have been publicly criticised by Richard's father for not sending*

*a wreath to the funeral and for not getting in touch.*

*'Richard's girlfriend, Joanna Thurston, has called me uncaring and selfish. She is expecting Richard's second child in March and they already had an 18-month-old daughter, Ruby.*

*'But I'm not surprised at the fury directed at me by Richard's family. If my 25-year-old son, or the father of my children had died as unexpectedly, I'd be angry too.*

*'The fact is that Bobby, Robert and I were advised that we should NOT attempt to get in touch with Richard's family.*

*'We were warned that in these harsh times even a message of regret could be misconstrued as an admission of liability or guilt.*

*'That apart, we didn't know how Richard's family would react to an approach from us.*

*We're a very private family and in similar circumstances – please God forbid – we'd want to be left alone to mourn.*

*'If there is one consolation it is that the comments are not being made about Robert, they are aimed at me.*

*'After 27 years as an entertainer, I'm used to criticism. I don't like it, of course, but I have to put up with it.*

*'But it is our Robert, 20 years old and very much an independent young man, who has to live with the fact that Richard Potter was killed, and his passenger, Mary Sholto-Douglas, was injured.*

*'It happened outside our house one warm evening last September. Since then we've all frequently wept real tears and not a day has gone by without us thinking of Richard.*

*'If l could turn the clock back I would, But I can't. And because I'm Cilla Black I can't even exercise my right as a mother to be with my son today.*

*'I'm not looking for sympathy. Please save all that for the family that Richard left behind.'*

Cilla's two Bobbys, father and son, were present to hear Coroner John Burton rule after a two and a half hour hearing that Richard

Potter had died accidentally in the collision with the Renault 5. Robert Junior stood solemnly in the witness box as his statement saying he pulled out into a clear road 'then heard a crash' was read out. It added, '*It was only when I got out of the car that I noticed the motorbike. It came from nowhere. There was a terrific bang and glass seemed to explode everywhere. I was aware something awful had happened I just didn't see him.*'

Witness, Michael Long, twenty-two, said he saw Robert come up to the junction. 'I remember thinking, Is that car going to stop?' The hurt and controversy did not end with the inquest. The Crown Prosecution Service (CPS) said a careless driving charge was being considered. Cilla cried herself to sleep that night.

Roy Potter said he was going to sue for damages – no matter what the CPS decided, 'The compensation we will be seeking will be very considerable. The money will be for the support of my son's child.'

Cilla was finally coaxed into saying something and responded, 'What happened to Richard was a terrible tragedy. I can't begin to express the feelings of despair I have had for his family. They will probably never get over the shock, but as Robert's mother I have also had to live with the shock and his feelings. I'd desperately hoped that the inquest verdict would be the end of everyone's ordeal. All we want is to be able to live normal lives again. That may sound selfish, because the Potter family has been shattered by their loss, and they can never get back what they had. But whatever the police and the courts decide, Robert will face up to everything with courage and we will support him and comfort him all the way.'

It turned out all the way to the Magistrates' Court at Beaconsfield, Buckinghamshire, where Robert Willis Junior pleaded guilty to careless driving. He was fined £250 and given five penalty points. The court result did nothing to assuage Roy Potter's feelings, and following the case he said, 'I can't believe the fine. I'm flabbergasted. The law is an ass. This is not a deterrent at all. He should have lost his licence for at least twelve months.' Magistrate Keith Hillyer said the sentence had only to be based on how the driving fell below what was to be expected of a 'reasonable and prudent driver'.

Cilla avoided the court hearing as she had the inquest, but even with her son dealt with by the criminal courts the case went on. Indeed, Cilla's son, the whole family, will always have to live with the death crash. Because of some of the comments surrounding it, Cilla insists that every Christmas the horror and tragedy of Richard Potter's death haunts them.

A civil settlement was finally reached two years after the fatal crash, with Robert Willis' insurance company and lawyers finalising a deal with Roy Potter's lawyers. It centred on compensation – at around £80,000 – for Richard Potter's partner, his daughter Ruby and Nathan, the son he never saw. Further costs of around £10,000 were also met. 'A million pounds wouldn't replace Richard,' said Roy Potter.

Later, he would say, 'None of the family feels vindictive towards Mr Willis, no one wants him hanged, but he was negligent and one would have thought he or his parents would have had the decency to express their sympathy directly to us.'

Some years after the accident, Cilla looks back, 'As well as everything else, it showed the worst side of being visible and recognised. My heart was really torn between the dead boy and my own child. There was no consoling Robert and still Christmas, the time when we're all together, is awful. That's when you remember. You can't take it away. You can't kiss him on both cheeks and make it better. As a mother, you can never go inside your child's head, but I can see when his face is darkening and he's thinking about it. He was only eighteen and he aged. He looked like an old man ... the rings under his eyes. But none of that is to detract from the other family.'

Robert Willis and Ben and Jack, who was with his mother on

16 July 1997, when she was presented with her OBE from the Queen, have all been given a privileged start in life. Their schools and colleges have been carefully chosen (Jack's early schooling was troubled until his dyslexia was diagnosed and dealt with) and their mother said, 'It was the best education that money can buy. I wouldn't let them go to boarding school because I wasn't having them not there on my days off. I missed out on education, Bobby and I both did, and I wasn't going to let it happen to our lads.'

What has happened is that Robert Willis who, like his brothers, had to earn his pocket money, has followed his parents into showbusiness. In 1998 he was his mother's manager, with his father still very much in the wings but concentrating on his other clients like Petula Clark for whom he landed a long 1990s London run in *Sunset Boulevard*. Cilla's Bobby was never too far away. She said, 'I like him in the building. If there's anything wrong he'll be down on the studio floor in a moment. That's it.'

Bobby Willis monitored every one of Cilla's performances from a private closed-circuit system wherever she hangs her pink *Woman's Journal* special offer bathrobe with the nylon patches on the shoulders.

Bobby Junior's first job was as an office runner for ITV's early morning breakfast show GMTV. He reacted to accusations of nepotism with, 'Mum is pleased I've got a job but it has absolutely nothing to do with my parents. I went for an interview like everyone else.' The job involved renting a London apartment and working twelve-hour days. There was still time though for 'being buddies' with Paul McCartney's artist daughter Mary: photo portraits by her have been shown in the National Portrait Gallery. Bobby is also close to Stella McCartney, the top fashion designer. Cilla wouldn't have minded her as a daughter-in-law but was, as always, careful not to say too much about personal family matters.

'I think it's terrific. They are just buddies. I find it quite strange, but youngsters today seem to be able to have a relationship without being sloppy. I blame it all on *Neighbours*. They just got together naturally at college. Robert was at Oxford Poly and made some great pals there. They didn't realise just who each other's parents were when they met. They became friends off their own bat. They both share the same sense of humour. He's very sensible – if anyone can be sensible about girls.'

Robert Junior, who graduated with honours in English and History from Oxford Poly in 1992, began working on his mother's career when he was about twenty. In 1990 she was Britain's biggest – and highest paid – television star, but she wanted more – especially respect. She had discarded a script for a television situation comedy but at her LWT office among what he calls 'her junk', the former literature student discovered it, 'I read it through and thought it was very good, took it home, showed it to Mother and the next thing I knew they had made a pilot for it.' Unfortunately, the show, *Follow the Yellow Brick Road*, featuring Cilla as a divorcée who imagines herself as a golden era movie star, never took off. Undaunted, her son just kept on writing his own scripts – and plays. He spent time with the Royal Court Theatre in London on a playwriting course but his parents never attended productions, 'Mother couldn't usually come along because if she did people would come up to her and want to talk to her – autographs and that kind of thing.'

His attitude in 1997 and into 1998 when he had taken over the running of his mother's office was a little like that offhand remark about 'autographs and that sort of thing'. It was an attitude his mother had worked for decades never to show; her power and popularity base has always been as 'approachable' Cilla, the girl-next-door, one-of-us Cilla. Her longevity rests on this. Her fans – and the demographic surveys show it – have grown older with her while she has added legions more with *Blind Date*.

In 1997 the normally co-operative Cilla had trouble with some arrangements for photographs for the *Sunday Times* in London. The newspaper's colour magazine said that when her regular make-up artist was not available they suggested using the renowned make-up wizard who had created the award-winning work on Ralph Fiennes in that year's Oscar cavalcade, *The English Patient*. When this was recommended to Cilla she responded, 'Am I really that bad?' The magazine said she preferred to cancel the photographic session. It did not endear her to writer Richard Johnson bm he saw the Cilla dichotomy, 'She loses her temper on set but, producing highly autographed programmes, she knows that it is her reputation that is on the line. And bad days only make her look more human.'

He then aimed for where he believed the blame for problems lay, 'Her son Robert runs her office in an offhand and lazy manner. Calls aren't returned, faxes and clothes go astray, shoots (photographic) don't always happen. As one source close to Cilla says, "Robert treats the media with contempt and it's slowly alienating her from the support she's always had in the tabloid press. And there lies the potential for disaster."'

For Cilla, the 1990s appeared to have been bought and paid for before they even got started. *Blind Date* was her insurance, a lavishly invested pension plan. Strangely, against her instincts, she had initially not wanted to host the series. She already had the hugely successful *Surprise, Surprise!* on her schedule, and didn't want to be overexposed. And, a new experience for Cilla, she was nervous.

The entire show rested on her ability to bounce the often ribald and sometimes too racy nuances around, perform a clever conjuring act with teams of over-eager 'Blinders' equipped with hormonal radar. Doubts over the generation gap between herself and the contestants, as well as her own complex schedules, made her wonder about the wisdom of taking on the pressures of *Blind Date*.

'It was something we didn't think would happen,' revealed Bobby Willis, adding, 'Cilla didn't really want to do it – she had to be persuaded. I don't think anyone involved imagined that *Blind Date* would run, well – it seems like for ever and ever ...'

*Chapter Eleven*

# BLIND LUCKY

*'I'm not in the business of offending anyone.'*
– Cilla Black, 1997

Bobby Willis was right. Neither Cilla nor anyone else could have predicted the success of *Blind Date*. It has become an intrinsic part of British life. Monday morning coffee breaks in home and office, and commuter chatter often dwell on why Geena from Doncaster picked number three from Cambridge when it was clear that number one from Southampton was the man of every sensible woman's dreams. Or not. Or whether or not Cilla's slip was, metaphorically, showing.

There is no precedent with such a format in the UK. Across the Atlantic, yes; just as for more than two decades Americans stayed up till 11.30 p.m. to watch Johnny Carson on the ninety-minute *The Tonight Show* five evenings a week, Cilla has become part of our weekly routine. One of the first images ITV broadcast in 1998 was Cilla wishing the nation Happy New Year. The newly ennobled Elton John, who had been so visible in the year of the death of Diana, Princess of Wales, had to wait his turn as the clock ticked past midnight just as, as Reg Dwight, he had had to wait for Cilla to pass his song on to Cliff Richard before his own career was given a chance. Television rather than music or the cinema bestows the popularity pecking order, makes and breaks the 'great' entertainment careers.

It is clear that Cilla Black will be eternally connected with *Blind Date*. For hundreds of thousands of people it is a huge topic in their lives, 'Cilla should have said this, done that, smiled earlier, told off the flash one, not allowed the tarty girl with the *enormous* cleavage to lean that far forward.' The content of the show is also questioned; just how far can and should the programme-makers go?

It is ironic that the big chance for Cilla, who is so British, so resonant of a particular UK way of life, should have its beginnings in America, the home of brash television. It was the agonising of John Birt, who was then LWT's Director of Programming, and was later to become a controversial Director General of the BBC, that led Cilla on to become the auntie-next-door and a television power-player. Birt wanted to get a version of a veteran game-show format on UK television.

American Chuck Barris, who invented the *Blind Date* concept, has made himself a multi-millionaire producing what he called 'popcorn for the mind'. Barris in the early 1960s was credited by America's entertainment moguls as having 'his finger on the pulse that beats historic'. He borrowed $20,000 to launch *The Dating Game* on ABC TV in 1965, and with its success became the producer of other game shows like *How's Your Mother-In-Law?* and *The Newlywed Game*. Of his original show he says, 'It was stupid and mawkish but never harmful. We stayed away from big prizes. If we'd introduced yachts it would have been horrible. They would have killed each other.

'I mean it. There is no limit to what people will put themselves through on television, what they will do for their fifteen minutes of fame.

'The ultimate game show would be one in which the contestant dies on air. I swear it's conceivable. The excitement gets pretty intense. If a contestant faints it's good for the show. Now, what if you discover that a contestant is carrying nitroglycerin pills and was going to kill themselves if they failed. Would you stop the show? I'm not sure.'

Barris, comments may seem outlandish but there is a precedent for TV being a life and death business. In 1997, after a *Surprise, Surprise!* style revelation and reunion on an American television show, a man went out and murdered a male neighbour who had confessed live on TV to lusting after him.

Barris, who acquired a personal fortune of more than $100 million with his game shows, retired to the South of France in 1989. He is an authority on the American format, especially about the perfect gameshow host. 'Any good wholesome American type with good teeth who looks good in a tuxedo and who older women can get their jollies over.'

His *Dating Game* was a major success on network television, until 1973 when it went into syndication which is a licence to print money. In 1984 Barris in a royalty-share deal sold the world rights of *The Dating Game* to the Fremantle Corporation, a giant programme production and distribution company and the world's largest supplier of game shows.

For the Fremantle Corporation *The Dating Game* was a bargain. 'All the great games are from the 1960s and early 1970s. There are no more than three or four of them and every successful game that's followed has been a variation of one of them,' said the company's president, Paul Talbot.

His business has more than eighty game shows running in

twenty-seven countries and a dozen of them (earning more than $20 million a year in licence fees) are based on *The Dating Game*.

As it turns out, the concept of *Blind Date* is almost as old as Cilla Black's career. When she was singing her first hits, Chuck Barris was making his first millions; an intriguing happenstance.

But you still have to make even a winning formula work. John Birt saw the potential – never imagining the idea would become part of late twentieth-century zeitgeist – and was in discussions to create *The Dating Game* for Britain. The same year as Barris sold the rights, Cilla was on a concert tour of Australia. There, she found work was getting in the way of a television show titled *Perfect Match*. It was broadcast five nights a week. A confirmed 'telly addict', she says she was hooked by it. 'I wondered, Why haven't we got it on the telly in our country?'

The answer was because Birt was wary of how the Independent Broadcasting Authority (IBA) would view such a risqué show being broadcast during the family viewing slot. 'I was worried that the IBA would think it was too smutty for a family audience.' A pilot episode was made, hosted by comedian Duncan Norvelle. His camp, Dale-Winton style was ruled 'confusing'. The IBA had questions: Did the couples need to kiss when the screen was pulled back? Couldn't they just shake hands? And – the big question – *did they have to stay overnight together*? It was an antiquated, Reith-like, no-sex-please-we're-British piece of broadcasting thinking. Half the world was being entertained by versions of *The Dating Game*: was Britain not game enough? Of course, she was! And even more receptive and willing than anybody could ever have predicted.

With hindsight, all the questions seem laughable but at the time they were very serious: success in an early evening Saturday time period was important financially and for prestige. Birt and company did not want criticism from the IBA or the Press or the public. They *did* want viewers.

The formula was a proven winner. The secret, ruled Birt, was in choosing the perfect host. They did not apply Chuck Barris' credentials – they wanted as vast an audience as possible, not just older women, getting their 'jollies' – but ruled out everyone from Julian Clary to Jeremy Beadle on the basis that either end of the sexual spectrum would not work because of the supposedly *subliminal* sex content of the series. Birt asked Alan Boyd, who was then LWT's Controller of Entertainment, 'Who's the most sexless person in television?'

Enter Cilla, from Stage Down Under. On her return from Australia, Cilla had approached Alan Boyd her LWT boss through *Surprise, Surprise!* – about *Perfect Match*. She maintains that at first she never considered the format for herself but she knows and likes successes: she liked the idea, laughed at it and regarded it as good entertainment. And, despite the warm reception of *Surprise, Surprise!* she was hungry. She was also lucky.

Echoing John Birt's appeal, Boyd told her, 'Who's the most sexless person on television? *You are!!!*

'You'll present it.'

Much about Cilla Black can be gleaned from her reaction to this. It was spelled out that only an ageing, seemingly longtime happily married mother of irreproachable domesticity, implicitly someone with a not too glamorous image, would be able to carry off a series which would succeed best on the level of its suggestiveness. It's why they mix comedians with strippers on stage – laughter takes away the threat and removes the raincoat brigade connotations.

In 1998 the 'Jewish Blind Date' was being created for Jewish Television (JVT), which was to be one of possibly 200 digital TV channels being launched by BSkyB. The twist on this was that the mother would be on stage throughout the show and have the final say on who goes on the date. She is also allowed to quiz the potential partners. 'With *Blind Date* the idea grows because the Jewish mother has got a tremendous reputation for doing everything she can to arrange a suitable partner for her children. Finding a partner is a major priority in Jewish life and a large part in the decision may go to the mother.'

No need for Cilla on that show then?

Gill Stribling-Wright, a producer of *Blind Date*, said, 'It would work without Cilla but she's ideal because she pitches it at the right level. She can flirt with the boys but slap a wrist at the same time.

'This sounds ghastly but it's a mother's role.'

And Cilla was delighted with it. She became a television Mrs Tiggywinkle in reverse: with her the prickly bits did not show on camera.

On 7 June 1985, Cilla recorded her pilot programme and on 30 November that same year, the foundations were laid, for a series which week after week during its runs has been watched by between eleven and fifteen million people. John Birt was happy with his choice, 'I suppose her chief qualities are the classic Northern virtues of warmth, good humour and the enjoyment of others; they allow her to oversee the show in a non-threatening, non-sexual way. She's like the friendly, older sister who wants people to go out and have a good time.'

The formula has not changed: a *Blind Date* picker quizzes three 'pickees' of the opposite sex who are hidden behind a screen. It's like Wimbledon with smut being lobbed and returned over the dividing wall. Supposedly on the basis of their answers, he or she chooses their date. The picker is shown the two people rejected before being teamed with their choice. The cameras gloriously record all this sexual manoeuvring with tactile Cilla buzzing around.

Randomly, the 'winners' then select a date location and with hardly time to collect their pre-packed ('just in case you're picked') suitcase they are off – with an LWT camera crew. When they return – usually for the next show – film of their antics, which can consist of anything from whispering sweet nothings to screaming abuse, is screened. Then, there is the 'bish-bash' in which they each and very separately say what they *really* think of each other. It can be excruciatingly embarrassing as well as extremely cruel. Sometimes egos have not so much been deflated as utterly destroyed.

Cilla doesn't mind. Win some ('he was hot'), lose some ('she was common'), it is all part of life's rich pattern. On television, anyway. There is also a grey area of British humour and tolerance which will allow Susan, who John has described as a 'right old boiler', to gamely say she will meet him for a drink if she's ever in Manchester. Or Mr Sex Appeal who's just been told that he hasn't got any by Rachel, to say they had 'a good laugh together'. And offering a wan grin as he says it.

From the start, *Blind Date* bridged class and age barriers, and that has often been visible on screen. Sex, lust, chemistry – call it what you will – can transcend class and cultural barriers from the West Country to Wigan. The first *Blind Date* wedding between an Old Etonian Londoner and a Midlands 'lass', a relationship that began as 'a jolly good bit of fun', proved that.

Or it might not. 'Good TV' can also be achieved from gross embarrassment and antagonism, especially the sexual variety. Donna, a cleaner from Rochdale, described her figure to Eddie from East London, explaining that her breasts were 'firm, big and very tempting'. Eddie was tempted. He picked Donna. Later, he said,

'The screen went back and it was a case of gutter from Ilford. She thought I was a snob and I thought she was one of those horrible Northern girls.'

Sociologists point out that class, as much as sex, is the focus of *Blind Date*. Will Darren from Dagenham pick Susie from Surrey in the battle-of-the-sexes lucky dip? The attraction, the magnet for the vast audience, is that the viewers are all-seeing, are aware of the choice. 'It's watching human behaviour in a harmless sort of way,' says Gill Stribling-Wright, adding, 'People tend to read all kinds of things into it but it's only a television version of what everyone does: date, chat-up. There are too many agony columns and you spend your life reading about sex. The British attitude to sex is bizarre through the keyhole stuff. What's the problem? Everyone does it and it's funny. Why all the angst?

I remind contestants that the show transmits early evening and they must endeavour not to be filthy. If they are, they should be bloody funny with it. It's like going to a party where people say, "He'll never score" or, "She won't get anywhere with him because he's a devil." You'll get all the filth you ever wanted to hear and sometimes it's incredibly funny, but I had to warn the younger ones not to be grubby. Old folks are good because they treat it as a joke and come out with some wonderful lines, but we missed out on the middle-aged group. Men in their fifties are either married or want a twenty-five-year-old.

'Part of the fun for a lot of the audience is "Did they make it, or didn't they?" '

Or, you could argue, it is *all* of the fun. Certainly, the banter with its carefully developed innuendo is aimed that way. The metaphor and pun are production values. Hazel from Lancashire revealed to Cilla that she had got into close proximity with Jason from 'Take That' on the 1994 *Blind Date* Christmas Special. Cilla knows the game, 'What happened then? Did he take that or what?'

And it doesn't have to be Christmas. *Blind Date* question, 'What sort of flower do you see yourself as?' Answer: 'A snapdragon. I could snap you up and I'm full of fire.' Maybe not the poetic romanticism of Elizabeth Barrett Browning, but the predictability of the encounters – male chooses female and vice versa, sight unseen – and the familiarity of it is made to work by the suspense.

Fans of the series will note how close the contestants who met a week earlier sit to each other on the sofa. Do they touch each other? Hate each other? One girl so disliked the man she picked, she turned down every inducement to return. But usually self-assurance overtakes such emotions. LWT does not allow the use of surnames now, in part to avoid would-be armchair stalkers.

Viewers at home can get just as involved as the hyped-up television participants.

When second names were used, a viewer tracked down David Beacroft through the telephone book. She said it was love at first sight. They married in 1988. This was one viewer who got what most of the audience want – a happy ending. The contestants all want to be stars, even if just for some TV moments. Cilla insists the choices they make are random, and contestants agree. One explained her choice, 'Number one was normal, number two was Welsh and number three was just creepy. So, I chose number one.'

Simple, really. Cilla finds sexual attitudes in what goes on, 'Men always choose the ones who sound sexy. They never listen to the answers. They like bimbo-sounding voices, not thick Northern accents.'

'The people I was always looking for were outgoing, eccentric and extrovert,' said Thelma McGough, who fits that criteria herself. A longtime *Blind Date* producer who was married to poet and former Scaffold star Roger McGough, but also dated Paul McCartney *and* John Lennon, she is known as 'Wonder Woman' at LWT, 'I always wanted the show to reflect young people. You have got to keep in touch. Youngsters are much freer in their attitudes and conversation. They're not afraid to talk sex – which I think is great.'

However, in case there are problems, would-be female contestants are asked if they object to going out with someone of different nationality or ethnic background. One girl said she had been asked to write down her sexual fantasy as part of her audition.

Before the show Cilla likes some time to herself to prepare and researchers often found they had to write down any questions they had for her and push them on pieces of paper underneath her dressing-room door. The first time Cilla meets the 'Blinders' is when she appears before them and the invited studio audience. They feel they know Cilla but she said:

'What they don't know is that if they go too far I'm going to slap them down like a little puppy. I'm a mummy dog, I never let up.'

*Chapter Twelve*

# SEX GAMES

*'I've just orgasmed.'*
– EXCITED *BLIND DATE* CONTESTANT

Cilla was not going to indulge in oral sex. Not on her television show.

She quickly censored ('Cilla-ised' she calls it) a male contestant laughingly engaging in what he considered saucy banter about the pleasures of oral sex.

Off-camera to her *Blind Date* audience Cilla will offer remarks which hover on that fine line between seaside postcard and more blatant 'adult' humour. She is canny enough to judge how far to go. Which, of course, is a big part of the ongoing suspense – and success – of *Blind Date*.

The content for every episode is as carefully styled as Cilla's hair, with its generous range of reds. Her favourite hairdresser, incidentally, is Wendy Craig, who almost always does her hair for the show. There have been clashes about the programme's style between Cilla, Bobby Willis and Thelma McGough. Cilla said, 'Thelma thought we needed to have more lively and sexier contestants, but I thought we had to stop going too far.'

This involved the editing out of the female contestant who clambered out of a racing car to yell, 'I've just orgasmed!' And of the string of too-naughty comments by 'Gay Count' Roberto Michieli, who won a trip down the Thames with date Jilly. As Tower Bridge lifted, Jilly said, 'Look, it's going up.' Antique dealer Roberto smiled into the camera, 'Well, it's the only thing that is tonight, sweetie.'

The challenge for the *Blind Date* team is to always make Saturday night feverish. And if the sex isn't up to it there is always the vitriol. Zoe McIntyre of LWT said, 'There's been a lot of venom spat out.'

Often because contestants like Alasdair don't get what they want. The Surrey lad was in a 'Euro' round and annoyed that all the pickees were foreign. He picked Valerie from Paris. 'Everyone fancies Valerie. All the boys, all the girls – she was fantastic.' A week later after their date Cilla asked about the '*Oooh La La*' and a sour-faced Alasdair responded: 'I didn't actually realise until number three that they were all foreign. That's when I twigged I'd been stitched up.'

On their date when Valerie went off to bed, Alasdair – to the astonishment of the studio audience and even 'mumsy' Cilla – stayed up drinking. 'I thought he would come but no,' said Valerie. Alasdair, a rugby-playing salesman, offered a little of the venom, 'The amusement-personality thing I look for in a woman wasn't really there.'

Valerie responded in kind, 'He's very selfish. He likes 'imself too much.'

Eileen was more emphatic about her date with David, 'I'd rather kiss a crab,' she said of her Caribbean encounter with the British Rail steward. They had won a date to Antigua and Cilla recalled, 'We called him Mr Thong. He said he was forty but I'm sure he was fifty if he was a day. On film during the bish-bash, he was sitting on a beach in one of those awful things that middle-aged men shouldn't wear in their wildest dreams.'

David and Eileen didn't get on. It was wonderful, compulsive and cringe-making television. The film of their Antiguan trip began with Eileen throwing David's hat at him and telling him to stick it up his backside. Talking to an LWT researcher she says, 'To me he's just a dirty old man. I'd be embarrassed to be seen with him.' At home the audience is laughingly embarrassed by all this. But there's more. David then enthuses about his ideal woman being, 'someone who is in awe of me'. He calls Eileen's perfume 'obnoxious'. She gives him a baby's dummy as a gift.

Not a lot of sexual chemistry there, then.

But for the LWT crew on the *Blind Date* trails, loathing or lust between the couples often present the same problem: keeping them apart. Zoe McIntyre says that researchers are often asked for moral support before the couple even reach their destination, 'And then we don't leave them together for too long. If they want to sleep together, of course, that's fine. They're over eighteen.'

However, not all of the viewers of *Blind Date* are. And because of that there is a gruesomely patronising nudge-nudge, know-what-I-mean buzz. Cilla talks about 'romance' and 'staying for breakfast' and 'things happening'. She is overly optimistic, according to Thelma McGough, 'Generally, there's a lot more talking about it than doing it. Given the restrictive climate of the 1990s people are less promiscuous, more cautious. More often than not it's the men who aren't on for it even if they fancy the woman. And if they don't like each other, people feel freer to be frank about not getting on.'

Which is arguably better television. There is nothing more fascinating than romance – especially between contrived, often mismatched couples – in particular romance that goes wrong. Or in the case of *Blind Date*, orchestrated situations where Eileen verbally and visually detests David and would rather be snuggling up to a shellfish.

Cilla insists, 'I'm a romantic at heart. I want them to get on, but there's devilment in me. I love it when they hate each other as well.'

Of course, at this multi-million-pound level of entertainment business it is television ratings, not love, that makes the world go round. There must be careful attention to the content so that it does not offend its huge numbers of viewers or the television watchdogs, and endanger what is one of television's most profitable projects.

Some situations are so obviously over the innuendo line they are easily dealt with – they are immediately cut out, clipped from the film that will be broadcast. Such 'out-takes' – once consigned to television's official rubbish heap – now find themselves edited into special videos like the 1997–8 *Blind Date* Christmas offering.

An example from a 1997 *Blind Date* recording: the last week's couple had spent their date in Jersey. How was it? The lad was a little eager, fast in pursuit: 'He kept coming too quickly,' the girl tells Cilla, to laughter from the audience. Cilla goes on, 'Would you handle it differently next time?'

The studio audience erupts into cheering and jeering at that. Cilla stares at the camera and snaps, 'That's definitely an edit.'

It is her remit to be the prude. Later, she would explain that particular incident, 'I do understand innuendo but not always at the time. If you do that leery look to camera it sets things back on the old road (official indictments for being too naughty). Children watch this show. I'm not in the business of offending anyone.'

But she does upset someone, somewhere, every time the show is broadcast, be it for the first time or in satellite syndication. And that is all because of the success of the show, the particular pull of the 'hook' of the series on which all else rests. As in life, people are never going to agree in the His and Her debate, 'What *does* she see in him? What *can* he see in her?' At least 20,000 hopefuls apply each year to undergo the humiliation of having everything from their body language to their body hair analysed by millions of viewers.

It doesn't matter if you are 'Frustrated of Roehampton' or TV newswoman Kate Adie or Radio Four *Today* stalwart Sue

MacGregor – both declared *Blind Date* addicts – there is never going to be a unanimously perfect *Blind Date* teaming, even the ones that have ended in marriage. In hospitals, factories, offices and workplaces around the country, even at 10, Downing Street, where Cherie Blair watches with her children, and at Buckingham and Kensington Palaces there are the ardent *Blind Date* followers. Prince William and Prince Harry watched the show with their mother, who rated it as one of her favourite television programmes and talked about appearing on the show as 'Delightful Di from Northamptonshire' following her divorce from Prince Charles. She talked of herself as the 'perfect' Blinder. It was, she declared, just an enormous amount of fun.

In the early days, Gill Stribling-Wright was at a London dinner party for a crowd of media people. 'Everyone was late and after a few drinks they all confessed they'd been watching *Blind Date*. They were reluctant to admit they watched a programme for pure enjoyment. There's almost a viewing snobbery.'

Cilla knew she had a hit when her then 16-year-old son Robert pleaded to go to a recording, 'My boys have never expressed any interest in my TV career, ever – even Basil Brush was competition. But every Saturday the whole family's hooked.'

*Blind Date* regularly goes head-to-head with the Saturday-night Lottery draw and consistently, even on rollover draws, brings in a bigger audience. The Lottery novelty had thinned out in the late 1990s, and millions of punters chose to watch Cilla Black's programme first and *wait* to discover if they had won the coveted jackpot; libido, even someone else's, beat the lust for loot hands down.

The audience for *Blind Date* stretches from toddlers to pensioners; the show has now been declared reasonably 'safe' by the nannies, mostly self-appointed, of good taste, if not the more precious critics who see it as testimony to dumbing down.

People who have appeared on the show now have children who aspire to being *Blind Date* contestants: it's a generational game. And Cilla is largely responsible for its popularity. For those aspiring to a long television career, she is a role-model and a heroine. When footballer Paul Gascoigne's wife Sheryl made her debut on Sky Television in 1998 as a talkshow host, the former secretary and model said the inspiration for her new career could be explained in two words: '*Cilla Black*.'

'Cilla is a weekly exhibition of what you can achieve by determination and personality and a willingness to learn,' said an associate, going on, 'But she has to make a lot of sacrifices for that continuing success. Like being tough.'

'Cilla only likes friendly people in the audience,' is how the warm-up man begins his spiel to the studio audience.'I need to know one thing. Are you a nice, lively, happy lot?'

The crowds who have waited and wondered about their chances of being on *Blind Date* – even just in the audience – are willing to agree to anything, now they have made it to the LWT recording studios. Many of them will tell you they have fantasised that contestants have fallen ill at the last moment, and that they have been plucked from the audience to take their place. 'I dressed especially sexy in case something like that happened,' said Carolann Johnson from Glasgow. Her friend Marilyn Brown from Southport, Lancashire, added: 'We spent most of yesterday getting our outfits *just right* so that Cilla would notice us.'

She – with the help of Bobby Willis – notices *everything*.

Canny Cilla was always aware of what a tremendous coup it would be if Princess Diana had appeared on the show. In the months before her death it had seemed, at least, a possibility. The Princess had also been in talks with Hollywood actor-producer-director Kevin Costner to co-star in a sequel to his successful film *The Bodyguard* – playing a princess in Hong Kong. Costner revealed that the Princess had asked for, and been sent, a script of the movie *Bodyguard Two*.

In retrospect, *Blind Date* would have been what she saw as a simple 'giggle'. No official letters were exchanged, but LWT were aware that something might happen. The *Panorama* interview had been against all the odds: unprecedented and totally unpredictable, in every sense. The royals had appeared on *It's A Knockout*, so why not Diana on *Blind Date*? Maybe it was not that preposterous a notion. And was she not, herself, in search of the perfect 'blind date'?

It is clear that the Princess was a true and loyal fan of the show, and of Cilla, who is careful about disclosing their conversations. She did not say they 'nattered' about *Blind Date* and revealed, 'She told me she adored a middle-aged chap with a red jacket and a medallion who we called the oldest swinger in town. "Where *do* you get them?" she asked me. I said, "Don't blame me, I don't pick 'em."

'She rings me up, saying, "You don't half get some dogs on that programme." '

Cilla, given her background, was mortified when at a charity function she saw Bobby Willis brush his hand against the Royal back, 'We were at a function when she made a beeline for him. He touched the small of her back and I thought, How can he do that? She's the future Queen of England!'

Cilla joked about that but denied naughty suggestions that his wandering hands nearly got him into even greater embarrassment. She said, 'He's got class, he would not have dreamed of putting his hand on her bum.'

Cilla, host in the 1990s of the most watched and talked about show on television, is certain that Diana, Princess of Wales, would have appeared on camera on *Blind Date* if she had lived. She says that the Princess asked her for two tickets for a recording, but elaborated: 'I thought she herself might be coming, but they were a Christmas present for two of her staff who were also fans.'

The two well-known faces first met at a charity football match. When Cilla was to be presented, the Princess said, 'You don't need to introduce Cilla. I know who she is.'

Cilla, a true believer in the Royal Family and the strength of it, was terribly upset when Diana and Prince Charles separated, 'I think it's a tragic situation. I love the Royal Family. It was when I watched the teatime news on the BBC that I began to fill up with tears. Anna Ford did a feature on the marriage from the start to finish and it really got to me. She showed them during the early days of their marriage – when everyone could see they were so happy. I feel so sorry for the Princes, William and Harry. They must be going through a terrible time. I hate to see any family break up like this.'

Like millions of others she avidly followed the life of the Princess, until Diana's tragic death in Paris in 1997. Cilla strongly identified with the pressures of bringing up sons and being so constantly in the public eye, and Princess Diana's divorce, despair and death were the more harrowing for her because of that.

But – and this trait may be inherited, or the result of her upbringing, or simply a case of having a sense of humour about herself and all around her – nothing seems to confound Cilla Willis for long. It's like that panto when she appealed to the audience for ideas on how to kill the baddie, and a 12-year-old boy in the audience yelled, 'Sing to him!' Which, of course, she did.

Getting on the show has become a national pastime for tens of thousands of people.

*Blind Date*, after all, offers something a little more than the Lottery. It offers love *and* money – the possibility of a date with destiny. This happened in 1997 for Beatrice Martinez, who found herself without a man but *with* a £12,000 *per week* modelling contract after appearing on the show. Beatrice, twenty-one at the start of 1998, was an assistant buyer with the House of Fraser department stores when executives, taken by her beauty and personality, more or less forced her to audition to be a 'Blinder'. She appeared on the show in 1996 and then again on a special edition in 1997, celebrating the 13th anniversary of the programme. Viewers voted her their favourite contestant.

Helen Illes, head of the MOT model agency and a *Blind Date* fanatic, watched the special show, 'After years in the business a light goes on. I knew she'd be a sensation but assumed she would be snapped up. I tried to trace her but didn't get very far.'

The *Blind Date* connection made a couple of Grand Prix turns: Beatrice's friend Misha Lee was an MOT model and Helen Illes elaborated, 'Misha told me she had a friend who should be a model and had been on *Blind Date*. I said, "Not the one in the finals?" It was fate.'

The House of Fraser who had twisted her arm – and were paying her £12,000 *per year* – lost their employee and the MOT agency gained a budding supermodel. By early 1998 Beatrice Martinez had a contracted list of assignments including television commercials and a Fiat advertising campaign. She had enjoyed a thoroughly worthwhile *Blind Date* experience.

Publicly, Cilla is shocked when 'revelations' appear about the *Blind Date* contestants, but privately her attitude is that it keeps the series constantly in the public consciousness. Stories will appear in the weeks before the series goes back on air. 'There is a reason for almost everything that appears about *Blind Date*, and it's usually to do with timing and getting the audience. On the surface it might seem like bad publicity but it's not.' said someone close to the show.

Indeed, the audience is there, much like a motor-racing crowd, to see a disaster rather than true romance blossom. It was 'great television' when Tony Maskell told viewers in 1992 that his date Sara Fellows couldn't keep her hands off him and he couldn't stand her 'black roots and white boots'. Offscreen revelations also boosted the ratings: Davina Mathews forgetting, in – 1995, to mention in her application form that she was a porn model. Or, in 1997, Hayley Dollery returning to discuss her date in the South of France, having been revealed as having many, many previous dates as a £130-a-night 'escort' girl.

Britain's obsession with Cilla and *Blind Date* has put the series into the media spotlight ever since it began. It is the television show which sweeps some people off their feet and also, it appears, eradicates their caution. As Andrea Tongue, softly spoken with waist-length blonde hair, found out when she thought she had 'won' the romance of a lifetime. All looked well at one time when the man of her choice presented her with a ruby and diamond ring at the start of 1997 and asked her to marry him. It was, she said in an interview, a shock and explained:

'I'd met Piers three months earlier on *Blind Date*. I'd done it for a laugh but I got really excited when I discovered I'd be picking. So there I was at the London studio with Cilla welcoming me on set. I was terrified, thinking, "Oh, God what have I done?" But as I asked my first question my nerves disappeared and by the time I got to my third question I was enjoying myself so much I wasn't sure which guy had said what. I had to base my decision solely on the answers to my last question, "If you were on *Blue Peter*, what would you have made earlier?" The last voice answered: "If you could see the tricks I perform with my magic wand made of loo rolls you'd know why I deserve my *Blue Peter* badge." Well, any man who knows the importance of a *Blue Peter* badge is the guy for me. "Number Two," I said confidently.

'When the screen went back I saw Piers and thought: Yes! He seemed perfect, like someone I could be friends with – possibly even more. When the envelope revealed we'd be going to the Niagara Falls, I thought everything was going to be great. The night before our flight, Piers and I sat in a hotel bar talking until 4 a.m. I don't fall for men quickly but I became hooked on Piers' sensitivity. I'd mentioned earlier that I wouldn't be able to sleep that night because I'd left my teddy bear at home. It sounds stupid, but it goes everywhere with me. Just as I was about to get into bed there was a knock at the door. Piers had called a twenty-four-hour shopping service and had a gorgeous teddy delivered to my room.

'The next day we arrived in Canada with the *Blind Date* crew. Piers and I were getting on brilliantly. Our hotel, right on the edge of Lake Ontario, was so romantic. That night after a posh meal we kissed for the first time. I liked the fact that Piers didn't rush me into having sex. I mean, it could have been so easy in such a fantasy-like location, but one-night stands aren't my thing and he respected that. Only one thing spoiled the holiday. One afternoon I decided to have a kip in my room before we went out for the evening. I'd been with Piers for every waking second since we'd arrived and I just needed a bit of time to myself. Just as I shut my eyes the phone rang. It was Piers, crying. I went straight to his room. The door was ajar and when I peered in I saw him lying on the floor in a foetal position, sobbing.

' "You just don't realise how important this relationship is to me, Andrea," he said. It was so bizarre. Up to that point everything had been so relaxed. Now, just because I'd wanted an hour on my own he was acting like we were a married couple getting divorced. I'd only known the guy for four days. Although he was twenty-seven I put my arms around him and comforted him like you would a baby and eventually managed to calm him down. Despite this hiccup the rest of the trip was perfect. Piers was great company – fun, thoughtful, kind – and I'd never been happier. I wouldn't say I was in love with him, but I was *very* fond of him. When we got home we exchanged phone numbers. Piers worked as a dental practice manager at RAF Leuchars in Fife, while I lived hundreds of miles away in Kidderminster. I knew it would be difficult, but as we'd shared this incredible experience I was determined to stay in touch. Piers seemed determined too.

'We spoke on the phone regularly, and a month or so after we met Piers arranged to come to Kidderminster to meet my parents. They booked a table at a smart restaurant but Piers didn't turn up. And he didn't call. I tried phoning him but he wasn't at home. It wasn't until the following day that I managed to speak to him. "Where have you been? I thought something terrible happened to you," I said. He claimed he'd sent me a letter on the Thursday explaining that he couldn't come but when it arrived it was postmarked Saturday. I was furious and that was it, "We've had a nice time but now it's over." I decided to forget Piers and concentrate on my studies.

'Our *Blind Date* was screened in December and I hadn't spoken to Piers since he stood me up so, after our first TV appearance, I took a deep breath and called him. It was as if nothing had gone wrong – we talked for hours just like we had in Canada. At one point Piers said, "Andrea, I'd really like us to see each other again." Before hanging up he promised to call me the following Saturday when our second appearance would be screened. He didn't and I felt betrayed a second time. What was his problem?

'Several of my questions were answered on Christmas Eve by a newspaper story headlined, *"Blind Date Rat Hasn't Even Sent Christmas Card To His Baby Girl – Anguish of Struggling Ex-wife."* Ex-wife? Baby? I immediately phoned Piers and demanded to know exactly what was going on. He swore he had wanted to tell me about his ex-wife right from the start but ... "the time was never right." Then he said something I'll never forget, "Andrea, I really want to make a go of this. I want us to be together properly. Will you give me a chance?" I know most people would have told him where to stick his chance but something made me want to help him.

'"OK," I whispered into the telephone. "But Piers, you have to be honest with me and tell me what's going on. If you need someone to stand by you then I will, but I have to know the truth about everything." He told me he'd divorced his wife but that they'd had a brief reconciliation twelve months earlier. He said he wasn't even 100 per cent sure the baby was his. I reckoned that everyone has a past and if I didn't give him a chance I'd never know if we could have made it work. And I knew we could spend some proper time together when he came to meet me the week before New Year. Finally, Piers arrived and it seemed as if everything was going to be OK. We talked everything over and then on New Year's Eve he popped the question. Just like that. As soon as he'd asked, he just burst into tears, "Andrea, don't turn against me. My mum and sisters have turned their backs on me, I couldn't bear it if I lost you too." Impulsively, I blurted out: "Yes." Yes, I would marry him. His ex-wife, his mother and sister had slagged him off in the Press and I didn't want to kick him when he was down by rejecting his proposal. My family are always there for me so I couldn't imagine what it must be like to be totally alone in the world. After New Year, Piers drove me home.

'I next saw him to do a newspaper interview. The producers of *Blind Date* had announced our engagement and Piers had suggested that by telling them our "love story" he could clear his name. I agreed. As soon as it was over Piers said he had to rush back to base. With that he gave me a quick kiss, stroked my hair and promised to call me later. When the story appeared it was chaos.

'*Blind Date* were thrilled. A lady wrote to me offering to design and make any wedding dress I wanted. Local companies offered to do my flowers and hold the ceremony and reception. I realised everything was getting out of hand – and Piers was nowhere to be found.

'A week later we were supposed to be meeting with people from *Blind Date* to discuss the wedding but – Surprise, Surprise, Cilla! – Piers failed to show. When I phoned him at the RAF base he hung up without saying a word. I was furious. How dare he? When he had needed someone I was there and this was how he repaid me? I felt so betrayed, and to this day I still don't know why he proposed to me, just to drop me like a leper. My friends say he did it to get himself good publicity. I'd like to think he proposed for the right reasons, even though I know I said yes for all the wrong reasons. But even if he hadn't wanted to go through with the wedding, why be so cruel by ignoring me?

'I don't regret going on *Blind Date* as it was an amazing experience, but I do regret accepting Piers' proposal. I should have said, "I'm not saying no, but let's give it six months and see how we feel." We weren't together long enough for a sexual relationship. I don't jump into bed with every boyfriend. I realise now I was naive. There were warning signs, but I was too caught up in the romance to notice them. The thing that gets me is that it was the bad luck of the draw. Imagine how things could have been different if I'd picked number three?'

The *Blind Date* auditions by the Thames in London are a free-for-all opportunity to meet a dream lover in front of millions of television viewers. Hopefuls arrive at LWT in search of romance and fame, some not even concerned about getting as far as the fifteen-minute interview. 'I didn't expect to get inside the door,' admitted 24-year-old Ruthie from Barking. 'I expected to find someone in the queue. In fact, there was one bloke I fancied. He came from round the corner in Dagenham.'

Debbie, another 24-year-old Essex girl from Colchester, had been sent along by her mother. 'She wants to get rid of me. When people find out where I'm from they say, "Oh, Essex Girl." I've had loads of real blind dates before, but they never worked out.'

Some hopefuls were considerably older than Ruthie and Debbie. Magician Sid Slavny was sixty-six when he went in search of true love. 'My wife died five years ago. I am a very romantic person and I hope to find someone here.'

Not so romantic is the LWT warning, '*Blind Date* is not a dating agency.' Application forms ask for interests, ambitions and idols, best and worst qualities. One applicant offered, 'I'm a sexual dynamo.' Another couple proved it – it's one of the *Blind Date* secrets – by eluding the chaperones and having sex in the LWT hospitality suite *before* the show was even recorded. Although the contestants are kept in different parts of the glass-fronted building, have separate eating and dressing areas to eliminate chance meetings between picker and prospective pickee, the system is not foolproof when the hormonal radar is on full alert.

The rules are set, and number one is no husbands, wives, steady girlfriends or boyfriends. The girls always outnumber the boys by two to one at auditions. Producer Thelma McGough said, 'Men seem to be more self-conscious, particularly as they get older. We find it difficult to encourage men over thirty-two to take part. Those who do are there for different reasons: some want to meet people, some just want to be on the telly. Some are exhibitionists. Some hope they can peddle their talents, but by far the majority just want to have fun.'

Fun, however, always seems to involve their fifteen minutes of fame as well as a week in the sun. Or Skegness. Couples are unaware of the location of their 'surprise' holiday when the envelope is opened. But whatever envelope they picked, the destination would be the same: arrangements have to be made in advance by the *Blind Date* crew. Some contestants recall arriving at their *Blind Date* hotel to be told, 'Oh, we knew you were coming a few weeks ago.'

There was a fuss once when *Blind Date* couples were being offered appearances as extras on the TV series *Emmerdale Farm*. Performers known as 'walk-on artists' who would be paid for such appearances were annoyed. Yorkshire Television, who produce *Emmerdale*, said *Blind Date* producers approached them with the idea, and as it meant free publicity for the farmyard soap opera, they went ahead. This was in the early days of the series, when *Blind Date* was already attracting huge ratings of ten to twelve million viewers per week. It then quickly achieved cult status and became a compulsory Saturday-night habit.

Despite its immediate success, some critics – and not just professional ones but those at home – found all those horrified reactions, off-the-cuff witty answers and satisfied smiles just a little too slick. Was this romantic Russian Roulette? Or were blanks being fired? These questions have haunted the series, almost as much as public curiosity about just how naughty things get behind the scenes. At the start Cilla went along with the nudge-nudge, know-what-I-mean aspects of it. The fun, she said, started when the contestants gather for the post-show party, there is a lot of telephone number swapping, kissing and cuddling – *not* always involving the so-called matched pair.' Yes, I've had to slap a few wrists and tell the lads to put the girls down,' Cilla said as part of the promotional patter. 'Everyone gets on great – except the people going off on the blind date together!'

She would put on her 'serious' look to discuss the success of the show, 'It's knocked me out. I just go in and have a laugh, and the more they make me laugh the more I know the show's a success. My make-up lady has a terrible time. I cry with laughter and all my mascara runs between takes.'

Early on, before it became clear to almost all that the majority of contestants were willingly involved in self-inflicted social horrors, it was criticised for exploiting the lonely by allowing ordinary people who have never been on television to make fools of themselves in front of millions. Cilla always disagreed, 'By the time the contestants get on the studio floor, they've been vetted and are fully prepared.'

Just how 'prepared' is the neverending question. Those who get to the London auditions are divided into groups of nine or ten and given 'thinking on their feet' sessions. The production team fire a series of questions which have already been used on the show, encouraging the would-be contestants to be witty and sharp in their replies, even lie if they want to. Most contestants have applied, others are chosen by LWT researchers who roam the country looking for 'talent'. The first rule is hammered upon again and again: you must be single, separated, or divorced. There is always the possibility that the contestant is lying to get on the show and does have a partner hidden at home. Producer Gill Stribling-Wright said that some people will always try to cheat. It is almost impossible to check up on all applicants, 'We just have to take their word for it.'

Audiences often wonder why the answers to the picker's questions are always quick and often quite clever. It's because both sides are given warnings of what to expect. 'We don't want to end up with egg on our faces on primetime television,' said Gill Stribling-Wright, explaining, 'We ask the picker to come up with ten questions, and between us we work out the best three. What might sound a hilarious question could prove impossible to answer and fall flat in front of the studio audience.'

Contestants are given clues of what the questions might be: hobbies, or their personality, so they have enough time to think about their replies. They often practise their responses to each other to test for reactions and also rehearse their lines. The cute number two with the nice line in chat-up on television might be useless when confronted by the same situation in real life. At LWT no one questions whether that is fair. The only question asked is, '*Is it entertaining?*'

In *Blind Date*, Cilla Black is hosting tightrope television, although contestant Steve Parks claims there is a giant safety net, 'The whole show is planned down to the last detail. It's even rehearsed beforehand. Those quickfire answers from the contestants aren't always what they seem. The producers can't afford to have people going blank because they record the show at one go. Me and the two blokes I appeared with spent the whole afternoon practising snappy answers to certain questions. By doing that we were able to get a vague idea of what our questions were going to be. But we weren't told what the girl did. What we wore wasn't left to chance. I was told to bring along several outfits for the show. I took three outfits and had to try them all on in front of the cameras so they could test what they would look like on a TV screen. They chose one of my outfits – a bright orange suit. But just in case a contestant didn't bring something right, the wardrobe was on hand to produce something.'

The strict segregation between the sexes can cause logistical headaches. Producer Stribling-Wright said, 'It's like a French farce. They arrive at different times, at different parts of the building. If someone goes to the loo we phone round to make sure it's all clear. If we didn't, then that lovely element of surprise and gamble would be gone.' What she *doesn't* say is that researchers will even go to the toilet with 'Blinders' as part of the chaperone regime, which is much stricter than that of the 'Miss World'or 'Miss Universe' contests!

But when the screen rolls back, the magic moment may have been faked. If something goes wrong – a camera angle, an invasive noise – the expressions of horror or delight have to be filmed again and edited into the show to be broadcast. If a contestant reacts with disbelief and horror, there is nothing she or he can do; they have contracted, in front of millions, to go on the 'date'. Once that screen disappears, that's it. Although some fixed dates immediately say it's not going to work, that their getaway will be a complete waste of time, no one has ever actually refused to go. 'Of course, it's great television if they slag each other off, but if it's pure venom, it's upsetting. I love it when they get along,' says Cilla. 'I insult the fellas and look after the girls. I'm a bit of a feminist on that side. I've got three brothers and three sons. I've always been in a man's world.'

Men are usually the most difficult 'dates'. Producer Stribling-Wright said: 'They all want to be pickers, not one of the three. They say they can't take being turned down in front of their mates. Women are more relaxed about it and don't take it so seriously.'

But it is a serious business, a flagship television series, one of the all-time moneymakers. And character showcase. Steve Parks, the contestant with the orange suit, was a disc jockey with an uncanny similarity to singer Lionel Richie. He won over the audience with his appearance during the second series, only to be revealed as a womaniser and a *Blind Date* sneak.

During the second series, *Blind Date* brought pensioners into the framework, 'Bobby and I were getting loads of letters from pensioners saying, "What about us?" and my heart went out to them. I love old people, they're so patient and have got so many funny stories to tell.'

The first couple, Evie and Gerald, were a hit, 'They were fantastic and so raunchy! Gerald said the greatest thing about it was that he'd made a friend. They talked non-stop, they had so much in common.'

Cilla speaks so genuinely of the special contestants and seems to mean it. At the first *Blind Date* wedding in late 1991 – an event witnessed by millions and millions of viewers – Cilla was there with her hat like a third mother-in-law. Many, including Cilla, thought she would be there at the consummation and after that the arrival of the firstborn, she appeared so emotionally entangled!

Cilla is different things to different people. It depends, not surprisingly, on her mood. Contestant Steve said, 'Cilla was nice to our group. She met us before the show for a quick greeting, and then afterwards she came to the hospitality room and chatted for about an hour. She was just like she is on TV, dead pally. She was drinking lager and was great to all of us.' But his friend Gary Mills said, 'I thought she was a bit standoffish.' His attitude reflects Cilla's ongoing dilemma: how *do* you please *everyone*? You cannot, of course, but Cilla has tried most valiantly over the decades to do so. With *Blind Date* she thought she had a greater advantage because of the 'opportunity of working with young people.'

At 5 p.m. Steve from Dudley in the West Midlands and the other contestants got ready in their dressing rooms. 'We were warned that we would start getting very nervous, but the time flew by until 7.30p.m. when the show started.'

The planning paid off when the show was recorded; it looked totally unrehearsed. Steve was picked by Clare McGrath and their 'prize' included the chance to make a parachute jump together from 600 ft and finished with a candle-lit dinner. Steve: 'It was a wonderful day. We were taken everywhere by chauffeur-driven Mercedes. I felt like a superstar – I kept talking to my mates on the car phone. Clare was a nice girl but, quite honestly, I'd have enjoyed myself whoever I was with. It was fun, just like after the show was recorded. The blokes and girls are kept in different places but, of course, the lads soon find out which hotel the girls are in.

'After filming, the fun really began. First we went to the hospitality room for free drinks. Then we were driven off – and it was party-time. Everybody was feeling great, like stars, so we went out to Stringfellows nightclub in London. I was tired from the excitement of winning so I only stayed ten minutes, but the others stayed on to chat with each other.

'The blokes said there was lots of smooching on the dance floor and afterwards ... well, let's just say that not everyone got back to their right hotel room.

'The best story I heard was from another contestant, Gary Mills, who'd been a *Blind Date* winner the week before me. To be honest, he didn't much like his date, Alison King, because she was a copper and flirted with all the Italians on their day out in Rome. He thought it was hysterically funny when he discovered she preferred another contestant.

'Gary told me that after he and several blokes came back from being on the town, they decided to play a practical joke on one of the other guys. They heard him take a girl into his room so Gary banged on the door and called out "Room Service!" Gary got a real shock when he found that the girl sitting on the sofa was Alison but he laughed when he told me. He wasn't jealous.'

When he returned to the studio with Clare to recount their 'date' to Cilla, Steve says he was more relaxed than the star. He wandered around LWT and enjoyed a game of snooker with comedian Bobby Davro in the entertainments room, 'One of the best things about being on *Blind Date* was the way everyone made you feel like one of the London Weekend Television stars. It was terrific.'

He found he spent more time with Davro than Cilla. As contestants prepare, Cilla stays in her dressing room. It is guarded by security men. In later years she only occasionally attended the after-show champagne party at the studios. Some of the contestants would be back the following week, and those close to Cilla argue that it is not disdain for the 'little Blinders' but a fear of appearing stale on camera, 'She operates better on the spur of the moment. That's why she insists on not meeting contestants until a few minutes before they walk on set.'

'It's very short and sweet,' said former contestant Tony Maskell. 'I would like to have seen more of her.'

Cilla is and has throughout her career 'sold' the approachable image; it is what audiences expect and also people who meet her in person. That counts more for the *Blind Date* contestants, but because of it many are surprised that there are rules to the game.

Cilla, it seems, is like a General on manoeuvres planning everything up to and including what contestants can and can't say. Zeno Nicolaou, from Redbridge, East London, recalled, 'It's a family show, so really risque replies are out. The girl I was on with played football and because I played rugby, I wanted to say something about odd-shaped balls. But they just wouldn't wear it.'

Tony, a gym instructor from Buckhurst Hill, Essex, said, 'I've appeared in an all-male dance troupe on the lines of the

Chippendales, but stripping down to your thong in front of a crowd of screaming women is nothing compared to appearing on *Blind Date*. Your brain freezes when you go in front of the cameras. When Cilla asks you which girl you want to date, you just say the first number that comes into your head.'

Laura Green, of Clayhall, Essex, said, 'The man who picked me was obviously disappointed. The two he turned down came out from behind the screen first. They were lovely – one a blonde with big knockers, the other with flowing auburn hair. Then I came out, and on the video you can clearly see him mouthing the words, "Oh, my God!" '

But it is Cilla's reaction that really matters. Zeno Nicolaou recalled, 'I was left in no doubt thatshe was the star, and was told not to try to upstage her. One chap, trying to be flash, told her, "Normally I don't like girls who wear too much make-up, but I'll make an exception in your case." You could tell she didn't like him. From them on, it looked like she was putting him down all the time.'

Cilla is indeed *the* star. Most who have been involved closely with her say she is 'best mates' with herself rather than with the television contestants. Anyone trying to grab the spotlight usually ends up out of it. Cilla has all the cards, principally the power of the editing machine, and whatever she says goes. Her wit can be sharp – cruel, even. Getting no reaction at all is much worse. Gaynor, from Great Eccleston in Lancashire, had expected applause when she slithered sexily out of her Santa suit to reveal hot pants and bra top during a recording of a Christmas Special. There was an embarrassing silence. Cilla managed to sneak out of the situation by moving on but Gaynor was left standing, an almost naked party pooper.

If Cilla fluffs a line or stumbles over an introduction it is filmed again. The contestants can make all kinds of fools of themselves and the cameras are left rolling.

The series, like Cilla, lives in two worlds. The public one is all upfront and spontaneous 'larfs'. The reality is a carefully rehearsed and choreographed image. Nothing is left to chance, everything is edited into its place. The rules are strict, the ruler stricter. Keeping Cilla happy is the most important thing.

Which is also the prime purpose of the contestants. Cilla is mainly interested in the show rather than the individuals. It works if they work – her way. 'It can get a bit regimented around the studios but everyone shrugs it off as the price of success,' said an LWT observer.

Part of that is distancing the audience from the reality. Couples who get to open the envelope are told to call their trip a 'date', not a holiday. On their return, what is shown is a shrewdly edited few minutes of footage and soundbites from usually more than an hour of film, often showing the pair at their worst. All involved admit chalk-and-cheese couples make better television, but there has to be a balance. One couple returning from a date in Turkey looked like lovers but it was all for the cameras. They had been encouraged by the producers to 'play up the romance'. What was unscripted was the man's involvement with Gaynor, of the Santa outfit, in a nightclub after the show!

At auditions it seems that some female hopefuls are really looking for love – so it is not just Cilla who wants a happy conclusion to some of the dates. The men are less romantic. All are involved in the most public dating game in the world.

'*If you are 18-plus, single and full of fun, why not come for an interview?*' says the *Blind Date* advertisement. First interviews often take place at the Connaught Rooms near the Strand in London. There are always a lot of girls with great tans and greater amounts of heavily sprayed hair. Closely-shaved, skin-pampered men wander around giving them the eye. It is rare to see a moustache or a beard. This is a Calvin Klein wannabe world. They must pose for a 'happy' Polaroid and are then given a number and a form with questions like: *What is your best quality? What is your worst? Who do you fancy and why? What is your party piece?* The master of ceremonies – a changing role – then announces to the room, 'Prepare to tell us about your most embarrassing moment!'

'They like your embarrassing moment to be something really smutty. That's what'll get you picked,' confided a blonde girl at the Connaught Rooms.

Jenny McCartney attended one such try-out and explained her experience: 'Seven of us, selected by raffle number, trooped into the interviewing room. A panel of two women and a man awaited us – the crack *Blind Date* interviewing squad. Chris O'Dell, master of the show, explained the drill. First, we would be individually quizzed on ourselves – our jobs, our preferences in men and, that most hallowed of all events, our most embarrassing moment. Then, we would each be asked to deliver an amusing response to the chat-up line, "My favourite instrument is the trombone. If you were a musical instrument, what would you be, and why?"

'I broke down and confessed to everything – some of it true, and plenty of it lies. I said I liked foreign men, short men, men who could dance a bit. But I had nothing at all against tall men either. A flicker of confusion crossed Chris O'Dell's face. I told a lame embarrassing moment, about festooning customers in a restaurant with beansprout salad. My responses began to get weirder, but somehow infused with a chippy, bolshy quality. I thought I saw one of the women on the panel scribble down a little, negative note.

'Then they moved on to Tracey. Tracey, a dancer, had once done a summer season with Michael Barrymore. She had been dressed to go on stage in a tiny khaki costume, so tight that it did not permit the wearing of knickers. Barrymore, wag that he is, playfully tugged at the costume before Tracey was due on stage. It came apart, leaving Tracey starkers, apart from her fishnet tights. That was more the ticket. To get on, you need to be game as a pheasant, and a glutton for embarrassing moments.'

Others who have been tried out recall similar experiences: sex and smut and booze are the main ingredients for the 'experiences'. Henry remembered, '"Tell us lots of stories about alcohol and nudity, the more the better," our group was told and they justified it with, "You'll have to tell them in front of millions when you're on the show so you might as well bare all now. We've been told to tone things down but I'll leave it to your own moral standards to judge how far you should go." It was clear that it was a case of the muckier the better. Light-hearted smut was rewarded with cheers from the panel of researchers whose task it was to weed out the no-hopers and send the rest on to the second audition.'

The second audition (getting there is very much a don't-call-us-we'll-call-you arrangement) is where it gets serious. The intent of the applicant is tested. Those with even a slight chance of meeting Cilla must provide a valid passport, which cuts out illegal immigrants as well as showing the ability to be involved in an 'international date', and must sign a form, much like an American visa application, to say that they have no criminal convictions nor appeared in pornographic films or naughty poses. And all applicants must write out a complete sentence saying they do not have a partner. *I do not have a girlfriend/boyfriend* ... is how it begins.

At one set of 'interviews', well-spoken blonde Anna-Louise pretended to be Princess Diana buying condoms. Clarissa, a former ballet dancer from Ascot and a keen amateur actress, 'played' Madonna presenting *Blue Peter*. If the applicants make it to the LWT studios on London's South Bank the pitch gets higher – and harder from the researchers, 'We want you to give it max. Don't hold back. The sexier the better. We want to know everything about your worst sexual experiences. We want to see just how prepared you are to make a fool of yourself, because you can't afford to be embarrassed if you want to go on *Blind Date*. We also want to see how freely you can talk about your private lives, because Cilla will want to know *everything*.'

Producer Kevin Roast has admitted, 'We're seldom out of the newspapers during the autumn for one reason or another.' What is expected is carefully explained and those trying out are clearly told, 'We own your performance. If you make a complete idiot of yourself, we'll still broadcast it.' Veterans of the show will explain that 'winning moments' are when Cilla gets a laugh at the expense of a 'Blinder'. There are always warm-ups at the second auditions and one session reflects the humour. History student James was asked to pretend he was Mr Motivator promoting baked beans. He touched his toes shouting: 'Never forget they are as good coming out as they are going in.'

There is an apparent obsession with condoms and the Royal Family in these 'play' sessions. Some wannabes are asked to be a stuttering Prince Charles buying condoms. Or impersonate footballer Paul Gascoigne reading the *Nine O'clock News*, Arnold Schwarzenegger tapdancing or Bruce Forsyth offering some naughty remarks at a wedding.

Sex is used as the final guillotine, the cut-off point. All applicants are closely questioned about their private lives. The message from the selectors is: You can't shock us, we've heard it all before. Some, like Alex, take them at their word: he gave an almost obscene geography lesson around a woman's body. The selection panel liked that although they will offficially insist, 'We like innuendo but not smut.'

Experiences suggest differently. It is the master and mistress of the obvious double entendre who appear to get on – literally. The odds have run over the years that one out of ten candidates gets to share the TV screen with Cilla. Those who do have vowed to do *anything* – especially with their date *even* if it is someone who turns them completely off. The final hurdle is when the applicants are asked to believe they are taking part in a 'real' show. An LWT production staffer sat in as 'Julie from Brighton' while Henry, a would-be contestant, practised being number one. He was told, 'Sell yourself and don't try to be too clever or patronising – girls don't like it.'

'Number one, what sort of first impression do you give girls on a date?' asked 'Julie'. 'Well, Julie,' said Henry, 'my friends think I'm a bit wild-looking because I worked as a cowboy in Venezuela. But, as you know, appearances can be deceptive. I'm not really a rough rider and I promise to handle your reins with great care.'

Later, Henry said: 'The panel seemed quite impressed for once and my innuendo earned me the highest praise from the producer, who asked me if I was sure I hadn't been on *Blind Date* before.'

There is one other reminder for possible 'Blinders' from the production staff, 'If you are chosen, you must tell us if you get a girlfriend – think how unfair it would be on your date.' Then, in an often-used throwaway line, an assistant will tell the groups, 'Obviously, if you just have casual sex we are not interested – unless you can tell us where to get some.'

Cilla, who doesn't want to offend anyone, and the others involved in producing the show are often surprised by what the contestants *do* get involved in. And usually – if it's wild or titillating enough – it will make the pages of the Sunday newspapers. Cilla's usual response is, 'I'm shocked.' It does, however, keep audiences wanting more and more *Blind Date*.

A typical *Blind Date* scoop involved Mark Joyce and Scott Coffey in a punctuation-free *Steamy Night of Lust and Four-In-A-Bed-Romp*. They palled up with two girl contestants at a drunken after-show party. This was all at the expense of LWT, who had also provided the drinks which got 'all of us going'. What made a mockery of the whole enterprise was that Mark's official date was asleep in the bedroom next door. He told his story:

'At the traditional party behind the scenes I met Scott, who'd been a standby contestant. We spotted Kate Bletchley and Nikki Eames, who'd both been turned down on the show, and fancied them. So we went in for the kill. I was delighted when Kate was rejected on screen because I thought she was a real babe and I knew I'd stand a chance later. She had a pierced belly button which was a real turn-on, and was wearing a skimpy little miniskirt and cut-off top which really showed off her figure. It left nothing to the imagination and I was all fired up. We got talking and she seemed to like me too. Then Scott chanced his luck with her pal Nikki. We went to a West End nightclub called Samantha's. I was having a good old kiss and cuddle with Kate in the disco. She told me I was cute and we were both really on a high from the show. We had plenty to drink and it really relaxed us both.'

As often happens, the contestants were booked into £115-a-night rooms at the Hotel Russell in London. Mark Joyce says the four of them sneaked into Nikki's room and began 'partying' in her double bed. 'I was lying under the covers with Kate, fondling and kissing. The other two were doing the same. After the buzz of the show we were after a good night out, some beers and some hanky panky. We were all on the bed for hours until early in the morning and we had a really good laugh. I didn't have full sex, but we did get intimate with each other. There was a lot of petting and frolicking going on.'

Kate said: 'We were just out for a laugh – I won't ever be seeing him again. It was just one of those ... blind dates!'

*Chapter Thirteen*

# MULTIPLE ECSTASIES?

*'Class, I haven't, but style I've got.'*
– CILLA BLACK, 1991

For Cilla the *Blind Date* phenomenon has been her passport to continuing mass celebrity. She has always been clever enough to know the source of her success is maintaining her relationship with her audience. Her gift is to handle her fame as if it has just arrived, is still a little bit of a shock. She says she does not put on 'airs and graces' and indeed it is rare to see a glimmer of them in her professional environment.

Cilla is one of a select group – which during the 1990s included Melvyn Bragg, Brian Walden, Denis Norden, Michael Aspel and Michael Barrymore – whom LWT regarded as franchise 'insurance'. With talent like hers involved, it was correctly believed that the fortunes at stake during franchise auctions would be safe. Cilla's insurance value just gets higher; her power base stronger, enabling her to pull strings and get her own way, if necessary. She is one of the most powerful people in television.

The 1998–9 series of *Blind Date* was given an even greater

production budget because it was such a flagship programme – and moneyspinner. It also got a new producer as well as new scriptwriters. Scriptwriters? Yes, for *Blind Date*, as much as any situation comedy, is carefully written, with special jokes formulated for every show, every contestant.

The overhaul for the fourteenth year of the series came partly as a reaction to a slump in ITV's fortunes. Surveys revealed that, on average, only a third of any daily television audience watched ITV. The BBC had nothing to boast about, for the defection was to the satellite channels. ITV in 1998 had dropped from 72 per cent (in 1994) to 65 per cent of commercial advertising revenue. In 1998, the new ITV boss, Richard Eyre, saw the future in regionalisation of programming, and making the most of successes like *Blind Date*.

In such circumstances, Cilla waited on the sidelines while Bobby Willis negotiated. In the television world it was rumoured that Cilla had worked out a 'longevity arrangement' worth millions of pounds which also involved her as a 'supervising producer' of *Blind Date* and as the 'talent spotter' of who would eventually replace her in front of the camera. Names ranged from Zoë Ball and Kirsty Young to even more established television females. Cilla and Bobby Willis, it seemed, favoured turning the host job around and making it a man like Eamonn Holmes of GMTV, who they regarded as another 'sexually unthreatening' figure who would attract an all-gender audience.

Cilla and Bobby Willis had a remarkable partnership and as a long-term team could take advantage of their history and their connections. When she was involved in her 'thirty years in showbusiness' celebrations in 1993, Cilla's anniversary album included duets with singers like Cliff Richard and Barry Manilow, who had a sell-out 1998 tour of the UK. Barry Manilow hadn't a clue who she was, until he got involved in the project. Cilla was surprised, 'Cliff I've known for a trillion years and I've sung with him on lots of old *Cilla* shows. I had met Barry too. I was cut to the quick when he told me he couldn't remember. In the Seventies I was doing an album in Los Angeles and I went out to dinner one night with Barry. It was only a small table, not many people. Can you imagine someone not remembering meeting *me*?'

She *has* been around a long time, and has been asked often about her greatest moments. The answer is always the same, 'Rubbing shoulders with and meeting the Royal Family. To me, that is the greatest thing.'

Like them, she has had to change. As has her celebrity vehicle. When *Blind Date* began, the winning couple would go out for a day only (the LWT people dubbed it an 'away-day' rather than a 'have-it-away-day') and the 'activities' involved more canoeing than canoodling and back before lights out. The early purpose was laughs, not shocks or surprises, but for millions it instantly became compulsive viewing.

Cilla and Bobby Willis knew they were on to a gold mine. Contracts were even more closely studied, schedules manipulated. Much as, in 1998, people continued to schedule Saturday nights out to allow a viewing of *Blind Date*. Back in 1987, it was boy-meets-girl and Cilla having multiple ecstasies. The early shows, especially with pensioners, seem in retrospect to be so tame: Edith, from Rochdale, was asked to select a beau from 'three lovely lads' who all qualified for free buss passes. 'They're trembling at the knees over there,' screamed Cilla. Edith liked swimming and John, from London, dreamed of being Tarzan. 'If I turned up for a date with purple hair, what would you say?' asked Edith. 'As long as you have some hair at all, I wouldn't be too bothered,' replied John. Alas, despite the swimming and tree-swinging interests they did not 'date'.

In The Beginning – and in ITV financial circles the series has taken on Biblical significance – it was like that, and yet it still brought in audiences which easily defeated *Coronation Street* and other populist shows in the ratings. More than eighteen million people were watching the early series and the popularity has 'thinned' rather than dropped. Television executives, even from rival companies, argue that given the competition from cable and satellite television, *Blind Date* has become even more popular, although the viewing figures are down on average four million a week on peak audiences. And no matter how much control Cilla or the producers impose, they cannot control the chemistry, the body language on the couch, of the couples who do or do not click. The intent may be Orwellian but often the result is more 'Mr Bean', with actions speaking louder than words. While Cilla would never call the series 'romantic' it has continued to be compulsive.

Before the show was established she said, 'I am not a comedienne, I never work out lines before I go on. It just comes naturally. I tried to stick to a script on the pilot and it came across as very false. For the second pilot my husband told me to be myself and it worked.'

But there has been much reworking over the years. The original Chuck Barris *Dating Game* premise was believed to be 'too vulgar' for Britain, a nation which in the early 1980s was deemed too innocent to really want to know if the couples had 'done it' or not. It was an absurd notion, for that was the vital question. And if not, 'They must hate each other, yeah?' The indecisive, the less than totally committed are as unwelcome as shrinking violets on *Blind Date*.

Cilla's increasingly difficult job over the years was to run a clean ship. She's got motherliness down to the fashion statement, reassurance to the pat on the calf not the thigh, control to the tight smile. Prurience is as much a British art form as *Carry On* film comedy. The fine art is knowing the limit for young viewers. *Blind Date* may not be the way parents want their sons or daughters to believe relationships begin, but it is closer to the real thing than textbooks. Cilla has, probably unwittingly, helped popular entertainment in Britain into more blatantly sexual times. In 1998 when one in twelve aged under twenty-five believed AIDS could be cured, and condoms were used if they were 'there' rather than seen as 'essential' by a growing majority of teenagers, she was the figurehead of a series which specialised in bringing together attractive, well-groomed and toned bodies. Other television game shows of the past had won huge audiences by giving away electric toasters – the commodity here was beautiful bodies. Bodies belonging to people who are willing to be humiliated, sacrificed in the neverending search for television entertainment.

'Cilla breezes through it all,' says a very close associate. 'It's numbers, numbers, numbers. It's, "How did I do? How did I look?" And after the show's been broadcast, all she wants to know is how many people watched. Well, they all do, don't they?'

In the late 1990s, it became clear that the purity of the early *Blind Dates* had been sullied. The idea of 'chance romance' was silly. The entire enterprise appeared too fabricated to audiences, even though they did not know that producers instructed – by word, writing and gesture – those 'picking' *who to pick*.

In 1998, all involved were so desperate to keep up the ratings that at every recording there was an urgency to match couples who would provide sexual sparks – in fact, any sort of televisual spark. Cilla and Bobby Willis sat in at such 'tactical' meetings with LWT executives.

'The concern was that most people would believe Cilla was conning them – which, of course, she was in a way,' said a television observer, adding: 'So, it was decided that the show should become more "real". For the series that was to be shown in autumn 1998, the plan was to *prove* to the public that it was all spontaneous.'

So a revamped format was devised: contestants would be

plucked from the studio audience at 'random' to take a place on a high stool and ask or answer suggestively. That, Cilla and the LWT executives decided, would take *Blind Date* soaring into the next century. And the 'random' couples, presumably without baggage, off on a dream 'date'.

For the new intake of producers and scriptwriters it meant planning ahead – and looking at the past. They are always on the lookout for some of the 'star' contestants of the past, people who for some reason caught the massive home audience's imagination.

Cilla has always talked up the show over the years, using carefully chosen anecdotes or 'sound bites' like, 'Many's the time a contestant has whispered to me, "I wish I'd picked the blonde girl instead," or, "The bloke I chose looks the worst of the three". One girl said the only way she'd like to contact her date again was through a medium. Yet he was such a nice Welsh lad and he said to me, "I don't know what I did wrong, Cilla. I was out with Miss Wales last week and she didn't think I was grotesque."

'I'm a total romantic and I love it when they get on, which unfortunately isn't very often. It makes compulsive viewing when they are rude to each other, but I wish some would hit it off.

'They are looking for fame. That's why they don't mind embarrassing themselves, but a girl almost burst into tears after her date told eighteen million viewers, "She's a pukka Sloane desperate to be an A-division yuppie." The girl was extremely upset because she never suspected he had despised her so much.

'The fellow on the show tend to go by the girl's replies. But girls live in a fantasy world, and most go for a sexy, romantic voice. Sometimes, when they're off-camera, the guys try to get round me by asking which girl they should choose, but I never try to guide them because that would be unfair. But invariably they ask me, "Oh come on, Cilla, which one?" It's usually the fellows who are indecisive.'

Cilla found herself a little indecisive, somewhat lost for words, when she was confronted about remarks she had made about the *Blind Date* contestants at an awards show. She had accepted her BAFTA award, after *Blind Date* was named as a 'significant and popular television programme', and grinning and happily waving it in the air, she proclaimed, 'I'd like to say a very big thank you to all those idiots who appear on *Blind Date*.'

That was in Glasgow in March 1995, and the effect was seismic. People could perceive 'Blinders' as 'idiots' for putting themselves through televised humiliation, but never Cilla; she is the genie of the piece, the one who can grant every wish. But here she was, slagging off the contestants.

Cilla was standing alongside Britain's busiest royal, Princess Anne when, gobsmacked, she received the unexpected *Blind Date* special award, and all but stopped the show with her remark before adding, 'I am there with you chewing my sofa on Saturday night, saying, "Oh God, I hope she doesn't pick number three." And she always does.'

At a dinner after the awards ceremony, a writer who attended said Cilla intimated she had got 'carried away'. Officially, Cilla said at the reception, 'It was a joke. Of course the contestants are not idiots! If they are idiots, the whole nation are idiots.' When asked if the Princess Royal enjoyed the programme, Miss Black replied, 'I know she does. She's there chewing the pillows on the sofa along with everybody else.'

LWT sprang into damage-limitation mode; they quickly issued this statement to the nation, 'All the people who appear on the programme are renowned for their sense of humour. We are sure they would take her comments in the humorous sense they were intended.'

Not contestant Jason Bate, of Falmouth, Cornwall, who went public with, 'I brought a bit of culture and was branded a pompous git as a result by one newspaper. I may have been eccentric but I am certainly not an idiot.'

It was *Blind Date* in the headlines again. Happiness for those who believe that there is no such thing as bad publicity. Cilla had remarked at the BAFTA evening that hers was a 'bread and butter' series but it had resulted in stunning viewing figures. An 'art' award – the BAFTAs are usually reserved for costume drama and 'quality television' – was another indicator in the change of attitudes not just of television audiences but of the British TV industry. Simply, they cannot afford to be snobby about commercial success for it makes possible more challenging enterprises.

But Cilla has always tolerated her critics and usually comes off best in the end. There was also the remark about her reportedly calling the female contestants 'a lorra dogs'. It caused outrage, headlines and surveys, which concluded that Cilla herself might be a bit of a barker herself among the celebrity crowd. The supposed remark was a subject she was quick to change when challenged, 'Ooh, I didn't, that was completely untrue but I'll tell you what I did say to one bloke who was a contestant on the show. He was slagging off the girls, so I told him he had the charisma of a mongrel with a head transplant. But they went and cut that out, I think.'

It is not a complete surprise to her that not everyone loves her, but her attitude has always been 'more fool them'. Comic actor John Sessions, who won praise for his late 1997 appearances in the BBC's four-part *Tom Jones* and celebrity creations in *Stella Street*, had contended that *Blind Date* was obscene and Cilla Black like a madam in a brothel.

Cilla could cope with that one, 'I'd love to be a madam in a brothel, honest. It might get rid of this straitlaced image I've had for so long. *Too* long. Yes, yes – *and* I'd take luncheon vouchers.'

The 'dogs' remark would not go away. She had indeed said to the audience at the LWT studios, 'Honestly, what a lorra lorra dogs we've had on recently. Let's face it, we've 'ad some right howlers on the show.' Then she described how the face of one good-looking male contestant dropped when he saw the girl he had picked. 'I felt so sorry for him – he turned down two good-lookers and picked the mongrel of the bunch.' The audience obediently laughed and she told them, 'Don't worry – there are no dogs on tonight's show!'

Susan Johnson, nineteen, who was in the audience, said, 'Cilla was really bitchy about the girls. She kept calling them dogs but she is not exactly an oil painting herself.'

The ensuing row reflected the interest in the show and finally LWT had to respond with, 'Cilla was a bit derogatory but it was only meant as a bit of fun. She had no intention to offend anyone. She likes some cheerful (off-the-cuff) banter with the studio audience before filming starts.'

There has always been much sensitivity about such an *in*sensitive format. When the series was felt to be lacking impetus after five years on the air, some researchers investigated the idea of a gay *Blind Date* special. Advertisements asking for contestants were placed in homosexual newspapers and magazines. They were looking into 'tasteful' ways of presenting such a show on primetime television. Young researchers regarded it as 'hilarious' but LWT executives used expletives to describe the plan. No gays - intentionally – on *Blind Date*. It was complicated enough for Cilla playing matchmaker to heterosexual couples: the demographics have always been against it.

In most countries, Britain especially, it is not proven that opposites attract. A UK 'census' showed the huge majority of married couples are born within ten miles of each other, and four out of five choose someone of the same race, level of parental income, religion and intelligence. More than 30 per cent of couples meet in local discos, dances and parties rather than globetrotting in pursuit of one of the 2000 million possible mates.

Men have the best odds: by the year 2000, for every 1000 men there will be 1035 women in the UK.

Which makes the *Blind Date* couples on a difficult dream to start with. Some couples do get on but the 'bish-bash' is often horrid. One girl reported back, 'I wasn't sure if this was supposed to be *Blind Date* or *Blind Drunk*. I had four drinks and he had thirty-two.' Another recounted, 'The only bit of contact we had was when I tried to throw him in the canal.' What about the man who moaned, 'She talked so much I thought she'd been vaccinated with a gramophone needle.'

Another forthright chap offered, 'I couldn't get over the way she just kept pouring smoked salmon down her cake-hole. It was like seeing *Jaws* on a dry rock.'

The researchers love it. Some call it *Grief Encounters*. Cilla plays diplomat, 'It's a bit like debriefing a bomber crew who have flown deep behind enemy lines – and sometimes there's been just as much flak. It's my favourite bit of the show, when the couples come back and sit on the sofa and listen to what they've said about each other after their date. It's usually possible to tell how they got on from the way they sit and how they use the cushions on the sofa.'

Why *do* people go on *Blind Date*?

'It was a laugh,' said Gina Mertakkas. 'I had no intention of winning. I thought they were looking for glamourpusses.'

'I thought it would be fun,' says Paul Boodell, a computer programmer from Oxford. 'It was a chance to be on telly and to win a free holiday. I'd also heard of contestants going out with three or four girls and I wanted to do the same.' He did!

'I really stumbled on to the show,' says Paul Nolan, the 'vision technician' (window cleaner) from Bournemouth. 'I went along to lend moral support to a friend and ended up auditioning myself. It was purely for a laugh. I had always been told that I should be on telly – I was the local clown – and so I made a big effort to make the most of the opportunity.'

The Independent Television Commission (ITC) believed the show was taking too many opportunities like that – and liberties. Early producers tried to say that looks were not a consideration in the selection of contestants. Plain and dumpy did not go on because it was 'performance literate' people who did, and they were 'too vain not to be glamorous.' It was a point of view but no explanation. The show, they insisted, was all about 'fun'.

Too much fun, thought the ITC in 1996, criticising *Blind Date* for its 'obvious sexual innuendo'. Cilla was hurt, 'I had a vicar in the last series. We must be doing something right. I do not think we would get members of the clergy on it, if that was true.' But sexual innuendo was part of the appeal? 'Well, after all, Frankie Howerd would not have had a career without *double entendre*. Where do you stop?' Cilla formally said she was concerned about the ITC's intervention, 'We will take it on board. We have had the little finger waved at us. Whereas before we monitored the content, now we will have to think twice about it.'

LWT's Kevin Roast said *Blind Date* had received only eighteen complaints during the previous series, and they already monitored content to comply with pre-watershed taste and decency rules. Cilla, distanced by the producers from the debate, did suggest all contestants are given a 'pep talk' about the limitations before they go on air, but also insisted that contestants had not got any 'racier' over the years. 'The boys are the naughtier ones – often because they haven't got their way. That's when I do slap their wrists.

'I don't want to be associated with anything offensive. I edit each programme as I go along. If I think something is a bit "iffy" or too near the knuckle, I turn to camera and say, "That's an edit." I have personally never had a single complaint, but now that I've had the headmaster's finger wagged at me, I will obviously take that on board.'

All involved deny that the show was 'spiced up' to combat the appeal of the Lottery on BBC 1. But 'spice', like beauty, is in the eye of the beholder. What one set of viewers enjoys, might offend another million or two. Some viewers and members of viewer councils have said they were concerned at various raunchy exchanges, references to 'legovers' and remarks like one from a man called Kevin, 'I'm a runner bean – pick me and you can run up my pole.'

Contestant Iris Meunier claimed the crew tried to persuade her to kiss her date on camera. She said a producer told her, 'It looks as if you did the business so make it look good.'

LWT countered with, 'They are not professional entertainers so their answers are a bit cheeky sometimes, but we don't consider them offensive.'

Cilla let her private upset over the ITC ruling overtake her normal discretion, which she observes even with close associates. She told a friend, 'I thought it was an unnecessary remark. You couldn't describe the show as smutty. I was watching *Supermarket Sweep* where Dale Winton was talking about a woman having no knickers on. Now that is 9.30 a.m. in the morning. I would never talk about knickers on *Blind Date*.'

There has never been any clear definition of what is and is not acceptable, or any pleasing everyone, by Cilla or *Blind Date*.

Any random sample of opinion will support that, like these comments from a series of interviews:

Congo explorer and author Redmond O'Hanlon: '*Blind Date* is an excellent example of Darwin's theory of sexual selection; it is very sexy and probably not rude enough.'

Clean-up television campaigner Mary Whitehouse was fair-minded, 'It mixes the cheap with the rich. Some of its stuff is an insult to viewers, some of it is delightfully innocent.'

Broadcaster Ned Sherrin, 'I adore it, but I'm waiting for Peter Tatchell to demand equal time for gay daters.' (In May 1998, Cilla's former *Surprise, Surprise!* partner Christopher Biggins was involved in pre-production of a gay *Blind Date*-type series for cable television.)

Former *Cosmopolitan* editor Marcelle D'Argy Smith, 'I find it gratuitously ill-mannered. I want to know if the contestants liked each other, not whether they got their leg over.'

Writer Christina Dodwell, '*Blind Date* is a tragedy for all the romantics of this world. I'm a traditionalist and believe falling in love takes longer than two statements. It used to be family entertainment but it stuns me now when I see it – it's really raunchy stuff. I wonder what goes through youngsters' heads when they hear what the contestants say.'

Father Jude Bullock, '*Blind Date* isn't on my list of favourite viewing, but I have watched it. It's trivial, a little demeaning to relationships, but not rude. Even if it was, it wouldn't particularly bother me. I'm against any type of censorship on television. If people don't approve of a programme, they can always switch over instead of getting hot under the collar.'

London dispatch-rider Darren Johnson, 'There's no way I'd describe it as too rude. There's no swearing, no one takes their clothes off and there's no violence.'

Housewife Rita Daley, 'It isn't rude at all, it's great fun. There are a hell of a lot ruder things on telly. I would prefer to watch *Blind Date* than all the bed-hopping and violence that you normally see.'

Solicitor John Marry, 'It isn't rude, it's pure rubbish. Nothing ever happens, the contestants just go off to the Canary Islands. They should do the whole thing topless including Cilla.'

Former convict and now writer John McVicar, 'The rudest thing about *Blind Date* is that monster, Cilla Black.'

Despite that sort of remark, Cilla has endured. 'You do get upset over a bad crit but I ride the storm. What keeps me going is that the public really enjoys what I do. That's why I do it. We are not in a vulnerable position, cashwise, any more. I love the wealth, I'm not knocking it, but I don't do what I do for the money and I never have done it for that, *believe me*. I do it for the fame, I do it for the adulation. I'm Mrs Showbusiness. I do it for that.'

Nicola Gill was looking for fame too when she took on the Cilla phenomenon. Gill was twenty-six and working for the tabloid *Daily Star* in London when she began her subterfuge to appear on *Blind Date* and complete a behind-the-scenes dossier. She did tremendously well, but it all boomeranged back on her, for Cilla was not pleased by her performance.

Gill had created a new identity when she attended the first *Blind Date* auditions at a hotel in Guildford, Surrey. She told everyone she was a temporary secretary who liked travel and sex, offering the researchers, 'I suppose I've been pretty naughty, but you're only young once.'

She attended a second round of interviews eight weeks later at LWT's studios along with nine other women in the same age group. Three months later she was told she had made it as a 'picker' and was given a researcher, Fiona, who began an ongoing inquisition. At all times Gill was concerned her 'cover' would be ripped away but she made it to showtime, to the filming of the programme. Before she sat on the high stool in front of the plain background next to the by-then infamous screen, she was given the Cilla 'protocol', the what-not-to-dos when 'Meeting Cilla'. Gill described it as like meeting the Queen. 'You must not: touch Cilla (unless she initiates contact); really kiss her (it's air kissing only); outsmart her (Cilla is the funny one); or say "Lorra Lorra" (It's not funny any more).'

Then she was 'on'. She said she was told which man to choose but misunderstood the signals (fingers held up as numbers as well as notes and mouthed words), and picked the wrong one – number three Paul Mankelow, an apparently amiable 32-year-old accounts manager from Nottingham. Off they went for a date on Skye.

By the time the show was broadcast she had celebrated a birthday and was working for *Cosmopolitan* magazine. Her former employers at the *Daily Star* were not happy that the coup she had instigated for them had gone elsewhere. Gill had brushed their complaints aside and breezed on confidently. It would be in the December 1997 issue of *Cosmopolitan* that she detailed her adventure.

She reported that Fiona the researcher stayed in the same hotel while the film crew were elsewhere. 'At every available opportunity,' she wrote, 'Fiona drags me aside and asks if Paul has kissed me yet. When I tell her he kissed me goodnight, her eyes light up and she demands, "On the cheek or properly?" She seems genuinely disappointed when I tell her it was just on the cheek.

'Later, when Paul informs Fiona that, even if we *were* sleeping together, he wouldn't share it with twelve million viewers, she retorts huffily, "But you can share it with me. Officially, no one gets drunk, smokes or shags on *Blind Date* – except, of course, most of them do." '

Two weeks later at LWT before the 'bish-bash' on the sofa with Cilla, Gill was repeatedly fed a line about liking surprises. Suddenly a cold-eyed Cilla turned on her, 'That was a load of fibs you were telling, wasn't it, Nicola? You said you like surprises. Well, I've a surprise for you. You're not a temp, are you? There must be hundreds of girls out there who would love a chance to come on this show, and you've deprived them of that chance. How do you feel about that, Nicola?'

There were nearly 500 people in the audience jeering at Nicola Gill. She says she blundered her way through and that afterwards Cilla was 'sweet'. Possibly, she knew Nicola might get her comeuppance.

The *Blind Date* programme and LWT have made much of the discovery, saying it was their faultless 'checking' procedures which led to Nicola Gill's lies being found out. In fact, a *Blind Date* researcher just happened to be at a party at which Gill was also present and her 'secret' assignment was talked about there. The deception was exposed, the Cilla 'Gotcha!' arranged after her date with Paul Mankelow.

Later, Gill said, 'Cilla was terrifying because she seemed to enjoy it so much. Even seeing a picture of her now brings me out in a cold sweat.'

However, even before the segment was screened in January 1998, and around the same time as Gill's *Cosmopolitan* article first appeared, there was more revenge for Cilla and the Blind Date team, as well as further humiliation for Gill, who up to that point had nevertheless looked as though she had still pulled off a popular coup. She just had not considered Paul Mankelow in her scheme.

When Paul read Nicola's remarks that she had admitted to having a boyfriend and that precluded any physical romance between them, he was hurt. For, he said, they had enjoyed a three-month love affair! She had at first admitted to having a boyfriend during their *Blind Date*, and after having unprotected sex (he said she turned down his offer to use condoms), explained the boyfriend was her fiancé. They continued their affair until he ended it, to protect himself, he said, because of his strong feelings for her. She returned to her fiancé, but suggested another weekend together before she got married.

A national newspaper heard of Paul Mankelow's feelings of betrayal – and he went public. 'In some ways I've sunk to her level by speaking out,' he concluded, 'and I'm angry with myself for that.'

His story, of course, put *Blind Date* once again in big headlines, only a couple of weeks before Nicola Gill's exposure on national television was to be screened. Another 'must see' show, especially among the snobby chattering crowd so disdainful of *Blind Date*. Yet another example of turning adversity to advantage.

*Chapter Fourteen*

# CHAMPAGNE AND TEARS

*'Nobody should be poor.'*
– CILLA BLACK, 1997

The success of *Blind Date* brought Cilla many new fans. When audiences saw her in panto following the first screenings of the show it was almost – just almost – like the early Sixties' days. Everyone wanted an autograph, to get a close look at the woman who controlled Britain's most popular television show.

Combined with *Surprise, Surprise!* the perception was that Cilla was on television all the time. She wasn't. There were concerts and tours and her own *Spitting Image* puppet. In 1988 it was her showbusiness Silver Jubilee and there was a concert at the Royal Festival Hall in London with her 'mates' like Frankie Howerd and George Martin.

A year later it was her twentieth wedding anniversary and she was still showing her legs in pantomime at every opportunity. She said, 'I keep going because of flattery. I like the idea that after years in showbusiness I'm still here and I'm still wanted. There must be somebody younger but they still want me and they pay me very highly for it.

'I shouldn't say this but it's money for old rope. Give me my eyelashes, my Polyfilla (make-up), my frock, show me my entrance and I'll do it. When my body clock tells me I've had enough I'll retire.'

With her thirtieth wedding anniversary looming that was still a very remote possibility. Her health, however, was a constant worry to her. Progressive bone disorders – known as the 'silent diseases' because they often have no symptoms and can escape detection for years – affect millions of mostly menopausal women. Death often results from fracture-related complications from the skeleton literally shrinking. Such scenarios are best not dwelled on in the early hours.

Cilla's mother's Brittle Bone Disease can be genetic, but Cilla cannot make herself discover whether she has inherited the debilitating condition. In 1997 she said, 'My doctor has given me this note to go and have a bone test myself. I haven't rung up to make an appointment yet. I am a bit like an ostrich with its head in the sand – I don't really like going to the doctor. I'm not frightened, I've had a great innings, but I wouldn't want to suffer, nobody would. At least I'm on HRT, that's very good for the bones.'

As well as Cilla's concerns that she might have inherited her mother's crippling osteoporosis, she gets angry at what she regards as the intrusion of age; she accepts the inevitable but will go on to friends about a future in which she will physically not be able to do as much as she wants. For someone who cherishes control it is a continuing annoyance. It does not inhibit her love of champagne and good wine and food, but she will have spells of being 'careful' with her intake. It is as much for herself, to keep up her high energy expectations, as for the cameras.

However, she is given to snacking, especially when she gets a bit low. It *is* hard work being Cilla Black and the smallest thing can set her off, upset her. She will munch on tinned salmon sandwiches or tiny cocktail sausages until she starts thinking about the sodium content and the body-bloating reaction. Those close to her say it is the worry that there might be hordes desperate to take her place. On every *Blind Date* there may just be someone who will impress as a TV 'natural' and – like Cilla following *Wogan* – get their big chance. It is Cilla's insecurity about her position which causes the most friction in her professional and personal relationships. She can go terribly quiet and brood for hours; it is better when she blows up all of a sudden because it is over as fast.

She and Bobby Willis had furious bust-ups in their years of marriage, but they always believed it was 'them' and 'us'. Few showbusiness partnerships, without the pressure of marriage as well, survived so long. There has been talk that their marriage was a sham, a 'business arrangement', but it seems unproven carping. 'They have too much invested in each other,' was the unromantic view of one friend.

Cilla said, 'We both work at the marriage. You have got to work at a relationship. There's no way you can sit back and say, "I'm happily married." It's not a one-sided thing. When you have children and the responsibility of raising them you have to be that bit less selfish.

'Having said that, if I was grossly unhappy with Bobby or he with me, I'm sure we would have done something about it years ago.'

They became Conservatives because they established a lifestyle and belongings to *conserve*. A fan of Margaret Thatcher, Cilla was in her forties before she voted – for the Tories. She has always feared the 'champagne socialist' label and has been quite open and strident about her political views. She's never loved Labour although denied she ever said she would leave the country if they took over; her policy with the New Labour crowd was 'wait and see' and she said, 'I've nothing against a Labour government and, if they do great things for the country, I will *personally* vote for them at the next election.'

She gets quite irate if people think she might 'retire' to Spain, be an exile like Gracie Fields or Sean Connery, 'I never said I would leave the country if Labour got in; it would be very foolish of me, for all my work is in this country. And where else could I live, with the roots I have had? I have never said it and I have never thought it. What I did object to was paying more tax than I earned during the Wilson government. It wouldn't bother me if income tax went up to 50 per cent. I *earn* a very good living and I thank God that I'm living such a charmed life.'

Prior to the Tony Blair-led landslide of 1997 she was a solid backer and campaigner for John Major, proclaiming at a 1992 election rally, 'He doesn't punish success, he promotes it.' She went on, 'I did vote for John Major and I feel mortified for him. He is not the grey person that he is painted. He's a sweetheart, very funny and a great leader. I think his Party let him down very badly.'

As Labour did Cilla. The socialist cause lost Cilla early on; the docker's girl won an award when Harold Wilson was in power at Downing Street, and doing the honours at the ceremonies, 'I said to him on stage, "When are you going to invite me to Number Ten for tea?" That was more than a blatant hint. I never got the invitation. My father was very, very upset.'

Cilla has a long memory, 'I know that even though I did the Royal Command Performance in 1964 it would have meant more to my father if Harold Wilson *had* invited me round to tea. I did get asked around later by Jim Callaghan.'

With John Major it was first-name terms, with Margaret Thatcher ongoing *simpatico* – a shared belief that they were absolutely right about everything even though they knew, and everyone else knew, they couldn't possibly be 100 per cent certain. It is all about being perceived to be *right*. She shook hands with Lady Thatcher at Number Ten and she would pronounce, 'I'm a capitalist. I support the Conservatives because I live like one.'

There were more personal matters than the changing political climate to concern Cilla in the early 1990s, when several traumatic events took place. One of the most devastating was the death in 1992 of Frankie Howerd, aged seventy-two, in an ambulance on the way to hospital after collapsing in his London home following a heart attack.

Howerd, Cilla's favourite Conservative, had created a unique comic character that served him from music hall, radio, films and television to a final cult status on the alternative comedy circuit while managing to remain the late Queen Mother's favourite comic, (Cilla was devastated at her death). He stuttered and fidgeted to fame, offering garbled innuendoes with a sly sidelong glance: 'Now missus – no, don't! – Oh, please yourselves ...' Howerd's delivery, never ad-libbed, grew out of a lifetime problem of stammering. It was from him that Cilla learned all about preparation, being ready for any and every eventuality: a guest who 'freezes', a camera that locks, an autocue that speeds up or slow down. Frankie Howerd had presented his own personality but magnified much, much larger than life. Cilla learned that.

Howerd, apart from her parents, is the person she misses most. They shared so much. He had confided in her – the woman who had been so naive about Brian Epstein's homosexuality – his problems over being gay. He had been a solace following her son's tragic accident. Some time after Frankie Howerd's death she said, 'When we had all that worry with Robert he was absolutely marvellous. He kind of turned the coin round. We kept on thinking about the poor dead boy and the family. Frankie said, "Well, it could have been Robert, think about that for a change." And it was frightening. Once he'd said that, it helped us a lot. I miss him dearly, and not just the laughs. He was my father figure. He hated me saying that, but he was the father I went to when not even my own husband could help, because he was going through the same problem.

'When you talked to Frankie, you felt a little bit of weight lift off your shoulders. In the early days, Bobby was a socialist, which used to drive Frankie mental. He'd say, "You're sitting in all this opulence, you champagne socialist. How are you?" I'd just sit back and then he'd have a go at me. In quieter moments with the family, especially when the kids came in to say goodnight, he'd really show his feelings. They'd give us a kiss and a hug and go to bed. Frankie said to me once, "I envy you. I really envy you." It upset me a lot because envy to me is worse than jealousy. It's envying somebody for what they've got. It's just that Frankie would have loved to have a family. We used to have very deep conversations, and he'd say, "Don't think I like being the way I am." He was very religious and he felt guilty. He'd say if there was a pill to take that would change his nature he would take it, which I found sad. Frankie claimed he was the father of all three of our kids anyway, it was one of his jokes. He had known them since they were babies and he loved them.

'After he died Robert said, "Do you think Frankie's sister would mind if I had his old tweed coat?" And she was delighted. Robert wears it sometimes and it still smells of Frankie ...'

As her son has the coat, she keeps her memories. She learned about respecting the past from her mother, who also taught her about business and conserving what you have; looking after yourself and your family. 'Big Cilla' was eighty-four when she died in 1996. Her final years had been difficult. That independent woman, a fiercely proud product of her time and place, could no longer lift anything; in the end her head was permanently tilted on one shoulder. Her death was horrible for Cilla, who reacted in a very normal way: you do anything but confront what happened, *believe* what has happened. Cilla was so aware of that, 'I did a show the day my mother died. People asked me afterwards how I could. Working was my solace. I wasn't being brave, I was being very much a coward. I was putting it off. I didn't want to be an orphan and that is what I was then. I miss everything about her.'

Cilla never lost the need for her mother's approval. Through the days of chasing Cliff Richard in taxis, to working with The Beatles, to becoming a television star and then the nation's most popular auntie, her mam was always there for comfort and support. It was a Northern relationship, so close in many ways, distant in others. There were no intimate chats about the birds and the bees, but home truths about walking tall and always being your own person and true to yourself and your family. Cilla's mother knew all about the nuclear family before they invented the bomb. When the clock caught up with her, Priscilla White would harbour no nonsense, no fuss. She wouldn't live with Cilla, and refused to have a nurse in her own home. It was silly, for the money was there. It was stubborn. But her distraught daughter understood, although finally, her mother *had* to have professional care.

For more than a year before her death in November 1996, Cilla's mother lived in a £280-per-week nursing home in Mossley Hills, Liverpool, having ordered Cilla not to 'go over the top'. She had insisted on staying in 'my Liverpool'. Cilla's brothers and extended family were there.

The family enjoy visits to Cilla's 'palace' in Denham and splashing out in every way, including skinny dips in her indoor swimming pool.

For them, said Cilla, it was like being in Hollywood. Or Disneyland. For her mother, terrified of the electric gates which reminded her of Rainhill Mental Home in Liverpool, it was much too grand. When she became too ill to look after herself she asked all the family to grant her wishes: typically, she did not want to be a burden to any of them. Cilla's family, very aware of her 'position', rarely say anything about her or their family, but in the case of her mother one did offer, 'Cilla was absolutely devoted to her mam and would never do anything to hurt or offend her. Her mother was a lady of great dignity and Cilla was very mindful of that. Her mother needed the kind of care and attention that a nursing home could give her, without taking away her pride or independence. She insisted on something simple. She was comfortable being where she was. She hated fuss.'

Cilla has often said she followed her mother's example, 'I've tried to do exactly as my mam did,' she said. 'She used to say to me, "If something doesn't feel right, if it embarrasses you, then don't do it." To the end my mam still told me off. She was as bright as a button. The will and strength was unbelievable. She was like a little sparrow, her mind was sharp and she never complained.'

At the hospital a nurse said, 'She got no special treatment because that was the way she wanted it. She was a wonderful lady, a real character who had no airs and graces despite her daughter's fame.'

Cilla could not have been expected to be so calm about her mother's death although running from the truth she did film an episode of *Blind Date* the following day. It took Cilla, usually so quick to publicly confront situations, some time to talk about her loss. When she did she explained the delay, 'I thought I would be OK because she had been ill for so long, but I was left in a terrible state of shock. I am still coming to terms with my mam's death even though she had been ill for some time and wanted to go. People have kept telling me it was for the best. She died on a Sunday and I was supposed to go into work on the Monday to film more *Blind Dates*. I didn't know how I was going to do it. I was in a trance; it just didn't seem real. I went to bed thinking that I would have to cancel the show the following day. I knew I would be in no state to go in.

'But that night, I had an incredible dream about my mam. I imagined that she had passed away in her bed and I was with her. But it didn't feel bad, it felt good and right. It was all very peaceful and calm. The following morning, I had a great feeling when I woke up. Bobby was worried that I would be too upset to do *Blind Date* and offered to call London Weekend to tell them. There would have been no problem because they expected me to pull out, but because of the dream I felt really great. I went in and did two of the best shows that I have ever done. I was glad to be able to go back to work. I don't know what I would have done without *Blind Date*. I think I would have just sat around and got very depressed.'

It would have been an easy trap to fall into. She knew her mother was desperately ill. She had made many flying trips from Denham Airfield to see her mother, but when it all seemed hopeless Cilla's brothers called to say their mother had brightened up, she seemed to be all right. She died a few hours later, with Cilla still in Denham. She says she will always feel guilty, 'Had I realised how serious she was I would have flown up there immediately. I don't know how many flights I had taken to see her when it looked serious. She had pulled back from the brink so many times. But when it actually happened, I had no warning at all. It took me completely by surprise.

'I am quite psychic and normally I know when something is wrong. I can sense it. I had spoken on the phone to my brothers earlier that day and they said she was fine. I think they were concerned over me worrying about her. But even they weren't with her at the end. They had been with her for some time, went out for a break and a pint and she just went. She was such a clever lady and I guess she didn't want to distress them.

'I couldn't believe how many letters I got from viewers; some have just been addressed to *Cilla Black*, *TV Star*, *Denham*. One came from a fan in America. How the news got over there, I don't know but it was very touching. My mam was around for me always. It's awful. I keep reaching for the phone – then remember that she's not there any more like she always was.

'When I left school I cried my eyes out and when I presented a *Surprise, Surprise!* show I cried my eyes out. My mam wasn't happy about that at all. She called me up and said, "You shouldn't have cried. Don't do that again. Keep a stiff upper lip." She was incredibly strong like that. She always said what she thought and encouraged me to do the same. She was very caustic but much more witty than me. I remember Bobby telling her he was going on a diet. Most people would have said, "You don't need to bother with that." But she looked at him and without batting an eyelid, said, "I would, if I were you." We were brought up on laughter and song. I used to go home when I had a day off and the neighbours would say, "You can sing, Cilla, but you should hear your mother – she's the real star."

'I was never allowed to let success go to my head.

'She adored anything I was on. She was a bigger fan of *Blind Date* than *Surprise, Surprise!* and would call me up with her views on the show. She hated the *Blind Date* with elderly people – and told me to get them off.

'People say to me, "She was a good age." I know they are trying to be kind, but there's no such thing as a good age. She was so active. Even though she was desperately ill, she was still the life and soul of the party.

'I still think, What has she done to deserve to die? I do miss her dreadfully. All of a sudden, in my early fifties, I'm an orphan. In a way, her death was the best thing for my mam because she was so ill. It was awful to see her the way she was, and one should have felt relief, but I didn't. I miss her sense of humour so much. When I used to go back up to Liverpool, the whole family would get together and we would have such a laugh. Now I worry that the family won't be so close any more.

'I still love Liverpool and I will go back sometime. I'll have to stay in a hotel now though because her house is gone. There's no point. Mam was totally crippled with osteoporosis and arthritis. She couldn't eat or swallow. It was so distressing to see her like that. And yet, she had the strongest heart of anyone I have known. It was unbelievable.

'Grief is a selfish thing and I had to come to terms with it. At first, nobody could even mention her name in front of me, but now I find myself sitting in my dressing room, saying, "Oh, Mother used to say that." I have to remember how she would say, "There's always someone worse off than you." Even at the end, she said: "It could be worse, I could have the dreaded cancer." I really had to find my strength from her strength.'

Her mother's death, the passing of Frankie Howerd, her own fiftieth birthday ... were all reminders of her own mortality. It had been hammered home in 1993 during the promotional celebrations of her thirty years in showbusiness. These involved an appearance on *Top of the Pops* with her song *Through the Years*. She had last appeared on the show in 1978 when she sang *Silly Boy*, and was followed on stage by a whole team of silly boys – the pivotal punk group The Sex Pistols. She played the appearance up in marvellous style, saying it would be more daunting than a Royal Command Performance. Then she played the generation card, 'I've got to get it out of my head that my boys will be watching and killing themselves laughing.'

She was more to the point with her memories of *Top of the Pops*, saying, 'I remember doing the show when I was twenty-two. I saw one male singer who was only thirty-five but I turned to Bobby and said, "What's that old man doing on *Top of the Pops*?" So, at the back of my mind was the dread thought that someone might say, "What's that old woman doing on *Top of the Pops*?"

'I don't know where the years have gone. We all shed our tears but I don't want to share that with the public because that's not my job. I'm a very private person in that respect. I don't want to share the bad times – I want them to see the good times.'

Privately, she has admitted to such bad times and also said, 'You know it's got to go downhill from here on. It's not from a looks or a career point of view – it's purely age. It is a difficult time.

'If nobody asked me for my autograph I'd be cut to the quick.'

Her sensitivity to her popularity is constant. She was upset by the reaction of some students to her 1994 invitation to become an honorary member of Liverpool John Moore University, the former Liverpool Polytechnic. She accepted on the basis of spending 'fifty-one years at the University of Life'. That cliché alone just increased the anger of the students, who opposed her planned inauguration in July that year because they argued it would 'devalue' their degrees. The university said it had offered the fellowship as a mark of respect for Cilla's achievements and to reflect that university's 'participation in the modern world.'

When news of the Cilla fellowship leaked out, a very Sixties demonstration took place. Politics student James Nolan was quoted at the time, 'We can't associate the host of *Blind Date* with anything academic. It's absolutely absurd. We have to work hard for three years to get our degrees and this devalues the whole thing.'

Cilla witnessed the student displeasure when she visited the campus and saw a 'demo' against her by students outside the Social Sciences Department. It is said that the words 'little snots' – or it could have been 'little swats' – were heard from her, but publicly she dealt with the situation admirably. She would not now be accepting the honorary fellowship, 'I am disappointed but I am not bitter. This is what we have a democratic society for. More power to the elbow.'

At other times she is not so tolerant. One *Blind Date* contestant, Debbie Kavanagh, reacted angrily after her television appearance.

'Cilla wants to make herself look good. She comes across as a nice homely girl but during filming she keeps on making her little bitchy comments every five minutes. I was embarrassed because they made me look a miserable cow. All the nice things I said about my date Ted were edited out and they left the nasty bits in. Cilla sided with Ted. She clearly thought he was great and couldn't understand why I didn't like him. She made various digs at me like, "Who do you want – Superman?" But I was determined not to let her get to me.'

The telephone salesgirl also made allegations about the *Blind Date* crew and their drinking habits, 'They must have the best job around. They spent about one hour a day filming and the rest of the time skiing, drinking and dining out.' The official line from LWT about that and all complaints about Cilla being 'bitchy' to contestants was and is, 'Cilla has a well-deserved reputation for her natural friendliness on and off the screen.'

But, as Nicola Gill discovered, she does not like to be messed about with, to be made to look a fool. She has privately gone berserk at researchers and producers if the *Blind Date* romantics turn out to be rogues. Teddy Maybank lied to Cilla when he went off with 'date' Claire, with Cilla predicting a 'future' for them; back home in Hove, Sussex, was his fiancée Joanna Schofield. He said, 'I did the show for a laugh. I didn't tell Claire I had someone else until the end of our day together. I think she understood. She's a lovely lady, and we got on really well.' When Cilla discovered the truth, she said, 'Obviously, we expect people to enter in good faith. It is sad that it appears Ted Maybank's motives were an attempt to gain television exposure.'

But Cilla began to get more and more fed up with the 'Blinders' who were economic with the truth about their love lives. In 1989 she said if they lied they could be sued. The warning followed Amanda Chimes revealing that she was not single but a married mother. Cilla only found out when it was too late to stop the 'foxy and single' Amanda appearing on screen. 'Cilla was furious about the lies and determined it would not happen again. She said she would take legal action for fraud against anyone who deceives,' was the word from an associate.

Cilla tried to play it as she did with the university students – coolly. In this case, it was icy, 'Contestants don't tell porkies to find romance – they do it just to get on the telly. They want to be stars even if it is only for a day. But viewers like to think couples paired up on this show might fall in love on their blind date. That would be a problem if a contestant who was married or had a steady relationship cheated their way on to the show. It could shock and upset their partner.'

The problem with the television dating game as with the real life one is that no one can ever be completely confident about another person's motives or character. During the run of the series there have been many bloomers.

In 1991 Leslie Edmondson talked Tracey Moore into believing he was the man of her dreams, the perfect gentleman. Before she agreed with him in front of millions of viewers, and he took her off for a free week in Rome, he did not tell her or Cilla he had also been to prison earlier that year for robbery and theft. LWT did not waste the trip – they screened 'highlights' of it, no matter the background. Edmondson, then a 24-year-old window cleaner, had spent three months in jail after he and three other men accosted a 16-year-old youth in an Oxford street, ordered him to strip, then took his wallet and watch. He also admitted robbing another youth of £10. His lawyer told the court he acted 'out of character'. But the judge described his behaviour as 'shocking and disgraceful'.

The *Blind Date* loophole was simple – it just was not possible to check on criminal records. Critics, of course, thought that should be one of the more necessary checks in the whole set-up. LWT said Edmondson applied to go on the show a month after leaving jail but told them he had no criminal convictions. 'He wasn't honest with us,' said the TV company, explaining, 'We don't rule out anybody who has done anything stupid when they were younger, but we don't want it to have happened that close to the programme being shown.'

Cilla has had a smorgasbord of embarrassments. Male model Tyrone Christie used a false name to appear on the programme for a second time. Claudia Tear set up a date at the aftershow party with a contestant she had rejected. She even phoned him from Amsterdam during her chosen TV date and talked about marriage. It seemed every 'Blinder' was possibly suspect before or after the blessed TV appearance. Nana Hughes had an abortion after being involved with another contestant's date. Both appeared on the same 1996 show.

There have been other troubling cases.

Contestant Johnny Law did not tell the *Blind Date* interrogators that he had once been tried for rape. A young mother had charged him with attacking her in his van. He was finally acquitted at Oxford Crown Court but was given a six-month jail term for failing to make a court appearance. Law insisted the woman consented to sex, then changed her mind. The jury had been told there was no medical evidence of rape. Cilla and LWT tried to distance themselves from the cases as much as possible, with the TV company saying Law had signed a statement that he had no criminal past. 'We knew nothing about this,' they insisted.

But no matter how often the embarrassments happen, there is always room for more headlines. Simon Parker, who was twenty in 1996, aroused public outrage when, facing a kidnap charge, he had his bail condition varied to enable him to audition for the series. Parker was allowed to defer reporting to the police by four hours so that he could take the screen test.

He had been granted bail on condition that he reported to Torquay police station daily between 5 p.m. and 6 p.m. Magistrates agreed to amend his reporting time to between 9 p.m. and 10 p.m. to let him apply for the show. Lawyer Andrew Cooper told the magistrates, 'He is due to appear in Bristol in an audition for *Blind Date*. It means he will not be able to report to Torquay police station. What we are applying for is for you to vary his bail conditions.' Ann Covell, Chairman of the Bench, told Parker, who with two other men faced three different charges, 'We're happy to agree.'

MPs of the day reacted for their voters. David Jamieson, Labour MP for Plymouth, Devonport, said, 'It is ridiculous. This should not have been granted.' Michael Stern, Conservative MP for Bristol

North West, said, 'The law is being made to look stupid by cases like this.'

The *Blind Date* producers enjoyed, for once, the embarrassment of the law rather than their own. One said, 'He applied in good faith; only about 10 per cent go through. He did not get through.'

Distinguished social commentators like Malcolm Bradbury have cogently deplored the *Blind Date* culture, but it has a tremendously popular appeal.

'Cilla gives people what they want. Why should she worry?' said a prominent producer of a successful television series, adding, 'It's the old saw – she didn't get where she is today by underestimating the public taste.'

She has, of course, film evidence to prove it.

*Chapter Fifteen*

# SEX SELLS

*'Large, a little less large, and large.'*
– BLIND DATE CONTESTANT CLAUDIA PATRICE WHEN ASKED TO GIVE HER VITAL STATISTICS

Cilla and *Blind Date* have contrived over the years to create instant television celebrities, from very self-indulgent 'cheeky chappies' to genuine characters who are magnetic by pure personality; then there are the others – those who you feel might just do anything on an adrenaline high … '

Cilla and the *Blind Date* team are well aware of what makes the programme work best. It is SEX. Sex sells. Sex and lust gone wrong sells even better. Sex that turns into recrimination and guilt is a right little belter. All this creates addictive, if often embarrassing television.

The unwritten code for the *Blind Date* productions is that the sexual element should exist every week. 'If they haven't got at least one couple genuinely at it then it's bad news,' said someone close to Cilla, revealing, 'The pressure is on everyone to see that a couple "click" in the sexual sense. It's not too difficult. They are often loaded up with booze and there's the excitement of the bright lights of London and staying in an expensive hotel.

'Look, Cilla's a millionairess because of all these people shagging. When you consider the basics, it's ... well, we must be careful. Let's just say it's showbusiness.'

Certainly, it's business. And a serious enough one for the behind-the-scenes people on *Blind Date*, from researchers to camera crews, associate producers to the make-up ladies, to whisper about the 'sex quota' required. Cilla and the producers do not object to the occasions when humour replaces sexual tension on the interview couch, but sex is the main focus. One-time suggestions about medical 'screenings' were dismissed as 'detrimental' on the basis that contestants were grown-up enough to practise safe sex in the AIDS era – and this despite lurid tales of rather spontaneous sexual action. A plan to issue condoms to contestants was quietly forgotten about, but LWT staff are 'armed for action' during the filming of the series. 'Silly not to be,' said one, redundantly explaining, 'That's what they've all come here for.'

Cilla expresses horror over Sunday newspaper revelations of couples making out with other than their chosen *Blind Date* partners. She dismisses it in an it's-all-a-bit-of-a-laugh sort of way. According to testimony, these sexual encounters usually involve lager, Stringfellows nightclub in London, more lager followed by wine, another nightclub, another bar, the hotel lounge, the hotel room mini-bar ... all paid for by LWT.

Karen Mason, a 'picker', said most of her fellow contestants had only one thing on their mind – and even that did not always work out the way it was planned. Her *Blind Date* Paul Nolan slept with another girl, 'Paul and I had already had a row and gone our separate ways, before the party we went to ended. When I arrived back at my hotel room I knew something was wrong. I could hear male and female voices giggling inside. The door was slightly ajar and I pushed it open. There, in *my* double bed, was Paul and this girl. They were under the blankets and Paul went purple with embarrassment. The girl squealed with fright. I went mad and screamed, "What the hell do you think you're doing? Get out of my room at once." I went outside and they hurriedly got dressed and walked sheepishly out. From that moment on I knew the whole thing was going to be a disaster.'

After the show, Karen and the rest of the 'Blinders' left the LWT studios. What happened next was, she was told, quite typical of what *happens every week*.

'We all met up at the girls' hotel – the Royal Westminster in London – and started boozing in my room. Everyone was getting tiddly and people were eyeing each other up. I must admit I went up to one of the contestants I *hadn't* picked – Guy Hardcastle, and told him I fancied him. We exchanged home addresses and telephone numbers. But Paul didn't seem to mind and we all headed for Stringfellows nightclub. By then everyone was out of their heads on booze. But Paul got angry when George Best paid attention to me. George was gorgeous. He came over, introduced himself, and joined our group. It was obvious he was making a play for me but I laughed it off.

'Paul was furious and started ignoring me. Eventually at 3 a.m., I decided to teach Paul a lesson. George and one of his mates invited me and another girl for an early breakfast. I gave Paul my bedroom key and told him to wait up for us. He just glared at me. George took us to a small cafe called Harry's and we spent a couple of hours chatting. I knew he fancied me but nothing happened. He was very polite, asked for my phone number and I promised to see him in a couple of weeks. Then he got a cab to drop me off at the hotel. It was then that I caught that rat Paul at it.

'I should have known: the moment I saw him I knew he was wrong for me. What a let-down when he came around the corner! He's only a short guy, and I'm six feet tall in my high heels; I towered over him. I much preferred Guy Hardcastle – I told Cilla he had a nice bum and I wish I'd chosen him. But Paul was the popular choice.

He delighted the audience with his impressions of showbiz personalities. When I heard him from behind the screen I thought, What a fantastic personality. He was very bubbly and the audience loved him. They'd have strung me up if I hadn't chosen him. They went wild with excitement when I said I was going for contestant number one.'

Karen says the animosity continued on their trip to America, 'One night I got revenge on him by going out on the town with a cowboy waiter called Whip. He slipped me a note during dinner with Paul. Paul was so busy talking about himself he didn't even notice. After we had all gone to our separate rooms I quietly went out again and had a few hours with this guy. He was very sexy and more attractive than Paul.'

Nevertheless, Cowboy Whip does not appear to have had the somewhat demonic sexual effect on *Blind Date* contestants as does a trip to Stringfellows in London. After Karen and Paul had recorded their 'date' recollections for the LWT cameras, they and other contestants went out for a second visit to ... Stringfellows! She said, 'A big gang of us went. All the lads were well tanked up, and the girls tiddly. Maybe it's my blonde hair, but the guys were swarming over me. When we all got back to the hotel we had a nightcap in my room. One girl – a contestant in next week's show – went back to her bedroom and suddenly Paul got up and followed her. The next morning you could cut the atmosphere with a knife. Thank God, that's the last I saw of him. I tried to be nice to him. I'd even prepared an album of photos of our trip but he just told me to stuff them.'

How can this happen when the *Blind Date* crew of 'minders' are paid to keep the boys and girls at least at ogling length? Karen said it is all for showbusiness: after *Blind Date* is recorded the rules, and apparently more than the gloves, come off.

'Before the recording they're absolutely paranoid. The boys have their hotel – and the girls another. Just before the show we're still kept on separate floors of the building. The producers take great pains to make it a complete surprise when we meet on air. But afterwards anything goes. We all have a few drinks in the lounge – and then we are on our own. It's obvious from the start who fancies who. It's all expenses paid and we want to take LWT for every penny. It must cost them a fortune. And there are more red faces the following morning than you see on the show. George Best? He pestered me at home to go out with him. I couldn't make up my mind.'

And, in the strange twists of television fame, Paul Nolan became one of Cilla's 'stars', had his fifteen minutes. He may not have impressed Karen, but his *Blind Date* appearances led to work as a disc jockey and some television spots. He said, 'All the others thought: This is going to make me a star – but I got on the show by accident because a girl I know was going in for an audition and I went along too. Obviously a lot of people liked me.'

Few, however, have made the big impression on *Blind Date* that Claudia Patrice did in 1989. She was five foot tall and weighing a generous fifteen stone when she appeared with Cilla, and was romanced on screen by a fellow contestant who worked for a kissogram company. Mark dressed up as Tarzan for his business work. You could not create a better set-up, and the *Blind Date* production people still talk of it as one of *the* best shows.

Claudia, from London but then an arts student at Cardiff University, played the game perfectly. She spoke her own – and the lines written for her – with feeling, 'I've never had a steady boyfriend in my life. When blokes see me they usually run in the opposite direction. They are just in awe of me because of the way I am. I dunno what it is ... it's because I just ooze confidence, I guess. They think to themselves, "My God, what a woman. I really want to meet her." But then they think I am going to immediately eat them up. Sometimes when they are drunk at a disco, they will approach me. They are a bit braver then, but I don't ever want to know.

'I haven't really had any serious relationship with anyone ever. And that's the way I like it.

'I don't rule out a sex-life entirely, but I've got my studies and my Student Union work. I'm into Chaucer and Shakespeare. I'm a little fierce with my three-inch nails and the rest of the look. I was a little dumpier even when I was at school and it was me that did all the chasing. But I didn't chase boys for kisses or whatever. I chased them to beat them up.'

Claudia was quick when asked about her vital statistics, 'Large, a little less large and large. I can't even bear to think what my measurements really are. I don't think I would be safe. Even before I appeared in Cilla Black's show, I couldn't walk down the street without being hassled or asked out by some weirdo.'

Claudia said she was sure she would be picked for *Blind Date* by Mark Millhouse when she heard the reaction she got from the studio audience, 'They were really behind me. It was amazing. I think they would have lynched Mark if he had picked one of the other girls. When he picked me up I thought, bloody hell, he must be strong!'

They went to Devon on a sailing trip 'date' and she nearly capsized a twenty-foot dinghy, found she was too large for her lifejacket and got trapped in the back of a Lada car. A *Blind Date* producer recalled, 'Claudia was a scream – literally. When she got into the dinghy she nearly tipped it over and started to scream her head off. Then the instructor screamed – because Claudia was standing on his foot. After their sailing, Claudia dropped off the back seat of the car taking them back to the railway station. As the car went down a 1-in-9 hill she rolled off the seat and got stuck between the front and back seats.'

It was all wonderful *Blind Date* television – even without the sex. Mark tried to keep his end up and for the cameras said, 'She kept throwing me on the floor and practising the kiss-of-life.' Claudia told it straight. 'I'm a very physical person but unfortunately there wasn't much of that aspect on our date. Mark was the perfect gentleman throughout.'

Cilla raved about Claudia's show – and demanded more of the same. 'She still gets tremendous pleasure from knowing a show has worked and is going to bring in the viewers. It is Cilla's life – it's all she seems to care for,' said a television associate.

Cilla also yearns for a 'touch of class' on the series which lives on a basic mix of sex, laughter, seaside postcard sex, humiliation, sexual innuendo and more sex. She was thrilled when it once seemed likely that a polo-playing friend of the Prince of Wales might give it some social uplift ... but you cannot plan on anything. When Cilla yelped out, 'Contestant Number One – Rupert from West London!' she was indicating Rupert Mackenzie-Hill, ex-Army (Special Forces in the Gulf) and strong of jaw and stride. Even former officers have to make ends meet. His two fellow contestants, Edward Farquhar and William Scott-Mason, were also former soldiers. Farquhar, who held a commission in the Life Guards, was once close to Princess Margaret's daughter-in-law Serena Linley and was in the same house at Stowe as Mackenzie-Hill, who was also with the Life Guards. Along with Scott-Mason, who served with the 13th/18th Royal Hussars, part of their work on Civvy Street involving being registered with the escort agency Sabre and Bearskin. They were men about town but still willing to compete for a television *Blind Date*.

They planned to pass muster and impress Cilla with a little seaside postcard humour. Food stylist Giselle Blake Davies was the 'picker' and asked, 'I spend 90 per cent of my spare time cooking. What would you do with the other 10 per cent?' The chaps, to Cilla's disappointment, forgot about the nicer aspects of countryhouse charades and the reply was that famous, 'Give you a good stuffing.'

Not inspired material. Neither was Mackenzie-Hill's jaunt to the Lake District with Blake Davis, granddaughter of the lead violinist of the Royal Philharmonic Orchestra. They spent their time driving a

Land Rover blindfolded and riding bikes. It turned out to be a very 'flat' encounter – one that couldn't be given more 'spin' by Cilla and her cohorts. Rupert was honest about that:

'She was a lovely girl but there wasn't any spark between us. I don't know why, it just wasn't there. Giselle looked all right but I must admit she was not the sort of girl I go for. I prefer girls who are more petite and preferably blonde. At our hotel, everyone else was about eighty and watched us wherever we went. Worst of all, Giselle and I had rooms on different floors. I don't think we could have slept together even if we'd wanted to. There was constant filming. Three hours after we arrived, we had to film the final dinner, in the middle of the afternoon! However, they could not have put on a better selection of activities for us. It was great fun but Giselle wasn't too happy. She definitely didn't enjoy the bike-riding. She had never done anything like that before and was rather nervous, while I've been riding all my life. Afterwards I had to go to bed early because I desperately needed some sleep. I suppose I didn't pay her as much attention as I should have done. It was impossible to feel really romantic. It didn't occur to me to try it on. It would have been inappropriate.

'There was one really romantic moment. We were in the Jacuzzi together with a bottle of champagne. The camera crew had finished and we had a few hours to ourselves. We walked down to the lake in our bathrobes with the champagne. By the lake, we kissed. I'm not sure why. It seemed to be the right thing to do at the time. I think Giselle and I got on very well. Maybe we haven't a lot in common, but I'm interested in all sorts of people. There's definitely no physical attraction between us.'

For once the stories almost matched. Except he was not too revealing about his bout of squeamishness. Her version of events, 'When the screen went back and I saw Rupert for the first time, I fancied him instantly because he's very nice-looking. On the date he had his moments – although I can't really think of any – when he told jokes, but I wouldn't say he was particularly sparkling company. Rupert hated being filmed; he clammed up every time a camera came near him. But I was pleased to discover that I loved it.

'When we were up in the plane the flight was quite turbulent and Rupert started to go green. The next thing I knew, he began throwing up. I felt very sorry for him, but in a way it was quite amusing because he had been so macho previously and told me he had done 200 parachute jumps. On the activities I cowered in the rain, but it was perfect for him. He could really show me up, which he definitely enjoyed doing. He's Rambo personified. To cap it all he went to bed at 10 p.m. while I stayed in the hotel lounge, because he was so tired out by the day's adventure activities!

'As the day went on I realised we'd end up as that cliché, just good friends. He liked talking about the Army and horses, and once you've heard one or two Army anecdotes, they tend to start sounding the same. We kissed once, but it wasn't very sexy. He's not really a sensual, tactile person at all – at least not with me. When the date ended, we both knew it was not going to lead to anything romantic, but we arranged to go out with the contestants I had turned down, because he knows them. A week later, we went out in a mixed group and it was fun. As I had suspected, the girls talked about guns and horses. It confirmed that we'd only ever be friends.'

What Cilla needed was some help, something different. It came from an unexpected location. In 1995 the Bishop of Manchester, the Right Reverend Christopher Mayfield, gave her his blessing. He agreed to allow the Reverend Simon Gatenby, vicar of Christ Church, Brunswick, Manchester, who plays the bongos and sets off his dog collar with a tattoo and earring, to appear on *Blind Date*. It was the vicar's way of 'reaching out' to Cilla's congregation. It was an act, as Cilla might put it, of blind faith.

For the researchers and producers it was indeed a godsend.

They had just the girl for the vicar – and they could see the headlines. Come in, Polly Alderton, who worked in a lawyer's office. Convent-educated Polly had also helped her bank account by stripping off her clothes as a kissogram girl and as a lingerie model. She had boasted to researchers that she had seven O Levels and added, 'I'm a 34DD. I'd nip out of the office to do a kissogram. I'd turn up in a pub and peel my clothes off to a basque, stockings and suspenders for £40 in the hand. The guys went wild; they loved it. I never got any complaints.'

You did not have to have won 'Krypton Seven' to see that the vicar and Polly had potential. But how could Cilla Fixit? 'They exploited Simon's naivety,' claimed Polly. She said she was 'steered' by production staff to pick Simon. They had both signed contracts with the show not to talk about it. Amazingly, she said, they were then fixed up for a photographic fashion layout for a newspaper. Polly, who wanted to work in television, was keen to do it. The 'profile' would show her well-bred background. Her father, retired Major Peter Alderton of the East Anglian Regiment, served in the Far East and in Northern Ireland, where she was born. She went to St Mary's Roman Catholic convent school in Colchester, Essex.

The fashion shoot was, however, nothing like the fun of appearing on *Blind Date*. She said, 'I absolutely loved doing it. Going in front of an audience with the lights on me gave me a great buzz.'

Things were a little less exciting for the vicar. Inspired by the production team, Polly gave a 'pain in the pulpit' interview. For millions of viewers' amusement she described Simon Gatenby as 'one of the vainest men I've ever met'. She said he told her that he had had eleven sunbed sessions before his TV appearance, shaved the sides of his head to hide his thinning hair, kept dozens of pairs of designer silk boxer shorts in his hotel room, and grandly talked of 'my PR man' (Jonathan Jennings, Press Officer of the Manchester diocese).

It was less than evangelical. The vicar, then aged thirty-two, was crucified. In a moment of clarity he wondered why – and explained why he had gone ahead, 'I've enjoyed the programme for ages and always wondered when I was going to see a bachelor vicar like myself on it, but it never happened. I asked myself what it would be like to go on as a vicar and what the response would be. And then I saw the advertisement for auditions for the programme so I went along. They took one look at me and seemed to be delighted, and so was I when they said I had been chosen. You see, I've never believed that priests should be anything other than themselves. Life is about fun. To me the Christian faith is about life in all its fullness, it's about enjoying life. God is not a party-pooper who says, "Thou shalt not do it." This was probably one of my reasons for wanting to go on the show, to give a positive message about Christianity, that even vicars can have a laugh and enjoy things.

'I have never gone about my life with a deliberate game plan. I've just been me. God has used me wherever I've been. I wanted to show all of this on the programme. I also wanted to have a laugh. Don't forget it's meant to be light entertainment and I've enjoyed watching it, even though you need the remote control to flick over when it gets too cringeworthy.'

Simon talked to friends in the Church and to his father Canon Denis Gatenby of Bolton and none of them disapproved. That was before Polly was displayed over two pages of a national newspaper in her 'profile'. In rather pleasant contrast to *Blind Date* mudslinging, Simon would not agree or disagree that he had been set up by the television series. Or lavishly reposed on sunbeds. 'I'm a priest and I believe in confidentiality. She may say what she wishes but I shall not retaliate. I'm not going to talk about personalities or shared experiences. That's not for me to do. I have a ministry here and I'm not going to get involved in that sort of thing.'

Was it Heaven sent (Polly was told, 'This is going to be on *The Best of Blind Date*) that the Rev. Simon was chosen? Or was there some 'creative' help? Polly says she had never seen the three men who were behind the studio screen. She got some directional hints, 'It was all in their answers. Before the programme I was asked about my likes and dislikes, and gave a list. I said I didn't like tunnels, bikinis, horses or show-offs. The only one who did not mention one of these in his prepared answers was Simon. I didn't want to ridicule him; I'm not anti-religious. It was how the LWT people wanted to play it. It's all about viewing figures, isn't it?'

And in that attitude she got into her mini-dress and posed, 'I was told they had some nice clothes and there was £1,500 in it. I stressed that I had nothing against Simon but we just didn't hit it off. There would be no romance.' Instead the headline read: *My Blind Date Vicar Was Too Fond Of Himself*. She says she felt concerned, 'All he wanted was to portray a trendy vicar image, but I realise he's been treated really badly. I was very naive ... but I thought that LWT were looking after us. When I called LWT to complain about the newspaper and how they had printed nonsense about Simon, and how awful I looked in the pictures, they tried to soothe me by saying, "You don't, you look lovely." '

LWT said, 'We are here to advise, to project and to protect.'

Liz Harris says she did not feel protected after 'winning' a date with Austen Turner. She says she was looking for romance. He was only interested in sex during their getaway in the skies above Buckinghamshire flying in gliders, biplanes and helicopters. Turner, apparently, had more down-to-earth thoughts.

'The trouble was that he thought he was God's gift to women and couldn't understand that I didn't fancy him. A researcher told me to go by my gut reaction after my first question. I asked a question and liked Austen's first answer so I chose him. When he came from behind the screen, I'm sure my face must have dropped. He was quite tall and slender but he had a bleached blond bob hairstyle. I thought, Oh God, I don't fancy him at all. I knew it straight away.

'Right from the start, he was trying it on. We had a party after the show and he was telling me he'd just ended a four-year relationship and he wasn't getting any sex. He kept talking about breaking up and saying his life was hard, and that he was sexually frustrated. I was stunned.'

But like so many on *Blind Date* shows, she wanted to make the most of LWT's hospitality. A majority of contestants appear to set themselves up for their critics – they never understand that there is no 'free' night at Stringfellows. Liz Harris could not resist an Italian restaurant, dinner and drinks with Austen Turner, and then went back to his room 'after having a lot to drink.'

Given the *Blind Date* culture she sounded surprisingly shocked as she recounted, 'I was lying on one of the single beds just chatting and I had on a dress that was very low-cut at the back. Austen came over and was trying to stroke my back and then began kissing my bare flesh. He kept touching me with his hands and rubbing them up and down. It was horrible. He thought he was being so ultra-seductive, but it was a real turn-off. But I couldn't really tell him to get lost because we had to get on for the sake of the programme.

'It was all rather childlike and foppish. He kept saying to me, "Oh, please kiss me." He tried to kiss me on the lips but I turned away and he kissed me on the cheek instead. I couldn't cause a fuss and storm out because we had the filming to do. So I pretended to sleep and actually fell asleep with my clothes on. In the morning, I dashed out of the room feeling very embarrassed. On the date we went to Henley Regatta and Austen met some friends by *chance*! I was standing near enough to hear what they were saying – and they were laughing and joking and asking him if he'd slept with me. He didn't deny it and gave the impression he had. I was very embarrassed.'

And then Cilla entered their lives in front of millions of viewers. The couple argued. She told Cilla he had tried to seduce her, but he replied, 'How can you lie in front of fifteen million viewers? I was the perfect gentleman.'

To Liz's dismay, Cilla got the studio audience going by saying, 'He's lovely, our Austen. Why didn't she fancy him?'

It was, she says, simply Cilla and showbusiness. The contestants were fodder to Cilla, 'I'm sure she knew because afterwards she gave me a hug and explained that some of what was said would be cut from the programme.'

One buxom contestant edited herself out of *Blind Date* in 1997. Charlotte Harrison likes small dresses, big hair and heels. Trekking in Nepal did not tempt her. With David Smith she was to take off on her *Blind Date* in a land which argues sensible shoes rather than fashion. So she did not disguise her feelings when she told the producers, 'I can't go, I can't go. I'm scared of flying – I always have been. I don't like foreign food and I don't like foreigners. It'll all be dirty – and what about all the diseases?' She then turned to her date, 'I'm sorry, David. You'll have to pick another girl or another holiday because I'm not going to Nepal.'

This situation had never happened before on the show, which had then been running for thirteen years. David Smith said, 'I thought it was just a big joke at first. Charlotte was a real stunner and I was so looking forward to our holiday. Then she did a runner and I never saw her again.' Cilla turned it around; when you don't follow her plans then the great revenge is humiliation. David Smith went off to Nepal and that particular episode was broadcast in January 1998. Viewers saw him solo sightseeing in Katmandu, riding an elephant and generally having a superb holiday. The Yorkshire park manager was prompted to pull out pictures of the girl who was intended to be with him, and in an over-rehearsed way say, 'See what you're missing, Charlotte?'

One of the show's associates commented, 'In situations like that it is often the idea to make someone who has not co-operated look daft. There's no mercy on *Blind Date*.'

But you get some *very* good-time girls. Hayley Dollery said she was a beauty therapist when she appeared on Cilla's show in 1997. Her date was Ben Hardcastle and the couple went off for five days to the South of France; he reported their trip to have been 'maybe passionate sometimes.' As it turned out, Hayley was familiar with such dates as she worked for an expensive escort agency. On television Ben Hardcastle told Cilla, 'There were a few kisses and cuddles. We had to make the most of it at the time so that's what we decided to do. I'm sure she did fancy me. What we had was like a holiday romance. We had a good time.'

Hayley, who had previously told Cilla that her favourite part of her beauty therapy was 'full body massage', described her time in France, 'On the first night, instead of sleeping we decided there was too much excitement so we went to my hotel room and had a few drinks and talked. You cannot get much better than this guy. I like Ben, but I don't fancy him. We will see each other again – watch this space.'

Later it was revealed that Hayley was not a beauty therapist but worked for the New Darlings Agency in Buckinghamshire. The escort agency advertises in newspapers and charges £30 to introduce clients to girls who, in turn, want at least £100 per hour for their time. After being labelled a call girl by a Sunday newspaper, Hayley reacted forcefully, 'I am *not* a prostitute. Men pay for my time – the sex comes free. I have only slept with a dozen of my clients and never on a first date. I only sleep with a bloke if I fancy him – *not* for money.'

It was in contrast to the innocent image she presented to Cilla (favourite *Blind Date* newspaper headline, '*My Porn Date*'), but Hayley was unrepentant. She worked, she said, with famous pop stars and businessmen.

'I have earned £5000 a week,' she revealed. 'My minimum target for one is £500 – and I can earn that with just one client. I get £100 an hour – the other £30 per hour goes to the agency. And as well as getting paid for my time, I get to enjoy a fantastic lifestyle. I've been to the best hotels, restaurants and nightclubs in Britain, all at the expense of other people. It's a great life.

'Men can buy my time but not my body. I was at a nightclub in London with my ex-boyfriend when this bloke walked up and said he'd give me £2000 if I had sex with him that night. I just laughed and told him to get lost. I don't need to sleep with men for money. I could never sleep with anyone I didn't fancy not for love *nor* money. If I fancy a bloke I will sleep with him, it's that simple. The sex is always on the house. I am uninhibited. I enjoy sex – and I have had some mindblowing sex with clients.

'I remember the first time. He was an accountant who drove a Mercedes and had a smart house in southwest London. He took me to Terence Conran's flash restaurant Mezzo in London for dinner, and then on to Brown's nightclub where all the big celebrities go. Afterwards he drove me back to his house for a coffee. He sat down on the sofa next to me and asked, "Is it OK if I kiss you?" It was fine by me – I fancied him like mad. He was tall, dark and had a good sense of humour. He was a wonderful kisser too. I always find that a big turn-on in a man. We ended up having really intense, passionate sex for about two hours.

'I might be a daredevil and I do enjoy sex. But I'm not into anything really kinky or weird. And I have always insisted on using a condom. It's important to look stylish and sophisticated when someone is paying £130 an hour for your time. I always wear my black silk stockings and suspenders and bodysuit underneath a designer suit, usually Moschino, with black stiletto boots. I think underwear is most important. I can't understand women who wear shabby undies. I think nothing of blowing £100 on a bra and knickers, and it always has to be silk. I do it for myself, not for men, but it does turn them on.

'I remember going out on a date with a hunky computer expert from London. We went out to dinner at Bolter's Lock, near Maidenhead, then he invited me back to his hotel for a drink. Over dinner, we had discussed whether he had any sexual fantasies – something I often do with my dates if I fancy them. It helps to put them at their ease, breaks the ice and usually raises a laugh or two. This man told me he liked to wear women's garter belts and stockings. I kept a straight face because I don't like my clients to think I am laughing at them. I had on a pair of very fine black stockings under my beige suit and he could tell because you could see the shape of the fasteners through the thin fabric of the skirt. I could tell he was excited and I was getting quite excited too.

'When we got back to the hotel, he poured me a drink and said, "Can I put your stockings on?" I was a bit taken aback and I started to laugh. I am very open-minded, but the way he blurted it out made me giggle. I reassured him that I wasn't laughing at him and said, "Whatever takes your fancy." Then I stood up and slowly peeled off my stockings and unclipped my suspender belt. I kept the rest of my clothes on while he took off his shoes, socks and trousers. I tried to help him put the stockings on but they laddered on his hairy legs and he had to take them off. It was hilarious – he asked me to help him put on the suspender belt but it wouldn't stretch around his waist and I had to hold it in place myself. He was very good-looking and I did fancy him, but I found the whole thing hysterical. I didn't have sex – I couldn't after that. I couldn't take it seriously.

'The guys I go out with are not sad, seedy types. They are all intelligent, attractive and wealthy. Most of them are in jobs where they don't have time to pursue a relationship. All I am doing is letting them enjoy the company of an attractive female. If good sex follows, that's my pleasure. I'm a bit of a control freak so I do like to be on top, that's my favourite position. That way I'm in the driving seat ... and that's how I like it. I pride myself on being openminded and uninhibited. I don't think there's anything wrong with these guys. Everyone has fantasies but not many have the guts to try them out.'

What Hayley Dollery had never fantasised about was being brought to the attention of the *News of the World*. The newspaper was keen to reveal her activities after she became a television personality by appearing with Cilla. *Blind Date* had become such a part of British life in the late 1990s that anything perceived to be out of order with the contestants made them legitimate targets. Although such stories bring all involved to the bottom of the media market feeding chain it has done nothing to harm the viewing figures of *Blind Date* or the circulation of the *News of the World*. Indeed, it enhances both. Where the publicity handshakes on such situations begin and end no one is willing to debate. But Hayley Dollery certainly provided Cilla's people with their headline for the week. The *News of the World* reported the story this way:

Blind Date *Hayley Dollery shamelessly strutted on to Cilla Black's smash-hit show last night ... and hid the secret of her sleazy sex and drugs trade.*

*But offscreen she is keen to get straight down to business and offered a* News of the World *undercover reporter five-in-a-bed sex.*

*'I could get a couple more girls if you want and you can get a friend,' she leered. We can have an orgy. Forget threesomes, let's go for fivesomes.*

*'I'll do anything. I don't mind spanking. I'm open to everything.' Hayley was also keen to brag about her bit of 'stardom'. One of the first things she told an undercover* News of the World *reporter was: 'I was on Cilla Black's* Blind Date. *I won it.'*

*Hayley conned millions of viewers – along with Britain's favourite hostess Cilla – into thinking she was a regular contestant when she appeared as a picker.*

*She managed to look delighted when she chose a fella to accompany her on a blind date to the South of France.*

*But the busy call-girl confessed to our reporter: 'I haven't got enough time for relationships with guys.'*

*Despite the huge risk of AIDS, Hayley also brags that she lets her customers perform some sex acts without a condom.*

*'I explore sex in so many different ways,' she smirked.*

*Hayley, whose unsuspecting sister Zoë is a special police constable, is just one of the high-class tarts on the books of an escort agency called New Darlings run by madam Michelle Canon.*

*Last week, our reporter, posing as a businessman, telephoned Canon at her luxury home in Buckinghamshire.*

*'We have a selection of ladies of all ages and groups, blondes and brunettes,' says Canon. Just tell me what type of girl you're looking for.'*

*She was quick to suggest Hayley for sex.*

*'There's a 19-year-old girl,' said Canon. 'She's tall, very long dark hair. She's over 5ft 10in in height with big brown eyes and a sexy figure ... 34–24–34.'*

*Continuing her sales pitch, the madam went on: 'Young Hayley is strikingly pretty and has a dead sexy personality as well. She's a self-employed beautician and is due to sign on at 3.30. She can be with you after that.'*

*Within an hour Hayley turned up at our reporter's suite at an hotel near London's Heathrow Airport.*

*She was wearing a fur coat over a beige suit and fishnet stockings.*

*Hayley discussed the £130 price for sex and explained: 'You normally charge a bit extra depending on the time and the punter.'*

*She had obviously decided that our reporter should cough up 'a bit extra' and charged him £250 cash including her taxi fare ... then suggested fivesomes.*

*When our reporter declined, she offered a drug-fuelled sex session.*

*What gear to you want?' she asked. 'I do cocaine. I'm thinking whether somebody will come and drop it off here.*

*'I know guys that do that, they've got loads. I'll get some for you tomorrow definitely. I'll pick it up later.'*

*Hayley then bragged about her TV appearance.*

*'I said if l had to launch my own designer range I'd call it "Leggy" just like me,' she said. 'Then Cilla asked me my inside leg measurement.'*

*Cilla, who has kept* Blind Date *at the top of the ratings for years with her special brand of warm humour, knew just how far to go. But in our reporter's hotel room, Hayley didn't. She hitched up her skirt to reveal black lace panties and matching suspenders.*

*On last night's show she told viewers, 'I spend my days waxing, filing and plucking.' Cilla carefully spelt out the word* plucking.

*Hayley chose Ben, a tall dark and handsome aspiring musician from Essex. But even that didn't satisfy her. We got on OK as friends but we didn't bonk,' she told our reporter.*

*For their* Blind Date *they were sent to Nice, Cannes and Monte Carlo. Their holiday report, which is prerecorded, is scheduled to be screened next Saturday.*

*'I had to spend five days with him,' she moaned. 'He had this faded* Starsky & Hutch *T-shirt on and I thought, How can I walk around with this guy?*

*The TV crew kept knocking on my door every morning asking if anything had happened.*

*They sent two breakfasts to my room, expecting him to be in bed with me, but he wasn't so I just ate both breakfasts.*

*They say if you don't get on you don't have to stay with each other, the most you have to do is eat together every meal-time whether you like it or not so they can film.'*

*Then she asked our reporter a question that she would never dare ask her TV suitors.*

*'Don't you ever wish, when you hear what men pay for girls, that you were a girl?' she said. 'Don't you ever think it to yourself?'*

*Today Hayley may wish she had never thought of it either.*

*Our dossier on her ... and her madam ... is available to the police and to Cilla.*

Details of how this particular contestant slipped through the 'vetting' were never available from LWT. And Cilla? She was always publicly more interested in *Blind Date* wedding bells. Privately, she was fed-up with such stories appearing in the newspapers: it was obvious that more stringent monitoring was required. What was entertainment on a Saturday night was not always palatable on Sunday morning.

Hayley Dollery was 'New Woman' incarnate for the programme's selection team: young, leggy, sexy, bright, cheerful – and not afraid to explain, in detail, her wishes. Sexual or otherwise.

Were the young women of the 1990s becoming too much for television, too mercenary, too predatory?

*Chapter Sixteen*

# WOMEN RULE OK?

*'Women in the days of* Blind Date *are not afraid to say what they think about men – or what they want from them.'*
– AUTHOR FAY WELDON, 1998

As the turn of the century loomed, the prospects for *Blind Date*, and for Cilla's role as its presenter, were being hotly debated was the programme past its shelf life? Did it still have that magical, elusive fizz that makes all entertainment work?

The television decision-makers, in particular Granada, are very aware that there is no escaping the popularity of Cilla and *Blind Date*. They are part of everyday conversation: in the 1997 cult British film *Shooting Fish*, one of the young characters takes revenge on a rival by breaking into his home and changing the video time to record Channel 4's *Dispatches* rather than Cilla's programme. In that particular Britcom movie, this is seen as incredibly evil.

The TV moneymen are acutely conscious of Cilla's audience awareness factor. There is one popular television joke about Cilla: she is a *cash cow*. Both she and Bobby Willis knew that when the cash stopped flowing from her enterprises, her engagements would cease. she also knows that she is pivotal to the future *of Blind Date* and keeping it the most talked-about programme in the UK. That was and is Cilla's gift, her easy involvement with the punters – the television-license-paying public – and, of course, those 'Blinders' with whom every week she gives an Oscar-winning performance.

Surprisingly, she is still shockable. In her early years, swearing and suggestive language was not commonplace in mixed company, certainly not in the front room and not on the wireless or, later, television. Her brothers did not swear in front of their father; The Beatles did not curse in her hearing. The backstage language and antics of her television contestants often requires only a dictionary, not an imagination. On screen over the years the *Blind Date* sofa exchanges have mixed the banal with the bawdy. Not always effectively.

From the beginning of *Blind Date*, the battle of the sexes has been evident. As the 1980s matured and moved into the young 1990s and onwards to the 21st Century, the attitudes of the 'Blinders' has reflected that of young people. Equality is all. A wally is a wally, no matter which gender. If anything, it has been the women who have taken over with the insults, the clever put-downs. There was much debate in early 1998 about feminism – had it gone too far? Cilla has been accused of many things, but not directly of being a feminist. Her background more than her generation stood her apart from such developments. But her show was a platform for the independent woman, confident and powerful and only really needing a man for 'fun'. Babies were available, as was so often pointed out, at the neighbourhood fertility clinic. Men? Who needs 'em!

That sort of feminine edge sidelined Cilla at times. She is a mother of three boys, sister of three boys, a traditionalist. Here she was overseeing one of the most popular television shows which won or lost on the relationship between the sexes. Author Fay Weldon, who says she resents her 'feminist' writer tag, offered her view, 'Everywhere I hear women talking of men as men talked of women in the Seventies: it wasn't nice then and it isn't nice now.

'I want women to stop the hatespeak. I never again want to hear a 'feminist' joke like "How many men does it take to wallpaper a room? – It depends on how thinly you slice them". Reverse the gender roles and you can see it is unforgivable. But women of the *Blind Date* generation are not afraid to say what they think. Nothing is more powerful nor more confident than today's young woman.'

Which is why, in some circles, *Blind Date* became known as *Women Behaving Badly* and became more and more like a sexual tennis match, with each player desperate to score the most points.

For instance, Alison said of Desa, 'I was expecting my answer to Prince Andrew and all I got was this hairy DJ from Birkenhead.' He countered with, 'There were a few things that annoyed me. One is that she had this high-pitched whining voice which drove me mad.'

And Wendy and Matthew? She said, 'I would rather have gone out with the horse. The bad things about him? His hair, his mannerisms, smelling of drink, the clothes he wears, the jewellery, his shoes, his attitude.' He said, 'Bad voice – very pushy, talks without listening, doesn't care what anyone else says.'

Simon and Mandy did *not* get on. Simon said, 'She had this really nice tiny face that I found quite cute and dinky, that sort of appealed to me. Just the smallness of her face, really ... that you could put your hands around and strangle it.' She revealed her taste, 'The lunch was very, very good. It was just a pity I had to share it with him.'

Romance? Forget it! And, increasingly, it was the women who were the most outspoken, difficult to control and gave off a sense of being a little dangerous. Which is why Cilla and the *Blind Date* machine got so excited over Old Etonian Alex Tatham and Susan Middleton, a down-to-earth contestant from Birmingham. Love, it seemed, could conquer anything, even the class barrier.

It began for Alex Tatham as 'a bit of fun.' The girl he met on *Blind Date* was so different from the usual mix at the débutante dances. Two years after meeting on TV the 'fun' turned serious and they planned to marry. 'Although their relationship was a bit tense at first, due to their different backgrounds, it's actually a really good match,' said friend Bill Russell, adding, 'They are both great characters with amazing senses of humour.' They would need all of it.

The wedding, in October 1991, was in every sense a production. For television it was an obvious ratings winner (more than seventeen million people watched), and Cilla and the team milked it. Almost dry. '*I'm delighted and I'm over the moon.*' That was Cilla, not the bride.

Alex was twenty-five and training to be an accountant; by 1998 he had become deputy managing director of a computer company. Sue was a year younger and working as a recruitment consultant. On *Blind Date* after he had chosen her as his date and the screen went back, he simply said, 'Superb.' Later, he recalled, 'We were immediately attracted to each other. I thought she was superb then and I still do. We were going out together because we met on a TV show. But we got married because we loved each other. We are so lucky because no other couple has that moment when they met for the first time on video.'

Their wedding plans were initially toasted in LWT champagne and gushes from Cilla. Finally, the magic had worked with the ultimate *Blind Date* payoff. They went from a medieval banquet in Ireland – their TV trip – to high-tech nuptials. And Cilla, keen as ever to turn a penny, got a bonus. In fact, there were financial arrangements all round. As well as Cilla's extra fee, the happy couple were paid. They had asked for £20,000 through an agency, but LWT refused. At one time it even appeared as though the wedding would go ahead in Pelsall in the West Midlands without being filmed for *Blind Date*. There were some executives at LWT who bristled at the money pay-outs but, aware of the audience appeal, the company finally compromised with a £10,000 payment to the couple.

The general feeling in and outside television circles was that, in the circumstances and given the return LWT would get in audience figures, that was reasonable. But had they not just agreed to a £1.5 million contract with Cilla? Why that extra £20,000? Her simple answer was that was the 'going-rate' for such an appearance. It was *her* time. Of the event, she gushed in her book *Through the Years*, 'Wild horses wouldn't have kept me away from that wedding.'

'A lot of people thought it was a bit rich,' grumbled a television executive, adding, 'It was felt that as Cilla had just signed a huge contract for a lot of money, she ought to go to the wedding as a guest, not get paid what amounts to an appearance fee.'

On the tenth anniversary of *Blind Date* – another ratings bonanza – Emily Tatham made her television début at five months old. There she was, the first *Blind Date* baby. Her parents had resisted suggestions to name her Priscilla after the woman who arguably brought them together. 'They were told it would be wonderful publicity, but they knew the baby would be stuck with the name for life. They were clever enough to realise it was just a one-off gimmick, something to get a headline,' said a TV associate.

Sue Tatham found she was pregnant toward the end of 1993, 'I'd always wanted children and after a couple of years of being married, the time felt right to start trying for a family. I was sick every morning for twenty-six weeks and at one point the baby was lying on my sciatic nerve, so for four weeks I could hardly walk. It was a nightmare! In fact, the last four weeks of my pregnancy were probably the best. And then our daughter arrived ahead of schedule.

'We went straight to the hospital, which isn't far from where we live, but then everything progressed rather slowly. Emily was born thirty-five hours later. Alex was with me all the time ... The name? Well, not Cilla. Or Priscilla. We'd had Emily Charlotte in mind since the early days and I think it suits her. It seems an age ago that I was single, looking for a boyfriend and going on *Blind Date* for a laugh. I didn't have to tell Emily how I met her Dad – I showed her on the video.' The tape has been rewound and rerun many times, and the family audience was increased in 1996 when their son Charlie was born.

By then Cilla had established a reputation for 'sad' hats. At the couple's wedding she had stolen the attention in a creation which alternatively was described by the then fashion mavens as 'a velvet Nazi helmet', 'a toaster' and a 'chamber pot', and one said: 'She has the dress sense of a colour-blind costermonger on speed but her taste is an important and endearing part of the Cilla persona. Who could relate to her in Jasper Conran? The garish jewels, sequined jackets and fuchsia talons symbolise Cilla's triumph over early adversity.'

It may have been a sense of this that dissuaded Anna Coverdale and Andrew Davies from inviting Cilla to their wedding in 1990. They planned to marry after meeting on *Blind Date* but, sin of sins, did not want publicity. It was only after their white wedding in Claines, Worcestershire, that they went remotely public. They had even insisted on no Cillogram. And, without the cameras, could it ever have been a real *Blind Date* wedding?

Life, it seemed, was full of surprises, even for Cilla. Clearly, she was *not* the person everyone would want to choose as their favourite wedding guest. Nevertheless, she certainly chose the hat she wore for the second 'official' *Blind Date* wedding. The titfer was big and green and looked like a tureen! This was about as poetic as things got. In 1994, Lillian Morris from Newcastle, then seventy-one, married David Fensom, a year younger, from Devon. The scriptwriters had enjoyed great fun with this couple. When the television screen had swooshed back she swooned, 'He's got bedroom eyes.' They had gone to Jersey on their *Blind Date*, kissed in the limousine, and he had proposed ten days later, 'At our age you have to savour every minute.'

The wedding took place in Tiverton. One guest said excitedly, 'I thought Tiverton had won the FA Cup when I saw the crowds. They weren't there to see Lil and Dave – it was Cilla they were after.' And there she was, arriving by limousine amid royal-style security and giving that Buckingham Palace wave. She was in a green suit which was a shade quieter than the hat. She got all the attention she wanted at the Register Office and then at the tiny church in Hemyock where the rector, the Reverend Tony Gross, attempted to enter into the television spirit of events:

'And for the wedding of Lillian and David we must thank God ... and Cilla.'

'I've never been compared to Him before,' Cilla said afterwards.

*Postscript*

# WALK ON

*'I'm alone but I'm not lonely, and I'm stronger.'*
CILLA IN 2002

In October 1997, there was a moment when Cilla's life appeared in serious danger. She and Bobby Willis had been to Liverpool and were flying into Denham Airfield, where weather conditions had worsened to a dangerous degree. They were both anxious to get home and unaware of the threat to their lives.

Conditions grew so bad the pilot considered diverting to Luton Airport – the usual procedure in such circumstances – but instead tried to 'chance it' to Denham. In the small world of domestic aviation the incident was gossip for some weeks. The pilot involved told colleagues, 'It was touch and go whether we made it or not. I don't think she was ever aware of how much trouble we were in. It could have been a right mess.'

Cilla was made very aware of the dangers only a few weeks later when, just as 1998 was beginning – on January 2 – a plane ploughed into the road near her home in Denham. Three people were slightly hurt in the crash and the access to her grounds was blocked for some hours.

It brought back memories of a 1970s turbulent flight to the South of France. 'They told us we had been downgraded from First Class, and I told Bobby that was an omen. I've never been downgraded in my life. I said, "We're all gonna die on this plane." As the flight began to get horribly bumpy I brought total chaos to the whole plane. I threw my safety belt off, stood up, and shouted, "God Bless Us, Happy Christmas, don't let us all end like this."

'I was standing there with my arms widespread, praying. At one point even the stewardess was down on her knees. I was standing there with my arms out appealing to God, when a woman came up to me and said, "Pull yourself together! Don't you know that we all look up to you as the second Gracie Fields?"'

She was also *first* of the British female pop stars to become a worldwide name, a leader in the UK renaissance of popular culture, Epstein's 'Fifth Beatle', John Lennon's 'Cyril'.

That achievement and those glorious days, like her present heights, cannot ever be taken away from her. Today's young comics have fun with the way she walks, and allude to her 'hostess frocks', in fact, Cilla wears immaculately tailored clothes designed for the well-to-do, middle aged woman. She is a survivor, an entertainer who has triumphed not just over the times but age itself. She has adapted and, in the ongoing circle of life, her time has arrived again. Proof that without the past, there is no future?

With the end of the 1990s the business of nostalgia was everywhere, especially in the world of entertainment, with the major focus on the Sixties. Michelle Pfeiffer was developing a Hollywood movie on the life and times of Marianne Faithfull. Starbound British actor Jude Law, who had delivered a remarkable performance in *Wilde*, playing the lover of Stephen Fry's Oscar Wilde, was the frontrunner as the lead player in a biographical film of Brian Epstein. There was talk of another Beatles' film along the lines of *Backbeat*, which had reflected on the group's beginnings. In 1997, seventeen years after the death of John Lennon, The Beatles, who had not recorded for a quarter of a century, earned £61.3 million – more than twice as much as The Spice Girls. In America that year they were placed fifth on the list of richest entertainers, trailing from the top Steven Spielberg, George Lucas, Oprah Winfrey and Michael Crichton; way below them were Michael Jackson and Tom Cruise.

In the mid-1990s much of The Beatles' work had been re-released in anthology albums with great fanfare and profit. In 1998 George Martin – the fifth Beatle – was partially deaf from his years of studio work and had decided to retire saying, 'I don't want to do things I am no longer good at.' He went out with the Fab Four. His last album was *In My Life* in which a varied group of stars including Sean Connery, Robin Williams and Jim Carrey re-recorded Beatles' hits. It was a significant farewell.

Britpop owed it all to The Beatles. Yes, The Rolling Stones (number twelve on the 1997 US earnings list) were an important landmark – but the Fab Four were the lads the girls could take home to Mum. For pop entrepreneurs, the magic trick was to find The *new* Beatles, again and again and again. So, we had The Bay City Rollers and Take That and Boyzone, Bros, The Pet Shop Boys and East 17 as well as The Monkees – 'The Fabricated Four' – and Sigue Sigue Sputnik, Milli Vanilli and all the others we can't recall or who never made it.

Arguably the mainstream British pop scene had not moved that far in more than three decades. Once the question was: Who's Your Favourite Beatle? Was it John, Paul, George or Ringo? In 1997, it was Who's Your Favourite Spice Girl? By the summer of 1998 it was being applied to the glamorous foursome called All Saints.

At Wolstenholme Square in Liverpool, after drinks at Mello Mello in Slater Street, the Saturday-night crowds lined up to get into the Superclub Cream. Many were from Liverpool itself, but just as many again had driven the three hours from London or come south from

Edinburgh and Glasgow. Their journey might have taken them down Scotland Road – now a motorway flyover. During the week there were coachloads of visitors from all over the UK; some came by ferry from Belfast or plane from Dublin – or even Paris, like Dior designer John Galliano.

Cream was indisputably the 'new' Cavern for the millennium: at John Moore University in Liverpool where they didn't want Cilla as an honorary anything – 70 per cent of the students said they chose their place of learning so that they could go to Cream. The fashions were different and the facilities superb compared to the early 1960s Cavern, but the aim was the same: to rock 'n' roll 'til you drop. Of course, it was also still about the dating game and in glitter, spray-on T-shirts and pants (the men), and bra-tops and tight shorts and skirts, as the young clubbers preened for attention.

Like clowns such as her friend Frankie Howerd, she wants to be taken seriously. To Bobby Willis it was always 'serious money', having a wife as one of the top ten female earners in the UK. To Cilla it has always been the applause – but also the need for everyone to realise that it is not just luck or a bubbly personality but hard work and talent that have kept her on top. In Cilla's world – Bobby Willis and her sons, especially Bobby Junior – there is much thought about the next century. She still has ambitions to be a star in America, but more possible is the family plan to create a television situation comedy for her.

That way the critics would still have her to kick around. They have happily knocked the mawkishness of *Surprise, Surprise!* and the prurience of *Blind Date* and in both cases with much justification. Critical and commercial success – and satisfaction – are bookends rather than bedfellows. Cilla craves both. After *Blind Date* was named as a 'significant and popular television programme' by the British Academy of Film and Television Arts (BAFTA) she commented, 'It's only taken thirteen and a half years for those people at BAFTA to get into *Blind Date*. I'm in with the elite. They obviously sat back and said, "This is one show that is never going to go away no matter how much we criticise it."

'Now. I've arrived.'

But this is a question of judgement, and that is because a snobbery still exists around Cilla. The Jo Brand breed of comics suggest we should laugh at sex, or at least the absurdity of the sex act. Cilla and her show do laugh loudly, but at the intrinsic silliness of what, in Cilla's day, was known as 'courtship'. It works because she has learned to stage-manage the ridiculousness of it all, of its elevated place in all our lives. It is remarkably clever stuff.

Coming up for forty years ago, Cilla Black arrived in London with a little help from friends like John Lennon in those remarkable Yesterdays. Now she lives in a different world. After she received her OBE at Buckingham Palace, a celebrity-focused glossy magazine sponsored a £10,000 riverboat party for Cilla and her guests, who included Christopher Biggins and radio personality Gloria Hunniford.

There was a chicken and salmon buffet. And a cake which was created by Jane Asher, the 1960s girlfriend of Paul McCartney who was with him on the day that Brian Epstein died and around when Cilla Black had her first number 1 hit with her second record *Anyone Who Had A Heart*. In 2002 it remained the biggest-selling single by a British female artist.

And the icing on the cake, as she says, has been meeting royalty. Vivienne Parry, a trustee of the Diana, Princess of Wales Memorial Fund, recalls an occasion, 'At one gala Dame Edna Everage (Barry Humphries as his most famous character) and Cilla turned up in the same dress. Thankfully, Cilla was able to send for another one. Diana heard the story and the first thing she said to Dame Edna was, "I like the frock." '

It has been quite a trip, her life so far. But Dame Edna, despite her dress sense, would not be Cilla's first choice to act out her life. She was asked in 1998 by a television magazine who she would want to play her in a movie. Without hesitation she chose Meg Ryan, the fizzy blonde actress from *When Harry Met Sally* and the romantic *Sleepless in Seattle*.

It was a good choice, for Ryan takes her work extremely seriously. She also enthusiastically enjoys her life and her family, but says she wants more: just like Cilla and Bobby, she says she doesn't see time as an enemy but *as an opportunity*.

By 1999 Bobby had found another opportunity for her. Always so media-aware, he has never been blinkered by geography. What works in America and Australia or Asia is likely to be successful in Britain; game shows have no cultural deterrent or geographical barrier. The difficulty in the new millennium was retaining some standards as what was becoming known as 'torture TV' took hold around the world, especially on the burgeoning digital and cable channels.

Bobby had seen the Japanese game show *Happy Family Plan*, a savage sort of entertainment where contestants are offered fabulous prizes *if* they succeed in a set challenge. Families on the poverty line are offered lifetime incomes and yachts if a key family member can perform the task. In Japan it is all or nothing – with everything resting on the shoulders of grandma or a child. It's comic and sadistic. The view from Bobby was, 'It's a competitive, all-embracing family show. Every member of the family, with all the children, will be able to take part.' He quietly bought the rights.

With Cilla in charge it became *Moment of Truth* and although it was toned down from the Asian version some critics still found it too cruel. In the UK show a family chooses from a range of prizes, takes on the challenges, and if they lose they get a booby prize.

There were no booby prizes for Cilla. She stood to earn more than £500,000 from the series but, most of all, it kept her where she likes to be – in the spotlight. While others retired or re-released former work, she was creating another series and trilling, 'I'm thrilled about doing something new. Everybody's excited about it.'

No one more than her. And Bobby Willis who had once again proved he would go to the end of the world for his Cilla. Tragically, he would not see just how far and how loved she was by television audiences. The lung and liver cancer which claimed his life robbed him of seeing just how strong a woman he had helped his wife become. She survived and many credit her sons with helping her do so; but anyone who knows Cilla Black testifies it is her own upbringing and inner strength that moved her to battle on, for, as Bobby enthusiastically believed, the show always has to go on.

And in it does. Cilla looks better and healthier than ever. She's trim and slim and, as she says, a 'grey babe'. Her priorities and life appeared to be in order and she now seems to have come to terms with the horrifyingly quick diagnosis and death of her husband. She has thought much about it and says, 'He fought for us. If he'd had his own choice, and we weren't there, he'd have decided, "I'm bailing out now." '

'Bobby had a great life. He did more in 12 months of his 57 years than most people ever do. If the boys get upset I say, "Your dad wouldn't have wanted this. Your dad would go mad if he could see you. Bobby's great legacy was laughter and this is how they remember him.'

'I'm alone but I'm not lonely. And I'm stronger. I've got no fear of cancer or getting ill. I used to be literally terrified of flying but now I absolutely don't care at all, because I think, "Well, if I go I'll be with Bobby anyway." I was talking to Michael and Mary Parkinson at Jimmy Tarbuck's son's wedding and we were remembering funny stories about Bobby. 'Mary said, "I can't imagine what it would be like without Michael or even think about it." And I said, "Mary, you must. Both of you have to think about this because Bobby and I just went on in oblivion, thinking we were going to be together till our old age. And I can't explain the shock when we were told about the cancer." There is absolutely no rehearsal for the effect of grief. The bad days still happen but I never know when they'll strike. That's grief and I'm used to it now. I've learned to accept it and I know that it will pass. I've got no solutions, except to say that you have to give in to it, but know that it's not going to be like that forever.

'In the beginning you think, "Please when is this pain going to stop." There were times when I actually cursed Bobby, I felt, "When is this going to end?" Grief and loss will always be there and I don't really want them to go away. They're the only thing I've got left, really, and I'm very protective of them. It's so private and when it hits me I just need to be on my own. I don't want to share it with anybody. I only want people to see the happy me.....

Today a memorial willow tree Cilla planted for Bobby Willis is thriving in the warm family home they established in Buckinghamshire. All who visit are invited to 'Come and see Bobby's tree.' The invitation, of course, is always from Bobby's Girl, from Mrs Willis. Cilla Black is who the world sees on stage or television. It has been an extraordinary performance.

# DISCOGRAPHY

### *Singles*

| Label/No | Title | Release Date | Chart Pos |
|---|---|---|---|
| Parlophone R5065 | Love of the Loved/Shy of Love | 10/63 | 35 |
| Parlophone R5101 | Anyone Who Had a Heart/Just For You | 2/64 | 1 |
| Parlophone R5133 | You're My World/Suffer Now I Must | 5/64 | 1 |
| Parlophone R5162 | It's For You/He Won't Ask Me | 8/64 | 7 |
| Parlophone R5225 | You've Lost That Lovin' Feelin'/ Is It Love | 1/65 | 2 |
| Parlophone R5269 | I've Been Wrong Before/ I Don't Want to Know | 4/65 | 17 |
| Parlophone R5395 | Love's Just Broken A Heart/Yesterday | 1/66 | 5 |
| Parlophone R5427 | Alfie/Night Time Is Here | 3/66 | 9 |
| Parlophone R5463 | Don't Answer Me/The Right One Is Left | 6/66 | 6 |
| Parlophone R5515 | A Fool Am I? (Dimmelo Parlami)/ For No One | 10/66 | 13 |

| | | | |
|---|---|---|---|
| Parlophone R5608 | What Good Am I/Over My Head | 6/67 | 24 |
| Parlophone R5652 | I Only Live To Love You/ From Now On | 11/67 | 26 |
| Parlophone R5674 | Step Inside Love/ I Couldn't Take My Eyes Off You | 3/68 | 8 |
| Parlophone R5706 | Where is Tomorrow?/ Work is a 4-Letter Word | 6/68 | 39 |
| Parlophone R5759 | Surround Yourself With Sorrow/ London Bridge | 2/69 | 3 |
| Parlophone R5785 | Conversations/Liverpool Lullaby | 7/69 | 7 |
| Parlophone R5820 | If I Thought You'd Ever Change Your Mind/It Feels So Good | 12/69 | 20 |
| Parlophone R5879 | Child of Mine/That's Why I Love You | 12/70 | - |
| Parlophone R5924 | Something Tells Me (Something's Gonna Happen Tonight)/ La La La Lu | 11/71 | 3 |
| Parlophone R5938 | The World I Wish For You/ Down in the City | 2/72 | - |
| Parlophone R5972 | You, You, You/Silly Wasn't I? | 11/72 | - |
| EMI 2107 | Baby We Can't Go Wrong/Someone | 2/74 | 36 |
| EMI 2169 | I'll Have to Say I Love You In A Song/ Never Run Out (Of You) | 5/74 | - |
| EMI 2227 | He Was A Writer/ Anything That You Might Say | 10/74 | - |
| EMI 2278 | Alfie Darling/ Little Bit Of Understanding | 3/75 | - |
| EMI 2328 | I'll Take A Tango/ To Know Him Is To Love Him | 7/75 | - |
| EMI 2438 | Little Things Mean A Lot/It's Now | 3/76 | - |
| EMI 2532E | Ask In Your Company/I Believe | 9/76 | - |
| EMI 2658 | I Wanted To Call It Off/ Keep Your Mind On Love | 7/77 | - |
| EMI 2791 | Silly Boy/I Couldn't Make My Mind Up | 5/78 | - |
| EMI 2840 | The Other Woman/Opening Night | 8/78 | - |
| Towerbell TOW 74 | There's A Need In Me/ You've Lost That Lovin' Feelin' (p/s) | 9/85 | - |

| | | | |
|---|---|---|---|
| Towerbell TOW 81 | Surprise Surprise/ Put Your Heart Where Your Love Is | 12/85 | - |
| Columbia 659698 7 | Through The Years/Through The Years (Orchestral Version) | 8/93 | 54 |
| Columbia 659698 4 | Through the Years/Through The Years (Orchestral Version) | 8/93 | - |
| Columbia 659698 4 | Through The Years/Through The Years (Orchestral Version)/The Feeling Just Gets Stronger (Through The Years)/Through TheYears (Do You Remember) (CD) | 8/93 | 75 |
| Columbia 659856 7 | Heart And Soul (with Dusty Springfield)/ A 10/93 Dream Come True (p/s) | | - |
| Columbia 659856 4 | Heart And Soul (with Dusty Springfield)/ A Dream Come True (cassette) | 10/93 | - |
| Columbia 659856 2 | Heart And Soul (with Dusty Springfield)/ Heart And Soul (A Capella Remix)/ Heart And Soul (Instrumental)/ A Dream Come True (CD) | 10/93 | - |
| Columbia 660013 7 | You'll Never Walk Alone Through The Years (p/s) | 12/93 | - |
| Columbia 660013 4 | You'll Never Walk Alone (with Barry Manilow)/ Through The Years (cassette) | 12/93 | - |
| Columbia 6600132 | You'll Never Walk Alone (with Barry Manilow)/ You'll Never Walk Alone (Hope In Your Heart Mix)/Through The Years (CD) | 12 /93 | - |

## *EPs*

| Label/No | Title | Release Date | Chart Pos |
|---|---|---|---|
| Parlophone GEP 8901 | Anyone Who Had A Heart (Anyone Who Had A Heart/ Just For You/Love Of The Loved/ Shy Of Love) | 4/64 | 5 |
| Parlophone GEP 8916 | It's For You (It's For You/ He Won't Ask Me/You're My World/ Suffer Now I Must) | 10/64 | 12 |
| Parlophone GEP 8954 | Cilla's Hits (Don't Answer/ The Right One Is Left/Alfie/ Night Time Is Here) | 9/66 | 6 |
| Parlophone GEP 8967 | Time for Cilla (Abyssinian Secret/ Trees And Lonliness/There I Go/Time) | 1967 | - |

| | | | |
|---|---|---|---|
| EMI 'Nut Series' EI 2698 | You're My World (You're My World/ It's For Series' You/Alfie/Love's Just A Broken Heart) (p/s) | 10/77 | - |

## *LPs*

| Label/No | Title | Release Date | Chart Pos |
|---|---|---|---|
| Parlophone PMC 12043 | Cilla | 1/65 | 5 |
| Parlophone PMC/PCS 7004 | Cilla Sings A Rainbow | 4/66 | 4 |
| Parlophone PMC/PCS 7041 | Sher-oo! | 4/68 | 7 |
| Parlophone PMC/PCS 7079 | Surround Yourself With Cilla | 11/68 | - |
| Parlophone PCS 7103 | Sweet Inspiration | 5/69 | - |
| Parlophone PCS 7128 | Images | 7/70 | - |
| Parlophone PCS 7155 | Day By Day With Cilla | 1/73 | - |
| EMI EMC 3031 | In My Life | 6/74 | - |
| EMI EMC 3108 | It Makes Me Feel Good | 3/76 | - |
| EMI EMC 3232 | Modern Pricilla | 6/78 | - |
| K-Tel ONE 1085 | Especially For You | 8/80 | - |
| Towerbell TOWLP 14 | Suprising Cilla | 10/85 | - |
| Columbia 474650 1 | Through The Years (with Cliff Richard, Dusty Springfield and Barry Manilow) | 9/93 | 41 |

## *UK Reissues and Compilation LPs*

| Label/No | Title | Release Date | Chart Pos |
|---|---|---|---|
| Parlophone PMC/PCS 7065 | The Best Of Cilla Black | 11/68 | 21 |
| World Record Club STP1036 | Cilla | 1969 | - |
| Regal Starline SRS 5044 | You're My World | 1970 | - |
| World Record Club ST1100 | Yesterday | 1971 | - |
| Sounds Superb SPR 90019 | Step Inside Love (Reissue of 'Sher-oo!') | 6/73 | - |
| Sounds Superb SPR 90062 | Cilla Sings A Rainbow | 1973 | - |
| K-Tel ONE 1085 | Especially For You | 1980 | - |
| EMI EMTV 38 | The Very Best Of Cilla Black | 1/83 | 20 |
| Music For Pleasure MFP415653 | The Very Best Of Cilla Black (Reissue of EMTV 38) | 5/84 | - |
| K-Tel ONE 1355 | Love Songs (Reissue of Especially For You) | 5/87 | - |
| Music For Pleasure DL113425 | The Anniversary Album (2 – LP) | 10/88 | - |
| C5 C5 547 | Yesterday | 1989 | - |

### *Soundtrack Albums*

| Label/No | Title | Release Date | Chart Pos |
|---|---|---|---|
| Columbia 33SX 1693 | Ferry Cross The Mersey (LP, includes 'Is It Love') | 2/65 | - |
| Castle Showcase SHLP 102 | Ferry Cross The Mersey (LP, reissue) | 4/86 | - |
| BGO BGOLP 10 | Ferry Cross The Mersey (LP 2nd reissue) | 3/88 | - |
| EMI DORIG 114 | Ferry Cross The Mersey (CD, Digipak) | 7/97 | - |

### *Exclusive Cassette*

| Label/No | Title | Release Date | Chart Pos |
|---|---|---|---|
| Starline TC EXC 100925 | Wonderful Tracks (compilation of 'Sing A Rainbow' & Surround Yourself With Cilla') | 1972 | - |

### *UK CDs*

| Label/No | Title | Release Date | Chart Pos |
|---|---|---|---|
| Telstar ONCD 5126 | Love Songs | 5/87 | - |
| EMI CDEMS 1410 | The Best Of The EMI Years | 6/91 | - |
| Columbia 474650 2 | Through The Years (with Cliff Richard, Dusty Springfield & Barry Manilow) | 9/93 | - |
| EMI CDEMS 1508 | Love, Cilla | 10/93 | - |
| Silva Treasury SILVAD 3004 | Cilla's World | 11/93 | - |
| Disky WM 860022 | Simply The Best | 1995 | - |
| EMI 7243 8 57053 28 | The George Martin/Abbey Road Decade - 1963 – 1973 (3-CD box set, with booklet) | 9/97 | - |

## *Flexidisc*

| Label/No | Title | Release Date | Chart Pos |
|---|---|---|---|
| LYN 995 | The Sound Of The Stars (avaliable via Disc &Music Echo, includes excerpts of Cilla in conversation with The Bachelors) | 1966 | - |
| V Enterprises 200 535-3 | Through The Years – The Cilla Black Story | 11/93 | - |

## *Exclusive Overseas Singles*

| Label/No | Title | Release Date | Chart Pos |
|---|---|---|---|
| SIR 200080 | M'Innamoro ('Step Inside Love' sung in Italian/Non c'è Domani (Where Is Tomorrow') (Sung In Italian) (Italy, p/s) | 3/68 | - |
| Private Stock PVS 45077 | Fantasy/It's Now (US only, no p/s) | 1976 | - |

## *Selected Overseas Albums*

| Label/No | Title | Release Date | Chart Pos |
|---|---|---|---|
| ST 2308 | Is It Love? (US LP, includes exclusive 'Heatwave') | 1965 | |
| Odeon OP 7577 | Sings A Rainbow (Japanese LP) | 1966 | |
| Virgin CICHCD1 | Cilla's World (Australian CD of children's songs) | 1990 | |
| EMI 157 2112 | The Best Of Cilla (Australian CD, reissue of 1968 LP) | 1990s | |
| EMI 43800 52 | The Most of Cilla (Australian CD, Includes 'I Don't Know How To Love You' & 'Across The Universe') | 1991 | |

# SELECTED BIBLIOGRAPHY

Best, Pete, and Doncaster, Patrick: *Beatle! The Pete Best Story* (Dell, New York,1985)

Black, Cilla, and Barrow, Tony: *Through The Years: My Life in Pictures* (Headline, 1993; Bluecoat, 1994)

Brown, Peter, and Gaines, Steven: *The Love You Make* (Macmillan, 1983)

Brown, Tony: *Jimi Hendrix, A Visual Documentary* (Omnibus, 1992)

Bugliosi, Vincent: *Helter Skelter, The Manson Murders* (Penguin, 1977)

Clarke, Donald: *The Penguin Encylopaedia of Popular Music* (Viking, 1989)

Clayson, Alan, and Sutcliffe, Pauline: *Backbeat, Stuart Sutcliffe: the Lost Beatle* (Pan Books, 1994)

Clayson, Alan: *Ringo Starr, Straight Man or Joker?* (Sidgwick & Jackson, 1991)

Cohn, Nik: *A WopBopaLooBop AlopBamBoom, Pop from the Beginning* (Paladin, 1970)

Coleman, Ray: *Brian Epstein, The Man Who Made The Beatles* (Viking, 1989)

Coleman, Ray: *John Lennon, (*Futura, 1985)

Davies, Hunter: *The Beatles, The Authorised Biography* (Heinemann, 1968; reissue Arrow, 1997)

Faithfull, Marianne: *Faithful* (Michael Joseph, 1994)

Garfield, Simon: *Expensive Habits, The Dark Side Of The Music Industry (*Faber & Faber, 1986)

Giuliano, Geoffrey: *Blackbird, The Life and Times of Paul McCartney* (Dutton, New York, 1991)

Giuliano, Geoffrey: *Dark Horse* (Bloomsbury, 1989)

Goldman, Albert: *The Lives of John Lennon* (Bantam, 1988)

Harrison, George: *I Me Mine* (Simon & Schuster, New York, 1980)

Ironside, Virginia: *Chelsea Bird* (Secker & Warburg, 1964)

Leigh, Spencer: *Let's Go Down, to the Cavern: The Story of Liverpool's Merseybeat* (Vermillion, 1984)

Lulu: *Lulu, Her Autobiography* (Granada, 1985)

MacDonald, Ian: *Revolution in the Head, The Beatles' Records and the Sixties* (Fourth Estate, 1994)

Martin, George: *All You Need Is Ears* (Macmillan, 1979)

Masters, Brian: *The Swinging Sixties* (Constable, 1985)

Miles, Barry: *Paul McCartney, Many Years From Now* (Secker & Warburg, 1997)

Moules, Joan: *Gracie Fields* (Summersdale, 1998)

Norman, Philip: *Elton* (Hutchinson, 1991)

Quant, Mary: *Quant by Quant* (Cassell, 1966)

Shrimpton, Jean: *An Autobiography* (Ebury Press, 1990)

Spencer, Terrence: *It Was Thirty Years Ago Today* (Bloomsbury, 1994)

Sutcliffe, Pauline and Thomson, Douglas: *Stuart Sutcliffe: The Beatles' Shadow* (Sidgwick & Jackson, 2001)
Thomson, Phil: *The Best of Cellars: the Story of the World-Famous Cavern Club* (Liverpool Bluecoat, 1994)
Tynan, Kathleen: *The Life of Kenneth Tynan* (Weidenfeld & Nicholson, 1987)